Hawkins County Tennessee

CIRCUIT COURT MINUTES

1822–1825

WPA RECORDS

Heritage Books
2024

HERITAGE BOOKS

AN IMPRINT OF HERITAGE BOOKS, INC.

Books, CDs, and more—Worldwide

For our listing of thousands of titles see our website
at
www.HeritageBooks.com

A Facsimile Reprint
Published 2024 by
HERITAGE BOOKS, INC.
Publishing Division
5810 Ruatan Street
Berwyn Heights, MD 20740

Nashville, Tennessee
The Historical Records Survey
January 16, 1939

International Standard Book Number
Paperbound: 978-0-7884-8805-4

W.P.A. RECORDS

The WPA Records are, for the most part, carbon copies of the original that was typed on onion skin paper during the Depression. Since these records were typed on poor machines by people who did not type in some cases and at the same time, they were read by persons not always sure of the older handwritten materials, the results are often less than perfect.

We have made every attempt to make as clear a copy as can be made from these older papers. Sometimes there are water stains and burned edges around the paper. This is the results of a fire at the home of one of the workers, Mrs. Penelope Allen, who was over most of the project. Sometimes, the index will be misleading in that they index by the middle name when a list of names are given in one family, i.e. "... the children of John Smith are, John, Jr., Mary Warren, and Oscar Sims. The indexer would list a Warren and a Sims in the index, when they should be Smith. Mountain Press has acquired a rather large number of finished and un-finished manuscripts. Many of these latter manuscripts are being typed and index now.

The WPA Records are now very scattered between the Tennessee State Library, various Public and Private Libraries and other collections. Some day, there is a hope that all of these can be collected and stored in one place. In spite of their many mistakes and problems, these are still the most complete collection of Tennessee records found anywhere.

TENNESSEE

RECORDS OF HAWKINS COUNTY

CIRCUIT COURT MINUTES
1822 – 1825

Prepared By
The Historical Records Survey
Transcription Unit
Division of Women's and Professional Projects
Works Progress Administration

Mrs. John Trotwood Moore
State Librarian & Archivist, Sponsor

T. Marshall Jones
State Director

Mrs. Penelope Johnson Allen
State Supervisor

Mrs. Margaret Helms Richardson
District Supervisor

. . . . .

Nashville, Tennessee
The Historical Records Survey
January 16, 1939

HAWKINS COUNTY

CIRCUIT COURT MINUTES
1822-1825

INDEX

Note: Page numbers in this index refer to those of the original volumn
from which this copy was made. These numbers are carried in the body of
the manuscript within parentheses, as (p 124).

Brooks, Littleton, 201, 202, 209, 221
Brooks, Thomas, 4, 16, 26, 68, 87, 209, 220
Brown, John, 179
Brown, Joseph, 128, 157, 195
Broyls, Lewis, 128
Bunch, Ben, 196
Bunch, Thomas, 40, 81
Bunden, Green, 173
Byram, Peter, 310
Burgess, Rebecca, 42, 93, 155, 195
Burgess, Wm., 42, 93, 155, 195
Burket, Wm., 85, 109
Burkheart, John, 35, 44, 56, 57
Burris, Jacob, 103, 232, 235, 236, 259, 263, 275
Burris, John, 284
Bussell, Ben I., 209
Bussell, Polly, 177, 210
Byrd, James, 166, 172, 176

C

Caiden, James, 166, 172, 176
Carden, James, 176, 186, 290,
Carden, Joseph, 134
Carden, Robert, 87, 118, 139
Careathers, Robt. E., 44, 89, 90, 103, 129, 185, 239
Carey, Patrick, 178, 251, 255, 260, 290, 297
Carmack, Cornelius, 112, 197, 200, 204, 218, 233, 241, 242, 282
Carmack, Wm., 95, 107, 141
Carmichael, Daniel, 3, 27, 50, 73, 88, 119, 297
Carpenter, Peter, 235
Carroll, Wm., 301
Carter, Hugh, 294
Carter, Wm., 58
Carver, Hugh, 128, 157
Chambers, 134, 151, 163, 176, 230, 234, 244, 248, 252, 254, 256, 259, 262
Chambers, Wm., 14
Charles, Hiram, 79, 172, 177, 182
Charles, James, 256
Cheek, Desse, 187
Chestnut, Henry, 225, 289
Chestnut, James, 209, 259, 262, 296
Chestnut, Samuel, 77, 96, 97, 99, 104, 149, 203
Chumly, Allen, 45, 48, 49, 161
Chumly, David, 45, 49, 162
Claibourn, Jones, 133
Clark, Henry, 168, 214
Clepper, Wm., 544
Click, Henry, 344
Click, Lewis, 1, 4, 9, 17, 34, 35, 36, 77, 79, 86, 87, 90, 96, 97, 99, 104,
119, 192, 230, 265, 277, 279, 282, 286, 288, 297, 298, 302, 308, 311
Click, Mary, 344
Cloud, Jeremiah, 136
Cloud, Joseph, 1, 9, 17
Cloud, Wm., 44, 56, 76, 187, 302
Cobb, Jesse, 119, 137, 274, 299
Cobb, Joseph, 17, 31, 40, 108
Cobb, Wm., 20, 22, 23, 65, 67, 70, 74, 81, 98, 109, 167

Cocke, John, 29, 60, 80, 104, 111, 116, 245
Cocke, Sterling, 14, 17, 21, 87, 193, 312
Cocke, Thomas, 35, 41, 44, 51, 56, 119, 148, 194, 201, 226, 277, 280, 313
Cocke, Wm., 43, 159, 165
Cockram, John, 35, 38, 63, 148, 158, 164, 172
Coffee, Benjamin, 151
Coffee, Joel, 151
Coffman, Dan, 82
Coker, Andrew, 201, 202, 209, 220
Cole, Richard, 197, 200, 204
Collins, John, 60
Collins, Vardi, 196
Colly, Thomas, 305
Condry & Cocke, 20, 43, 79, 108, 188, 197, 210, 237
Conway, Edward, 30, 31,
Cooper, Christopher, 99
Cooper, David, 14
Cooper, James, 214, 268, 307
Cooper, Lydia, 99
Cooper, Nancy, 14
Cox, George, 278
Cox, John, 34
Cox, Thomas, 127, 187, 208, 218, 220, 302
Crabb, Joseph, 402
Craighead, Benjamin, 60
Crawford, Andrew, 2
Crawford, Robert C., 285
Crawford, Susannah, 285
Crawford, Thomas, 2
Crawkey, Henry, 151, 164, 218, 242, 286
Creech, Jesse, 171, 200, 261
Crews, Jacob, 87, 90, 96, 209
Creyton, Itson, 12
Critz, John, 96, 131, 148, 216, 279, 308, 310
Critz, Philip, 7, 122, 124, 148, 166, 172, 176, 235, 237, 252, 255, 280
Cross, Asabel, 238
Crowbargers, 87, 88, 90, 113, 131, 178, 179, 216, 252
Crowley, Wm., 57, 138, 148, 155, 158, 191, 233, 279, 282, 310, 317
Curry, Samuel, 17, 18, 32, 230

D

Dalzell, Francis, 39, 69, 86, 134
Dalzell, Nancy, 224
Daniel, Wiley, 236
Davis, Asa, 296, 310
Davis, Benjamin, 119, 279, 280, 308, 310
Davis, Hezekiah, 263, 268, 270, 305
Davis, John, 120
Davis, Rosey, 44, 56, 76
Davis, Solomon, 123
Davis, William, 88, 94, 152, 209, 218, 223
Deadrick, David, 196
Dean, Andrew, 180
Delap, Robert, 13, 14, 16, 21
Den, John, 7, 8, 9, 10, 11, 12, 15, 20, 26, 28, 29, 37, 38, 39, 40, 42,

47, 55, 62, 68, 79, 81, 86, 100, 103, 121, 123, 134, 137, 143, 149, 154, 161, 187, 188, 190, 193, 194, 197, 201, 207, 208, 210, 237, 243, 268, 274, 280, 283, 307, 317

Denny, John, 160, 164, 172, 176, 254, 256, 259, 262

Derrick, Andrew, 237, 238

Devalt, Jacob, 131

Dickard, Michael, 178

Dodson, Charles, 189

Dodson, James, 96, 122, 124, 207, 248, 252

Dodson, Reuben, 189

Dogan, John, 5, 35,

Dunn, John H., 59, 218

Dyche, Christian, 128

Dyche, William, 36

Dyer, Joel, 20, 43, 79, 108, 188, 197, 210, 237

Dykes, John, 3, 36

E

Eidson, Creighton, 151, 163

Elkins, George, 192, 215, 241, 242

Ellis, Elijah, 83

Ellis, John, 277

Elrod, Peter, 19, 24, 124, 125, 133, 134, 139, 155, 203, 209, 228, 241, 242, 304

Elrod, Wm., 52

Emberson, Hezekiah, 125, 183, 200, 202, 229, 247, 249, 312

Embree, E., 24, 55, 58, 138, 170, 189, 227, 229, 238

Emmerson, Thomas, 120, 283

Epperson, Hopson, 178

Epperson, Shad, 186, 193, 195, 204, 209, 218, 286, 297, 307

Epperson, Thos., 297

Etter, James, 44, 96, 132, 134, 141

Evans, Fleming, 86

Evans, George, 60, 80, 116, 187

Evans, Rhode, 60

Evans, Sally, 60

Everett, Eppy, 17, 56

Everett, Joseph, 126

Everhart, David, 179, 208, 220

F

Fain, Nicholas, 165

Falkner, Elijah, 290, 303, 310

Farris, Jacob, 26, 87

Farris, Leneas, 26, 68, 87, 90

Feltner, Jacob, 11, 18

Feltner, Robert, 8

Fen, Richard, 193, 207

Finch, Aaron, 89

Finley, Alexander, 110, 183

Finley, Samuel, 7, 11, 28, 39, 42

Fisher, Walter, H., 179

Fitzpatrick, 122

Flanagan, B. P., 30, 31

House, George, 263, 273
Howe, Catharine, 54
Howe, Jacob, 54
Howel, Ed, 9, 47, 62, 318
Howell, Henry, 80, 116
Howel, James, 4
Howel, Jesse, 17, 64, 73, 100, 164, 218, 282, 297, 311
Huffmaster, Joseph, 1, 9, 17, 122, 124, 166, 176, 230, 265, 279, 286, 290, 297, 303, 308, 309, 311
Humble, Jacob, 55
Humble, Jesse, 240
Hunt, Timothy, 87, 90
Hunter, Alfred, 217
Huntsman, Grief B. 297

I

Ingram, Thomas, 313
Innis, Wm. 285
Ireland, John, 43
Isorn, Isaac, 132
Itson, Craton, 163

J

Jack, John F. 60, 104, 111, 240, 245, 291
Jackson, James, 50, 87, 90, 96
Jackson, Robert, 4, 17, 50, 79, 129
James, Wm. 252
Jenkins, Oliver, 67
Jenkins, Olliver, 286
Jenkins, Wm. 106
John, Jones, 252
John, Phoneas, 128
Johnson, Asahel, 59, 85, 120, 135, 139, 164, 223, 257, 291, 297, 312
Johnson, George, 44, 56, 115, 174, 204, 241, 242
Johnson, James, 39, 51, 56, 64, 73, 77, 79, 88, 91, 94, 96, 104, 230, 265, 282, 286, 288, 298, 303, 311
Johnson, John, 1, 9, 17, 38, 56, 77, 95, 97, 99, 119, 186, 279, 308, 310
Johnson, Larkin, 223
Johnson, Pleasant, 122, 134
Johnson, Robert, 134, 175, 243
Johnson, Thomas, 25, 59, 64, 68, 85, 103, 114, 120, 153, 174, 219, 222, 226, 250, 253, 278
Johnson, Wm. 152, 160, 164, 209, 224
Jones, Addison, 135
Jones, Benjamin, 214
Jones, Claibourn, 141, 143
Jones, Elijah, 181, 187, 195, 315
Jones, Isaiah, 143, 198, 205, 248, 268, 292, 301
Jones, James, 18, 32, 100, 112, 152, 153, 160, 166, 172, 176, 199, 205, 248, 255, 258, 292
Jones, John, 140, 141
Jones, Jonathan, 178, 222, 258

P

Pace, John, 214
Pack, John, 257
Paine, Isaiah, 60
Paine, Orville, 311
Paine, Wm, 183, 312
Painter, Levy, 87, 90, 197, 200
Parker, Aaron, 138, 192, 233
Parker, Caleb, 8, 9, 29, 34, 74, 80, 114, 168, 276, 288, 314
Parks, Orish, 232
Parsons, Joshua, 82
Parsons, Peter, 97, 106, 116, 129, 175, 183, 223, 266, 268, 304
Patrick, Charles, 61
Payne, Charles, 61
Pearson, Michael, 103, 174, 250
Peck, Jacob, 40, 164
Pentland, Aphraim, 256
Peoples, John, 216
Perkins, Simeon, 318
Phail, Malcom B. 69
Phipps, Wm. 64, 73, 122, 230, 247, 265
Porter, Alex, 226
Porter, Alexander, 193, 277, 280
Porter, Nimrod, 102
Powell, Samuel, 36, 39, 44, 52, 59, 64, 75, 145, 147, 153, 156, 159, 160, 165, 176, 195, 232, 279, 283, 290, 298, 304, 311, 318
Powel, Sol, 5
Preston, John, 121
Price, Henry, 234
Pride, Samuel, 255, 260
Proffit, David, 17, 28, 37, 40, 43, 81, 100, 121, 123, 135, 137, 143, 149, 164, 188, 234, 317
Province, Henry, 164
Pryor, John, 69, 84, 89, 126, 159, 161, 212
Pryor, Wm. 26, 45, 47, 53, 93

R

Randolph, John, 162
Rector, John, 262, 273
Redd, John, 13, 106
Red, Mary, 169
Redd, Walter, 13, 106
Reed, Andrew, 18, 32, 100, 112
Reese, John, 88, 290
Reese, Joseph, 302, 310, 313
Reese, Wm. 129
Renfroe, Robert, 66
Reynolds, Henry, 25, 289
Reynolds, Isham, 74, 80, 167, 208, 209, 220, 225, 252, 274, 276, 288, 289, 303, 314
Reynolds, John, 51, 56, 64, 73, 77, 95, 97, 148, 181, 186, 208, 230, 279, 232, 286, 297, 298, 310
Reynolds, Sam, 57, 71, 184, 255, 275
Reynolds, Wm. 84, 191
Rhea, John, 157

T

Tannehill, Wilkins, 159
Taylor, James, 129, 159
Taylor, Thomas, 152, 153, 156, 195, 204, 209, 244, 248
Taylor, Wm. 229, 245
Terry, Kiffle, 236
Thompson, David, 173, 215, 256
Thompson, George, 298
Thurman, Ben, 51, 64, 73, 209
Thurman, Dickenson, 119, 127, 141, 153, 156, 241, 252, 256, 259, 262
Thurman, Elisha, 112
Thurman, Wm. 78, 112, 134
Tipton, Jonathan, 164, 166, 184, 224
Traylor, John C. 169
Trigg, Abraham, 11, 63, 105, 286
Trigg, Joseph, 63
Tucker, George, 255, 262
Tucker, James, 218
Tyler, John, 214

V

Valentine, Sevier, 317
Vaughan, James, 227, 230
Vaughan, John W. 127, 152, 156
Vernon, Abraham, 8, 88, 94, 153, 156, 208, 220

W

Walker, Elizabeth, 171, 173, 214, 223, 256, 261, 291, 297, 302, 312
Walker, James, 113, 200, 213
Walker, Jesse, 171, 261
Walker, Wm. 297
Wallen, Elisha, 99
Wallen, John, 13, 99
Waterhouse, R. 108, 117, 142, 152, 182, 311
Weare, Stephen, 158, 166
Webb, Lewis, 139, 257
Webb, Susannah, 258
Weems, James, 143
Wells, John, 119
Wheeler, Oliver, 212
White, George, 118, 134, 175, 180, 185, 266,
White, James, 168, 241
White, Jonathan, 91
White, Thomas, 286, 288
Whitesides, Wm. 28, 37, 81, 149, 188, 284, 317
Wilbourne, Stephen, 1
Wilds, Morgan, 305
Williams, Aaron, 4, 18, 32, 35, 38, 39, 51, 52, 63
Williams, Etheldred, 12, 40, 43, 81, 124, 137, 143
Williams, George, 18, 32
Williams, James, 122, 132, 186, 244, 262, 279, 280, 308, 310
Williams, Jane, 78, 112
Williams, John, 218
Williams, John W. 38, 51, 52, 207

HAWKINS COUNTY

CIRCUIT COURT MINUTES
1822 — 1825

(p1)   At a Circuit Court begun and held for the County of Hawkins at the
Court House in Rogersville on the first Monday of April in the year of our
Lord one thousand eight hundred and twenty two and the Forty sixth year of
American Independence.
        Present The Honorable Edward Scott-Judge.

        Gabriel McCrow Sheriff of Hawkins County returns into Court his Ven-
ire Facias Executed upon the following persons, to wit, James Long Esq
John Moore John McAnnally, Hezekiah Hamblen Christion Morell Michael McCann,
Joseph Huffmaster, Joseph Busell, John Reynolds Esq. John Johnson Esq. Samuel Wilson, George Hale, John Mitchell, Larkin Willis, Joseph Baker, Lewis
Click Esq. Stephen Wilbourn William Alexander James Francisco, Joseph Cloud,
William Bradley, Nicholas Long Clinton Armstrong, and Joel Gillenwaters-
Out of the foregoing persons were drawn as Grand Jurors for the present Term
of this Court, to wit.
1. John Johnson
2. John Mitchell
3. Joel Gillenwaters
4. John Moore
5. Joseph Huffmaster
6. Lewis Click
7. Samuel Wilson
8. Joseph Cloud
9. Hezekiah Hamblen
10 James Francisco
11 George Hale
12 John McAnnally
13 John Reynolds
        Whereupon the Court appointed John Johnson Foreman of the Grand Jury
who were severally sworn and being charged by the Judge withdrew from the
Bar.

        Monday April 1st, 1822 (p2)
        Robert W. Gillenwaters Constable was sworn to attend on the Grand
Jury the present Term.

        On affidavit filed. It is ordered that Nicholas Long be discharged
from serving as a Juror the persent Term

        JOHN F. JACK)   Garnishment Andrew Crawford being summoned as Garn-
             vs.   )   isheron the Execution issued in this
        JOSEPH CRABB)   suit returnable to the present Term of
this Court to appear & C now on this day the said Andrew Crawford personally appeared in open Court and being duly sworn deposeth and saith that he
owes the defendant Joseph Crabb nothing and further saith that Thomas Crawford of Knox County did owe said Crabb one note of hand for One hundred
Dollars to be paid in cash-one other note of hand for Fifty Dollars to be
discharged in house Carpenter work and one other note for Thirty five doll-

ars to be paid in corn, Oats, Rye or any kind of Grain and that be this deponent understood by said Crabb that he said Crabb had assigned said notes away but did not understand to whom and that he knows of no other debts or property in the hands of any other person belonging to said crabb.

Ordered by the Court that Larkin Willis be excused from serving as Juror the present Term.

STATE)   Benjamine Mowl (p3) William Moulton and John Dykes,
vs.)   surrendered in open court the body of Thomas Lee the
THOMAS LEE)   defendant in discharge ot themselves as appearance Bail
for said defendant. Thereupon said Thomas Lee was ordered into Custody of the sheriff and the Bail discharged from any further liability.

DANIEL CARMICHAEL)   This day came the Plaintiff in his proper per-
vs.)   son into Court and dismisses his suit and there-
WILSON ROACH)   upon Wilson Roach the defendant comes into open
Court and confesses Judgment for the costs. It is Therefore considered by the Court that the Plaintiff recover of the defendant his costs in this be-half expended and that Execution issue accordingly.

THOMAS MEE)   This day came (p 4) the parties by their attornies
vs.)   and thereupon came a Jury to wit Michael McCann Jos-
JAMES FORGEY)   eph Russell, William Bradley, Thomas Hamblen, Charles
P. Miller, Robert H. Jackson, James H. Howel, Jacob Miller, William Clepper Benioni Harris, Thomas Brooks, and Aaron Williams who being elected tried and sworn upon their oath do say we find that the defendant did assume and take upon himself in manner & form as the Plaintiff hath complained and assess the Plaintiffs damage by reason of nonperformance of said assumpsit to ninety five dollars besides costs. It is therefore considered by the Court that the Plaintiff recover against the defendant the sum of Ninety five dollars the damages aforesaid by the Jury aforesaid in form aforesaid assessed together with the costs by him in this behalf expended & the def't in May.

MARY CLICK Serv. &)   This day came the defendants by their att-
MATHIAS CLICK Serv.)   orney and moved the Court for a Rule to
Executrix & Executor)   shew cause why the appeal in the nature of
of HENRY CLICK Dec'd)   a Writ of Error in this case should be dis-
vs.)   missed which rule is granted by the Court
LEWIS CLICK, JOHN COX)
and FREDERICK AKEARD)

JOHN DOGAN)   It appearing (p 5) to the satisfaction
vs.)   of the Court from the representation of
SAMUEL WILSON)   the attornies of the parties in these
)   suits that the matters in controversy
)   in said suits had been referred to the
THOMAS GILLENWATERS & Co.)   arbitration of Absalom Kyle, Cleoe Moore,
vs.)   George Hale, William Alexander and John
JOHN DOGAN)   Johnson and that the parties had mutually bound themselves to each other by bond made under their hands and seals to stand, to abide by and perform the award of said arbitrators and also that the award of said arbitrators should be the Judgment of this Court. It is therefore ordered by the Court that said award be entered of record which is in the words and figures fol-lowing, to wit.

We the undersigned arbitrators chosen to settle the matters in dispute

between John Dogan on the one part and Thomas Gillenwaters, Sol Wilson, A.
Looney & Sol Powel of the other part, in three suits one brought and now
depending in the Circuit Court of Hawkins County by said Dogan vs. said
Gillenwaters, Wilson, Looney & Powel, one brought by said Company of Gillenwaters, Wilson, Looney and Powel before a Justice of the Peace & now depending in the Circuit Court of Hawkins, and one other brought by said Co
of Gillenwaters, Wilson (p 6) Looney & Powel in the County Court of Hawkins and now the said arbitrators having heard testimony respecting all of
said several suits on both sides and having maturely considered the same
do award that said Dogan has no cause of action against said Gillenwaters,
Wilson, Looney & Powel the said suit brought by him against them and that
he the said Dogan shall pay the costs of said suits and that said Gillenwaters, Wilson, Looney & Powel has a good cause of action against said Dogan in the said suit brought by them against him in the County Court of
Hawkins but they having agreed not to ask any damages do award that said
Dogan pay the costs of said suits and we do further award and order that
said Dogan pay to the said Gillenwaters, Wilson, Looney & Powel the sum of
sixty four dollars in the suit brought by them before a Justice of the Peace
& now depending in the Circuit Court of Hawkins & also the costs of said
suit. Given under our hands and seals this 1st of June 1821.

> Geo. Hale (seal)
> A. Kyle (seal)
> Cleoe Moore (seal)
> Wm. Alexander (seal)
> Jno. Johnson (seal)

It is therefore considered by the Court that Gillenwaters, Wilson, Looney
& Powel recover against the said John Dogan the sum of Sixty four dollars
in the suit brought by them, before a Justice of the peace together with
the costs in both suits expended.
The Court adjourn until tomorrow (p 7) 8 O'clock A. M.

> Edw Scott

Tuesday 2nd April 1822.
The Court met according to adjournment.
Present The Honorable Edward Scott—Judge.

MOSES McCONNELL and	)	James Bootman who heretofore had been sum-
THE STATE OF TENNESSEE	)	moned as a witness on behalf of C. Eskridge
vs.	)	Kenner the defendant in the suit being sole-
C. ESKRIDGE KENNER	)	mnly called came not but made default. There-

fore on motion of C. Eskridge Kenner by his attorney It is considered by
the court that the said C. Eskridge Kenner recover against the said James
Bootman the sum of One hundred and Twenty five dollars agreeable to an act
of Assembly in such case made and provided unless sufficient cause of his
disability to attend be shown at the next Term of this Court after notice
of this Judgment.

JOHN DEN LESSEE of	)	This day came the parties by their attornies
ROBERT WRIGHT	)	and thereupon came a Jury to wit, William Brad-
vs.	)	ley, Michael McGann, Robert Nall, William Mar-
SAMUEL FINLEY	)	tin, Moses McGinnis, James Sanders, John Shough,

Bennoni Harris, Gregory Smith, James Forgey, Philip Critz and C. Eskridge
Kenner who being elected tried and sworn. The Plaintiff by his attorney
(p 8) says he will not further prosecute this suit but suffers a non suit
therefore it is considered by the Court that the plaintiff be non suit-
that the defendant go hence without day, and recover his costs in this behalf expended for which Execution may issue.

JOHN DEN LESSE of)

SARAH LAWSON) This day came the parties by their attornies and
vs.) Ejectment) thereupon came a Jury, to wit, William Bradley,
CALEB J. PARKER) Michael McCann, Robert Nall, William Martin,
Moses McGinnis, John Shough, Bennoni Harris, James Forgey, Phillip Crits,
C. Eskridge Kenner, Robert Brice and Jacob Fettner who being elected tried
and sworn upon their oath do say we find that the defendant is Guilty of
the Trespass amd Ejectment in manner and form as the Plaintiff against him
hath complained and assess the Plaintiffs damage to six cents. It is therefore considered by the Court that the Plaintiff recover against the defendant his Term aforesaid yet to come of and in the said Tract of land called
& c and the sum of six cents by the Jury in form aforesaid assessed for
her damages which she has sustained by occasion of the Trespass & Ejectment
aforesaid together with the costs by her about her suit in this behalf expended and the defendand in mercy & c.

JOHN DEN LESSE of) This day (p 9) came the parties by their att-
EDWARD HOWEL) ornies and the Plaintiff by his attorney says
vs.) he will not further prosecute this suit, but suf-
WILLIAM GRAHAM) fers a non suit. It is therefore considered by
the Court that the plaintiff be non suited that the defendant go hence without day and recover his costs in this behalf expended for which Execution
may issue.

CALEB J. PARKER) This day came the parties by their attornies and
vs.) Trespass on) thereupon came a Jury, to wit- John Johnson, John
the case) Mitchell, Joel Gillenwaters, John Moore, Joseph
SARAH LAWSON and) Ruffmaster, Samuel Wilson, Joseph Cloud, Hezekiah
others) Hamblen, James Francisco, George Hale, John Mc-
Annelly and Lewis Click who being elected tried and sworn upon their oath
do say we find that Sarah Lawson is not guilty in manner and form as the
Plaintiff against her hath complained but we find that George Lawson and
Wiley Lawson are Guilty of the Trespass in the Plaintiffs declaration mentioned and assess the Plaintiffs damage to Twelve dollars besides costs.
It is therefore considered by the Court that Sarah Lawson one of the defendants go hence without day.

JOHN DEN LESSE of) On motion (p 10) of defendant by John A. Mc-
SARAH LAWSON) Kinney his attorney for a Rule to show cause
vs.) why a new Trial should be granted, which is all-
CALEB J. PARKER) owed by the Court.

JOHN DEN LESSEE) This day came the parties by their attornies
of WILLIAM BRADLEY) and thereupon came a Jury to wit, Clinton Arm-
vs.) strong, Michael McCann, Robert Nall, William
THOMAS SPROUL) Mortin, Phillip Critz, James Sanders, Gregory
Smith, Moses McGinnis, Charles P. Miller, John G. Winston, Robert Brice
and Thomas Hamblen who being elected tried and sworn well and truly to
try the issue Joined, In the progress of this suit the Hury from rendering their verdict are respited until tomorrow.

ABRAHAM B. TRIGG) By consent (p 11) of the parties It is ordered
vs.) by the Court that a Commission issue directed to
JOHN LYNN) any Justice of the peace for Washington County
in the State of Virginia to take the depositions of James C. Trigg and
Peter J. Branch on behalf of the Plaintiff which depositions when taken to
be read in Evidence on the trial of this cause and that he give the defend-

ant Twenty days notice of the time and place of taking the same.

The Court adjourned until tomorrow 8 O'clock A. M.

Edw. Scott

Wednesday 3rd, April 1822.
The Court met according to adjournment.
Present the Honorable Edward Scott, Judge.

JOHN DEN LESSE of)
ROBERT WRIGHT)
vs.)
SAMUEL FINLEY)

On motion and affadavit a Rule is granted the
Plaintiff to show cause why the Non suit should
be set aside.

A Deed of Conveyance from James Kirkpatrick to Richard Mitchell for
one hundred and sixty acres of land lying in Illinois Military Boundary
was proven in open Court by the oath of Jacob Fettner and William Lyons
and ordered to be certified for registration.

JOHN DEN LESSEE of)
WILLIAM BRADLEY)
vs.)
THOMAS SPROUL)

This day (p 12) came the parties by their attornies and thereupon came a Jury, the same who
were respited on yesterday from rendering their
verdict, to wit, Clinton Armstrong, Michael Mc-
Cann, Robert Nall, William Martin, Phillip Critz, James Sanders, Gregory
Smith, Moses McGinnis, Charles P. Miller, John G. Winston, Robert Brice and
Thomas Hamblen upon their oath do say we find that the defendant is not Guilty of the Respass and Ejectment in the declaration mentioned as by pleading
he hath alledged. On motion of the Plaintiff by his attorney a rule is granted to show cause why the Verdict rendered in this cause should be set aside.

JOHN DEN LESSEE of)
WILLIAM BRADLEY)
vs.)
THOMAS SPROUL)

Orville Bradley
The Bail for the prosecution in this cause on
motion is released from his Bond and John A.
McKinney Esquire comes into open Court and under-
takes as prosecution. Bail in this case that if the plaintiff shall fail
in prosecuting his suit he will be responsible for the costs and damages t
that may be adjudged and awarded for failure.

JOHN KING & others)
vs.)
WILLIAM ALEXANDER)

By consent (p13) of the parties by their attornies it is ordered by the Court that a Commission issue directed to any two Justices of
the peace for the County of Henry in the state of Virginia to take the depositions of Lewis Franklin, Walter Redd, Thomas Sterling, John Wallen,
and John Redd which depositions when taken to be read in Evidence on the
trial of this cause on behalf of the plaintiffs and that Thirty days notice of the time and place of taking said depositions be given to the adverse party.

STATE)
vs.)
ROBERT DELAP)

The defendant by the order of the Court was brought
to the bar and by his attorney moved on his affidavit to change the Venire in this cause, and the Court
being advised thereon was of opinion that the Venire could not be changed
to which opinion of the Court the defendant excepts in law and tenders a
Bill of Exceptions which was signed and sealed by the Court- Thereupon the
defendant was remanded to prison.

A Deed of Conveyance (p 14) from David Cooper and Nancy Cooper his wife
to Dicks Alexander for one hundred and sixty acres of land lying in the
Arkansas Territory the execution of which was acknowledged in open Court
by David Cooper and thereupon the Court examined Nancy Cooper separate and
apart from her husband touching the execution of said Deed of Conveyance
on her part and the said Nancy acknowledged that she had executed said Deed
of Conveyance of her own free will and accord and not by reason of an threat
compulsion or constraint of her said husband. It is therefore ordered by
the Court that said Deed of Conveyance be certified for registration. The
Court adjourned until tomorrow 9 O'clock A. M.

Edw. Scott

Thursday 4th, April 1822.
The Court met according to adjournment.
Present the Honorable Edward Scott—Judge.

STATE) Harmon Thompson and William Chambers who being summ-
vs.) oned as witnesses in this cause in behalf of the State
ROBERT DELAP) and being solemnly called came not but made default
and thereupon on motion of Sterling Cocke Solicitor General for Judgment
against the said Harmon Thompson and William Chambers & c. It is therefore considered by the Court that the (p 15) State of Tennessee recover
against the said Harmon Thompson and William Chambers the sum of Two Hundred and Fifty dollars each agreeable to act of the General Assembly in
such case made and provided. Unless sufficient cause be shown of their
disability to attend at the next Court after notice of this Judgment.

STATE) John Newman and Timothy Sexton who being heretofore
vs.) summoned as Witnesses in this suit on behalf of Rob-
ROBERT DELAP) ert Delap the defendant and being solemnly called
came not but made default and on motion of Defendant by his attorney. It
is ordered by the Court that Robert Delap recover against the said John
Newman and Timothy Sexton the sum of two hundred and Fifty dollars each
agreeable to act of the General Assembly in such cases made and provided.
Unless sufficient cause of their disability be shewn at the next Term of
this Court after notice of this Judgment.

This day appeared in open Court Samuel K. Kinnard and produced his License
to practice as attorney in the Several Courts of Law and Equity of this
State and took the oaths required by law and was admitted as an attorney
of this Court.

STATE) This day came (p 16) the State by the attorney Gen-
vs.) eral, and Robert Delap the defendant being brought
ROBERT DELAP) to the bar - present also his Council and thereupon
came a Jury to wit, Thomas Brooks, John Mills, John Mitchell, Joel Gillenwaters, George Rogers, Jacob Fettner, Thomas Barrot, Clinton Armstrong,
John McAnnally, William Armstrong, John Beal senr and Lazarus Spiers - who
having been tried & elected by the Prisoner Robert Delap - and sworn well
and truly to try the issue of Tennessee the state against the said Robert
Delap - Do upon their oaths say that Robert Delap the prisoner at the bar
is guilty in manner and form as charged in the Bill of Indictment - Thereupon the Court remanded the s'd Prisoner into the Custody of the Sheriff.

The Court adjourned until Tomorrow 9 O'clock.
Edw. Scott

Friday 5th, April 1822 (p 17)

The Court met according to Adjournment.
Present The Honorable Edward Scott Judge.

JOSEPH COBB Admr.) This day came the parties by their attornies
de bonus non of) and thereupon came a Jury, to wit, John John-
the Estate of) son, John Moore, Joseph Huffmaster, Lewis Click,
ABRAHAM MIFFERLY) Samuel Wilson, Joseph Cloud, Hezekiah Hamblen,
vs.) James Francisco, George Hale, Samuel Curry,
DAVID PROFFIT) Eppy Everett and Robert H. Jackson who being
elected tried and sworn well and truly to try the Issues joined upon their
oaths do say we find all the issues in this case for the defendant David
Proffit. It is therefore considered by the Court that the Defendant go
hence without day and recover against the plaintiff his costs by him in
this behalf expended.

STATE) This day came the state by Sterling Cocke the Attor-
vs.) ney General and with the permission of the Court
DAVID OWENS) enters a Nolle proseque.

JOSEPH ROGERS) By consent of the parties, time is given to make
vs.) Trespass) up the pleadings and that this cause be continued
JESSE HOWEL M) until the next term of this court.

STATE) This day came (p 18) the state by the Attorney Gen-
vs.) eral and with the permission of the Court as to the
JOHN A. McMINN) charge in the Indictment contained against the said
John A. McMinn enters a Nolle Prosequi.

JAMES JONES) This day came the parties by their attornies and there-
vs.) upon came a Jury, to wit, William Bradley, Clinton,
ANDREW REID) Armstrong, Isham Mills, Samuel Curry, Aaron Williams,
Robert Gamble, George Williams, Thomas Hamblen, Jacob Miller, John McWilliams, William Altum and John Mills who being elected, tried ans sworn well
and truly to try the following Issues - to wit - Is the spring included in
the Grant to James Jones and in the Survey of Andrew Reid the same spring
mentioned in the Entry of Andrew Reid of No 553 on which such Survey was
founded?
Did Hugh Blair ever make an improvement at said Spring included in
said Survey of said Andrew Reid and grant to James Jones?
Was the Entry of the Caveatee notoriously known (p 19) claimed
and surveyed for Andrew Reid at the time of the Caveators first survey and
Grant, and was the same known to the said Caveator?
Did Hugh Blair make an improvement on the Cedar fork of Lick Creek
including a Spring prior to the time of Caveaters Entry?
Did Hugh Blair have more than one Improvement on said Cedar fork of
Lick Creek including a Spring at and prior to the time of Caveatees Entry?
Had the Caveator notice of the Caveatees Entry at the time of the
several surveys upon which he obtained Grants?
Was said Improvement generally known in the neighborhood as the one
made by said Blair at the time of Caveatees Entry?
Upon their oaths do say - from rendering their Verdict are respited
until tomorrow.

A Deed of Conveyance from Peter Elrod to John A. Rogers for one hundred and
sixty acres of land lying in the state of Illinois Military Boundary was
acknowledged in open Court by the said Peter Elrod and was ordered to be
certified for registration.

JOHN A. ROGERS vs. SAMUEL WILSON senr.	)	On motion (p 20) of the defendants by their attorneys to renew the several orders made at the last term of this Court for taking depositions in these suits. It is therefore considered by the Court that the said Several orders made at the last term of this Court for taking depositions in these suits be renewed and that commissions issue accordingly.
JOHN A. ROGERS vs. SAMUEL WILSON Jnr.	)	
JOHN A. ROGERS vs. ELI BOYAKIN	)	
JOHN A. ROGERS vs. WILLIAM COBB	)	
JOHN DEN LESSE of CONDRY and COCKE vs. JOEL DYER	)	By consent of the parties by their attorneys this cause is continued until the next term of this court.
ROBERT NALL vs. JOHN S. HILL	)	By consent of the parties by their attorneys this cause is continued until the next term of this Court.

The Court adjourned until tomorrow 9 O'clock A. M.

Edw. Scott

Saturday 6th, April 1822 (p 21)
The Court met according to adjournment.
Present The Honorable Edward Scott, Judge.

STATE vs. ROBERT DELAP	)	Indictment as accessary of the Murder of Eve Martin.

This day came the State by Sterling Cocke Esqr the Attorney General who prosecutes for the State in this behalf and the Defendant Robert Delap in proper person being brought to the Bar in pursuance of the order of the Court and being asked by the Court if he had anything to say why the Judgment and sentence of the Law should not be pronounced upon him according to the Verdict of the Jury rendered against him on Thursday the fourth day of this Term. And he saying nothing further than as heretofore. Whereupon all and singular the premises being seen and by the Court considered and fully understood. It is by the Court nowhere considered and adjudged that the said Robert Delap for such his offence be taken to the Jail of Hawkins County there to remain in person until Friday the seventeenth day of May next and from thence be taken to the common place of Execution in Hawkins County and there between the hours of Ten in the morning and Four O'clock Post Meridion be hanged by the neck until he is dead – And that the Sheriff of said County of Hawkins be charged with the execution of this Judgment.

And it was further considered (p 22) by the Court that Robert Delap pay the costs of this prosecution for which Execution in the name of the State may issue.
In the progress of this cause the defendant by his attorney tenders his

Bills of Exdeptions and prayed that the same may be signed and sealed
which is done accordingly and thereupon prays an appeal in the nature of
a Writ of Error to the Supreme Court of Errors and Appeals to be held
for the first Circuit at the Courthouse in Rogersville on the first Monday of May next. Which appeal is granted by the Court.

JOHN A. ROGERS) On motion of the Plaintiff by his attorney
vs.) to renew the several orders made at the last
SAMUEL WILSON Senr) Term of this Court for taking depositions in
) these suits on behalf of the plaintiff. It
JOHN A. ROGERS) is therefore considered by the Court that the
vs.) said several orders made at the last Term of
SAMUEL WILSON Junr) this Court for taking depositions in these suits
) be renewed and that Commissions issue according-
JOHN A. ROGERS) ly.
vs.)
ELI BOYKIN)
)
JOHN A. ROGERS)
vs.)
WILLIAM COBB)

LIJAH KINCHELOE) On affadavit (p 23) of the defendant. It is or-
vs.) dered by the Court that a Commission issue direct-
JOHN A. ROGERS) ed to any two Justices of the peace for Edgefield
District in the State of South Carolina to take the deposition of Levi al-
ios Eli Morgan which deposition when taken to be read in Evidence on the
trial of this cause on behalf of the defendant and that Thirty days notice
of the time and place of taking said deposition be given to the Plaintiff.

JOHN A. ROGERS) On affadavit of the Plaintiff It is ordered
vs.) by the Court that a Commission issue directed
SAMUEL WILSON Senr.) to any two Justice of the Peace for Limestone
) County in the State of Alabama to take the de-
JOHN A. ROGERS) position of William Scott and tat a Commission
vs.) issue directed to any two Justices of the Peace
SAMUEL WILSON Junr.) for the State of Alabama to take the deposit-
) ion of John Galbreath that a Commission dir-
JOHN A. ROGERS) ected to any two Justices of the peace for St
vs.) Stephens State of Alabama to take the depos-
ELI BOYAKIN) itions of - Frances H. Gaines, John Morriset
) and Henry Henderson that a Commission issue
JOHN A. ROGERS) directed to any two Justices of the peace for
vs.) Cincinnati in the State of Ohio to take the
WILLIAM COBB) deposition of William Henry Harrison and that
a commission issue (p24) directed to any two Justices of the peace for
the County of Buffaloe in the State of New York to take the depositions of
John G. Camp which depositions when taken to be read in Evidence on the
trial of these causes, on behalf of the Plaintiff by giving the adverse
party forty days notice of the time and place of taking said depositions.

E. EMBREE surviving) On affadavit of Amis Grantham one of the
partner of ELIHU EMBREE) defendants in this cause. It is ordered
vs.) by the Court that a Commission issued dir-
AMOS GRANTHAM and others) ected to any two Justices of the peace for
the County of Lee in the State of Virginia to take the depositions of Pas-

cal Hamblen, Thomas Roberts, John McKinney Junr., David Lawson, Daswell Rogers and William Roberts and that a Commission issue directed to any two Justices of the peace for Surry County in the State of North Carolina to take the deposition of Callihan Moore which depositions when taken to be read in Evidence on the trial of this cause on behalf of the defendants by giving the Plaintiffs Thirty days notice of the time and place of taking said depositions.

A Power of Attorney from Thomas Martin to Peter Elrod was acknowledged in open Court by said Thomas Martin and ordered to be registered.

MICHAEL McGANN)
vs.)
FRAZIER BRINLEY)

On motion (p 25) of the Plaintiff by his attorney to renew the order made at the last Term of this Court for taking of depositions in this suit on behalf of the Plaintiff. It is therefore considered by the Court that said order be renewed and that Commissions issue accordingly.

THOMAS JOHNSON)
vs.)
JACOB HACKNEY)

On affadavit of the Plaintiff It is ordered by the Court that a Commission issue directed to any two Justices of the peace for Hawkins County State of Tennessee to take the deposition of Henry Reynolds which deposition when taken to be read in Evidence on the trial of this cause on behalf of the Plaintiff by giving the adverse party Five days notice of the time and place of taking said deposition.

HOUSEN KENNER)
vs.)
LEWIS STURGEON)

On affidavit of the Plaintiff It is ordered by the Court that a Commission issue directed to any two Justices of the peace for Greene County in the State of Tennessee to take the deposition of John Dogan which deposition when taken to be read in Evidence on the trial of this cause on behalf of the plaintiff by giving the adverse party Five days notice of the time and place of taking said deposition.

JOHN DEN LESSEE of)
THOMAS BROOKS)
vs.)
JACOB FARRIS and)
LENEOS FARRIS)

On (p 26) affadavit of the defendant It is ordered by the Court that a Commission issue directed to any two Justices of the peace for the County of Hawkins in the State of Tennessee to take the deposition of Housen Kenner which deposition when taken to be read in evidence on the Trial of this cause on behalf of the defendant and that he give the Plaintiff Five days notice of the time and place of taking said depositions.
And it is further ordered by the Court that Hezekiah Hamblen Esqr. Survey the land in dispute and return Three plots thereof to the next Term of this Court.

STATE)
vs.)
WILLIAM PRYOR)

Forfeited Recognizance.
This day came the State by the Attorney General and William Pryor being bound in Recognizance in the sum of one hundred dollars for his appearance to this Court and being solemnly called came not but made default and hath forfaithed his recognizance. It is therefore considered by the Court that the State recover against the said William Pryor the sum of one hundred dollars unless he appears at the next Term of this Court and shew sufficinet cause why this Judgment should not be made final and that Scire Facias Issue against him and John A. McKinney and George (p 27) Hale being bound in recognizance in the sum of Fifty dollars for the appearance of said William Pryor at the present Term of this Court and being solemnley called to bring into Court the body

of said William Pryor as they were bound to do or they would forfeit their recognizance brought him not and wholly made default. It is therefore considered by the Court that the State recover against the said John A. McKinney and George Hale the sum of Fifty dollars each unless they appear at the next term of this Court and shew sufficient cause why this Judgment should not be made final and that Scire Facias issue against them.

JOHN A. ROGERS vs. SAMUEL WILSON Senr.	By consent of the parties It is ordered by the Court that this suit be refered to the arbitration of William Lyons and George

Hale with leave to choose and umpire and their award returned under hand and seal to be the Judgment of this Court.

A Power of Attorney from Daniel Carmichael to Luke Lea Esq was acknowledged in open Court and ordered to be registered.

MOSES McCONNELL and the STATE of TENNESSEE vs. C. ESKRIDGE KENNER	This day (p 28) came the defendant by his attorney and sets asice the forfeiture taken against James Bootman a witness in this suit on a former day of this Term on the payment of costs.

JOHN DEN LESSEE of ROBERT WRIGHT vs. SAMUEL FINLEY	Rules to set aside the Non Suit - And now on this day came on to be argued the rule to set aside the Non Suit entered in this cause and Council being heard as well for as against the rule and

the premises considered and understood.
It is therefore considered by the Court that the rule be made absolute and the Non suit be set aside and It is further considered by the Court that the defendant recover against the Plaintiff the costs of this term expended for which execution may issue

JOHN DEN LESSEE of WILLIAM WHITE- SIDES vs. DAVID PROFFIT	Rule for a New Trial. The rule for a New Trial granted at a former Term of this Court is made absolute and a New Trial granted.

JOHN DEN LESSEE of SARAH LAWSON vs. CALEB J. PARKER	Rule for a New Trial. (p 29) This day a new Trial haveing come on to be argued and council being heard as well for as against the rule and the premises considered and fully

understood. It is therefore considered by the Court that the rule be discharged- From which opinion of the Court the defendant excepts in law - and tenders his Bill of Exceptions and prays the same may be signed and sealed which is done accordingly - and thereupon prays an appeal in the nature of a Writ of Error to the Supreme Court of Errors and Appeals to be held at the Court House in Rogersville on the first Monday of May next, - gave Bond and security for the prosecution thereof and the appeal by the Court granted.

JOHN DEN LESSEE of WILLIAM BRAD- LEY vs. THOMAS SPROUL	Rule for a New Trial on cause shewn to the Court. It is ordered that the rule for a new trial be made absolute and a new trial granted.

JOHN A. ROGERS)   On affidavit (p 30) of defendant It is ordered
vs.   by the Court that a Commission issue directed to
ELI BOYAKIN)   any two Justices of the peace of Selma in the State
of Alabama to take the deposition of Edward Conway that a Commission issue
directed to any two Justices of the peace in —— County East Tennessee to
take the deposition of Robert P. Flenagaan which depositions when taken to
be read in evidence on the trial of this cause on behalf of the defendant
and that he give the Plaintiff Thirty days notice out of the State and Ten
days notice in the state of the time and place of taking said depositions.

JOHN A. ROGERS)   On affidavit of the defendant by his Attorney.
vs.   It is ordered by the Court that a Commission
SAMUEL WILSON Junr.)   Issue directed to any two Justice of the peace of Selma in the State of Alabama to take the deposition of Edward Conway that a commission issue directed to Any two Justice of the peace in
—— County East Tennessee to take the deposition of Robert P. Flanagan
which deposition when taken to be read in evidence on the trial of this
cause on behalf of the defendant and that he give the plaintiff Thirty
days notice out of the State and Ten days in the State of the time and
place of taking said depositions.

JOHN A. ROGERS)   On affidavit (p 31) of defendant.
vs.   It is ordered by the Court that a Commission issue
WILLIAM COBB)   directed to any two Justice of the peace of Selma
in the State of Alabama to take the deposition of Edward Conway that a Commission issue directed to any two Justices of the peace in —— County East
Tennessee to take the deposition of Robert P. Flanagan which depositions
when taken to be read in evidence on the trial of this cause on behalf of
the defendant and that he give the Plaintiff Thirty days notice out of the
State and Ten days notice in the State of the time and place of taking said
depositions.

ELIZABETH STOLEY)   Petition for Divorce.
vs.   This day the plaintiff by her Attorney comes into
JOHN STOLEY   open Court and dismisses this suit. It is therefore considered by the Court that the defendant go hence and recover against the Plaintiff his costs in this behalf expended.

ANDERSON HICKS)   Petition for Divorce.
vs.   This day came the Plaintiff by his attorney and
JANE HICKS   the sub poena that issued in this cause being returned, Executed and the defendant being solemnly called to come into
Court and answer the Petition filed against her or the same will (p 32)
be taken as Confessed and heard exporte and the Court proceed to decree
accordingly.

JAMES JONES)   This day came the parties by their attornies and there-
vs) Caveat)   upon came the same Jury that was respited on yesterday
ANDREW REID)   from rendering their Verdict, to wit, William Bradley,
Clinton Armstrong, Isham Mill, Samuel Curry, Aaron Williams, Robert Gamble,
George Williams, Thomas Hamblen, Jacob Miller, John McWilliams, William
Altum and John Mills who being elected, tried and sworn well and truly
to try the following Issues to wit
1st Issue - Is the Spring included in the Grant to James Jones and in the
Survey of Andrew Reid the same Spring mentioned in the Entry of Andrew
Reid of No 553 on which such survey was made? Upon their oaths do say
"It is not".
2nd Issue - Did Hugh Blair ever make an improvement at said Spring includ-

ed in said Survey of said Andrew Reid and Grant to James Jones, upon their oaths do say? - No satisfactory proff that he did.

3rd Issue - Was the Entry of the Caveatee notoriously known claimed and surveyed for Andrew Reid at the time of the Caveators first Survey and Grant and was the same known to the (p 33) said Caveatory - upon their oaths do say - From the evidence, we do not find that it was.

4th Issue Did Hugh Blair make an improvement on the Cedar fork of Lick Creek including a Spring prior to the time of Caveatees Entry ? - upon their oath do say - He did at the Blue Spring now Newmons Spring.

5th Issue - was said Improvement generally known in the neighborhood as the one made by said Blair at the time of Caveatees Entry? - upon their oaths do say- "It was"

6. Issue Did Hugh Blair have more than one improvement on said Cedar Fork of lick creek including a Spring at and prior to the time of Caveatees Entry? upon their oath do say - but one on Cedar fork now called Newmans fork.

7th Issue - Had the Caveator notice of the Caveatees Entry at the time of the several surveys upon which he obtained Grants? upon their oaths do say from the Evidence we do not see that he had when he made his first survey. The Caveatee moved he set aside the proceeding of the Jury on producing his own affidavit and the affidavit of Newmon but the Court was of opinion that they ought at least to see the best evidence of the existance of the facts alluded to in the affidavits and of their existance could be deemed material and Issue might ordered at any time before final Judgment. The present motion with Liberty to shew at any time before final Judgment that the Caveatee in Justice ought to have a new Trial.

CALEB J. PARKER vs. SARAH LAWSON and others	On Demurres (p 34) It is ordered by the Court that this cause be continued until the next Term of this Court for further argument.
MARY CLICK Serv. and MATHIAS CLICK Serv. Executrix and Executor of HENRY CLICK Dec'd vs. LEWIS CLICK, JOHN COX and FREDERICK AKEARD	In this cause it appearing to the satisfaction of the Court that the appeal in the nature of a Writ of Error was taken before final judgment rendered in the Court below. It is therefore considered by the Court that the appeal be dismissed and that the defendant recover against the plaintiff their costs

in Court expended & that Execution may issue & c.

Court adjourned 'till Court in Course.
Edw. Scott

Monday 7th October 1822 (p35)
At a Circuit Court begun and held for the County of Hawkins at the Court House in Rogersville, on the first Monday of October in the year of our Lord one thousand eight hundred & twenty two and the Forty seventh year of American Independence.
Present - The Honorable Samuel Powel - Judge.

GabrielMcCrow Sheriff of Hawkins County returns into Court his Writ of Venire Facias.
Executed on the following persons to wit, John McWilliams, Absalom Looney, James Johnson, Esqr Isham Mills, George Rogers Esqr Joseph Baker Esqr,

John Burkheart, John Reynolds Esqr. Nicholas Long, Jackson Smith, Hezekiah Hamblen, John Johnston, Edward Lee, Andrew Galbreath, Serv, Samuel Wilson Esqr., Thomas Cocke, Lewis Click, Joel Gillenwaters, Aaron Willimas, Robert D. Young, Thomas Lee, Michael McCann, John Young Senr, John Cockram, George Hale & Jacob B. Groves out of the foregoing Venire Facias the following persons were drawn as Grand Jurors for the present Term, to wit,

1. George Hale
2. Samuel Wilson
3. John McWilliams
4. Absalom Looney
5. Nicholas Long
6. John Johnson
7. Aaron Williams
8. John Cockram
9. Jacob B. Groves
10 Michael McCann
11 Thomas Lee
12 Hezekiah Hamblen
13 Joel Gillenwaters

Whereupon Court appointed George Hale Forman of the Grand Jury (p 36) who were severally sworn and being charged by the Judge withdrew from the Bar.

Jesse Spiers Constable was sworn to attend on the Grand Jury the present Term.

> STATE   )   William Dyche, John Dyche & Robert Lee being bound
> vs.   )   in Recognizance for the appearance of Thomas Lee
> THOMAS LEE)   at this Term surrenders the body of the said Robert

Lee in open Court in discharge of Themselves as Bail for said Thomas Lee. Whereupon the said Thomas Lee was ordered into custody of the Sheriff.

Joseph Baker, Jackson Smith and Lewis Click returned on the Venire Facias as being summoned as Jurors to the present term of this Court and being solemnly called to come into Court and not appearing. It is ordered by the Court that the said Joseph Baker, Jackson Smith and Lewis Click be fined in the sum of Twenty Five dollars each for such their default unless they appear at the next Term of this Court and shew cause why Judgment should not be made final and that Scicre facias issue.

> JOHN DEN LESSEE of)   On affidavit (p 37) of the defendant It is
> ETHELDRED WILLIAMS)   ordered that a Commission issue directed to
> and others   )   any Justice of the peace for Cocke County Tenn-
> vs.   )   essee to take the deposition of David Stuart
> DAVID PROFFIT   )   which deposition when taken to be read in Evi-

dence on the trial of this cause on behalf of the defendant and that ten days notice be given to the plaintiff of the time and place of taking said deposition and that this cause be continued until the next term of this Court.

> JOHN DEN LESSEE of)   On affidavit of the defendant It is ordered by
> WILLIAM WHITESIDES)   the Court that a Commission issue directed to
> vs.   )   any Justice of the peace for Cocke County in
> DAVID PROFFIT   )   the State of Tennessee to take the deposition

of David Stuart which deposition when taken to be read in Evidence on the
trial of this cause on behalf of the defendant and that ten days notice
be given to the plaintiffs of the time and place of taking said depositions
and that this cause be continued until the next term of this Court.

JOHN DEN LESSEE of) This day (p 38) came the parties by their
JOSEPH RUSSELL   ) attornies and thereupon came a Jury to wit,
vs.) Ejectment   ) Samuel Wilson, John McWilliams, Absalom Loo-
ZACHARIAH STACEY   ) ney, Nicholas Long, John Johnson, Aaron Williams, John Cochram, Jacob B. Groves, Michael McCann, Thomas Lee, Hezekiah
Hamblen and Joel Gillenwaters who being elected tried and sworn upon their
oath do say we find that the defendant is Guilty fo the Trespass in Ejectment mentioned and assess the plaintiffs damage to six cents.
On motion of the defendant by his attorney a rule is allowed him to shew
cause why a new trial should be granted.

ARTHUR G. ARMSTRONG) Ordered by the Court that this cause be con-
vs.   ) tinued until the next term of this Court the
JOHN WRIGHT   ) Judge being related to the plaintiff.

MICHAEL McCANN) This cause is continued until the next term of
vs.   ) this court the Judge having been employed as
FRAZIER BRINLEY) counsel.

JOHN DEN LESSEE of) On affidavit (p 39) of the defendants It
FRANCIS DALZELL &) is ordered that this suit be continued un-
WILLIAM SIMPSON   ) til the next Term of this Court.
vs.   )
GEORGE STIPE Senr.)
& GEORGE STIPE Junr.)

JOHN DEN LESSEE of) This day came the parties by their attornies
ROBERT WRIGHT   ) and thereupon came a Jury to wit, Samuel Wil-
vs) Ejectment   ) son. John McWilliams, Absalom Looney, Nich-
SAMUEL FINLEY   ) olas Long, John Johnson, Aaron Williams,, John
Cockram, Thomas Lee, Hezekiah Hamblen, George Rogers, James Johnson and
Isham Mills who being elected tried and sworn are respited from rendering
their Verdict until tomorrow.

The Court adjourned until tomorrow 9 o'clock A. M.
                         S. Powel

Tuesday 8th October 1822 (p 40)
Court met according to adjournment.
Present The Honorable Samuel Powel Judge.

JOHN DEN LESSEE of) On motion of the plaintiffs by their attorney
RUTHERFORD WILLIAMS) It is ordered by the Court that a Commission
and others   ) issue directed to any Justice of the peace of
vs.   ) Grainger County Tennessee to take the deposit-
DAVID PROFFIT   ) ion of Henry Bowen which deposition when taken
to be read in Evidence on the trial of this cause and that ten days notice
be given to the adverse party of the time and place of taking said deposition. And that a Commission issue directed to any Justice of the peace of
McMinn County Tennessee to take the deposition of Thomas Bunch which deposition when taken to be read in Evidence on the trial of this Cause and

that Twenty days notice of the time and place of taking said deposition be given to the defendant, & by consent of the parties the deposition of Thos Bunch to be taken at Joseph Cobbs tomorrow & without notice.

ARCHIBALD McKINNEY)   On motion of the defendant by his attorney.
vs.   )   It is ordered by the Court that a Sub- poena
JOHN McCOY   )   duces tecum issue to Joel Gillenwaters Esqr. o
to bring into open Court immediately the papers in this suit tried before him.

JOHN F. JACK)   Garnishment (p 41)
vs.   )   John Kenndy and Jacob Peck being summoned as Garnish-
JOSEPH CRABB)   es on the Execution issued in this suit returnable
to the present term of this court to appear & c. Now on this day person-ally appeared in open Court John Kennedy and being duly sworn deposeth and saith that he does not owe Joseph Crabb anything nor has he anything in his hands belonging to the said Crabb nor does he know of any property in the hands of any other person belonging to said Joseph Crabb.
Also personally appeared in open Court Jacob Peck and being duly sworn de-poseth and saith that he had undertaken with Joh Crabb that in the event of Joseph Crabb being cost in this suit he said Garnisher would pay Fifty dollars of the cost and further saith that he has never had any of the money or estate of Joseph Crabb in his hands - but cannot gainsay Judg-ment against him for the sum of Fifty dollars. It is therefore considered by the Court that the Plaintiff John F. Jack recover against Jacob Peck the Garnisher the sum of Fifty dollars and also the costs in this behalf expended and be in Mercy & c and that John Kennedy be discharged from his Garnishment.

A Deed of Conveyance from (p 41) William S. Owen and Elizabeth Owen his wife to Ewel Moore for Two hundred and three acres of land was proven in open Court by the oaths of Charles McAnnally, Thomas Cocke and Clem Moore.
Whereupon the Honorable Judge having examined the said Elizabeth Owen separate and apart from her said husband who acknowledged that she did Execute the said deed freely and voluntarily of hew own accord without any threat persuasion or coersion of her said husband. It is therefore ordered by the Court that said deed be registered.

A Deed of Conveyance from William S. Owen and Elizabeth Owen his wife to Ewel Moore for ---- acres of land was proven in open Court by the oaths of Charles McAnnally, Thomas Cocke and Cleon Moore. Whereupon the honor-able Judge having examined the said Elizabeth Owen separate and apart from her said husband who acknowledged that she had Executed the said deed freely and voluntarily of her own accord without any threat, per-suasion or coersion of her said husband. It is therefore ordered by the Court that said Deed be registered.

JOHN BLEVINS   )   The death of Robert Gambill is suggested in abate-
vs.   )   ment of this suit by his attorney.
ROBERT GAMBILL)
& JOHN BEAL   )

JOHN DEN LESSEE of)   This day came (p 42) the parties by their
ROBERT WRIGHT   )   attornies and thereupon came a Jury, to wit,
vs.) Ejectment   )   the same Jury who were respited on yesterday
SAMUEL FINLEY   )   from rendering their verdict came into open

Court and upon their oaths do say we find that the defendant is not Guilty of the Trespass in the declaration of ejectment. It is therefore considered by the Court that the defendant go hence and recover of the Plaintiff his costs by him in this behalf expended and that Execution issue for the same.

WILLIAM BURGESS &	On affidavit of the defendant.
REBECCA BURGESS	It is ordered by the Court that a Commission
his wife	issue directed to any Justice of the peace of
vs.	Green County to take the depositions of Jane
ALEXANDER SEVIER	Russell and Lorinda Russell and that ten days

notice be given to the adverse party of the time and place of taking said deposition and that a Commission issue directed to any Justice of the peace of White County in this State to take the depositions of Joseph Holt and Jesse Lincoln which depositions when taken to be read in Evidence on the trial of this cause and that Twenty days notice be given (p 43) to the adverse party of the time and place of taking said depositions and that this cause be continued until the next Term of this Court.

JOHN DEN LESSEE of	On motion of the plaintiffs attorney.
ETHELDRED WILLIAMS	It is ordered by the Court that a Commission
and others	issue directed to any Justice of the peace of
vs.	--- County in the State of Mississippi to take
DAVID PROFFIT	the deposition of William Cocke which deposit-

ion when taken to be read in Evidence on the trial of this cause and that Forty days notice of the time and place of taking said deposition be given to the adverse party.

JOHN DEN LESSE of	By consent of the parties this cause is contin-
GANDRY & COCKE	ued until the next Term of this Court.
vs.	
JOEL DYER	

A Deed of Conveyance from John Ireland to James Shields for Twenty Six acres of land was proven in open Court by the oaths of John Moore and Gabriel McCraw and was ordered to be registered.

MOSES McCARMEL &	This day (p 44) came the parties by their
the STATE of TENN-	attornies and thereupon came a Jury, to wit,
ESSEE	John Reynolds, John Burkhart, Andrew Galbreath
vs.	Thomas Cocke, John Moore, Preston Blevins,
G. ESKRIDGE KENNER	Thomas Gillenwaters, James L. Etter, William

Armstrong, George Johnson, Samuel N. Bradley, & Robert L. Coreathers who being elected tried and sworn upon their oaths do say we find for the defendant—
On motion of the Plaintiff by attorney a Rule is allowed him to shew cause why a new trial should be granted.

ROSEY DAVIS	The Plaintiffs death being suggested by her attor-
vs.	ney.
WILLIAM CLOUD	It is considered by the Court this suit be revived

in the name of Archibald McCoy administrator & c.

Court Adjourned until tomorrow 9 O'clock A. M.
S. Powel

Wednesday 9th October 1822 (p 45)

Court met according to adjournment.
Present The Honorable Samuel Powel Judge.

A Deed of Conveyance from James Spencer to Francis Gamble for Three hundred and twenty five acres of land was acknowledged in open Court and ordered to be registered.

STATE) Forfeited recognizance.
vs.) This day came the State by the attorney General and
WILLIAM PRYOR) Allen Chumley and David Chumley being bound in recognizance in the sum of Two hundred and fifty dollars each for their personal appearance at the present term of this Court to give Evidence in behalf of the State against William Pryor and being solemnly called to come into Court came not but made default and forfeited their recognizances. It is therefore considered by the Court that the State recover against the said Allen Chumley and David Chumly the sum of Two hundred and fifty dollars each unless they appear at the next term of this Court and shew sufficient cause why this Judgment should not be made final and that Scire Facias issue against them respectively.

ANDERSON HICKS) Petition (p 46) for Divorce.
vs.) In this case the petitioner having heretofore filed
JANE HICKS) his petition praying for a Divorce from the Bands of Matrimony subsisting between him and his wife Jane Hicks and it appearing to the satisfaction of the Court that a Copy of his said Petition had heretofore been served on the said Jane Hicks and she had been regularly served with a subpoena calling on her to appear and answer the said Petition and the said Jane having failed to appear and answer the same and the Court having proceeded to the examination of testimony touching the facts charged in said petition and the Court being fully satisfied from the testimony that the said Jane has been guilty of wilful and malicious absence and desertion from the bed and board of the said Anderson Hicks for more than two whole years next before filing the said petition, the Court being satisfied that the petitioner was a Citizen of the State of Tennessee more than one whole year next before filing his said Petition. It is therefore considered ordered adjudged and Decreed by the Court the the Bonds of Matrimony heretofore subsisting between the said Anderson Hicks and his wife Jane Hicks be and the same is hereby Decreed void annulled and for nothing held and that the said (p 47) Anderson Hicks from his said wife Jane be and he is hereby forever Divorced. It is further ordered by the Court that the petitioner pay the costs in this behalf expended.

JOHN DEN LESSEE of) On motion of the Plaintiff by his attorney a
EDWARD HOWEL) Rule is allowed him to shew cause why the non
vs.) suit entered at the last term of this Court
WILLIAM GRAHAM) in this cause should be set aside and placed
upon the docket for trial.

STATE) Forfeited recognizance
vs.) The defendant William Pryor being bound in Recog-
WILLIAM PRYOR) nizance for his appearance at the lat term of this Court and being solemnly called to come into Court came not and forfeited his recog. and now on this day personally appeared in open Court and prays that the forfeiture entered against him may be set aside and for reasons disclosed in the afficavit of the defendant. It is ordered by the Court

that the forfeiture entered against the said William Pryor at the last term of this Court be set aside on the Payment of costs.

STATE) Forfeited (p 48), Recognizance.
vs.) The defendant John A. McKinney and George Hale
JOHN A. McKINNEY) being bound in recognizance at the last Term of this Court for the personal appearance of William Pryor and being solemnly called to bring into Court the said William Pryor brought him not and forfeited their recognizance and now on this day comes into Court and prays that the forfeiture entered against them may be set aside, and for reasons appearing to the satisfaction of the Court, It is ordered that the forfeiture entered at the last term of this Court against the said John A. McKinney and George Hale be set aside on the payment of costs.

STATE) Forfeited Recognizance.
vs.) This day came the State by the Attorney General
ALLEN CHUMLEY) and Allen Chumly being bound in Recognizance, in the sum One thousand dollars for his appearance to the present term of this Court and being solemnly called to come into Court came not but made default and both forfeited his recognizance. It is therefore considered by the Court that the State recover against the said Allen Chumly the sum of One thousand dollars unless he appears at the next (p 49) Term of this Court and shew sufficient cause why this Judgment should not be made final and that Scire Facias issue against him.
And David Chumly and William Blackburn being bound in recognizance in the sum of One thousand dollars Jointly and severally for the appearance of said Allen Chumley at the present term of this Court and being solemnly called to bring into Court the body of the said Allen Chumly as they were bound to do or they would forfeit their recognizance brought him not but wholly made default. It is therefore considered by the Court that the State recover against David Chumly and William Blackburn the sum of One thousand dollars unless they appear at the next term of this Court and shew sufficient cause why this Judgment should not be made final and that Scire Facias issue against them.
Personally appeared in open Court John A. Aiken and Tristram D. Knight – attornies at law and took the oaths to support the Constitution of the United States of the State of Tennessee and of attornies of this Court and thereupon they were severally admitted to practise as attornies in this Court.

STATE) This day came (p 50) the State by the
vs.)Assault & Battery) attorney General and with leave of the
JAMES M. JACKSON &) Court enters a Nolle Prosequi and there-
ROBERT H. JACKSON) upon James M. Jackson came into open Court
and confesses Judgment for the costs. It is therefore considered by the Court that the said James M. Jackson pay the costs in this behalf expended for which execution may issue.

DANIEL CARMICHAEL) This day came the Plaintiff by his attorney
vs.) and dismisses his suit and thereupon James
JAMES M. JACKSON &) M. Jackson came into open Court and confess-
ROBERT H. JACKSON) es Judgment for the costs. It is therefore
considered by the Court that the Plaintiff recover against the said James M. Jackson his costs by him in this behalf expended and that Execution issue & c.

STATE) This day came the State by the Attorney General and the

vs.   )   defendant in his proper person and having here-
ABSALOM HAWORTH)   tofore been charged on the Bill of Indictment plead
Not Guilty and put himself on the County and now on this day came (p 51) ,
a Jury to wit, George Rogers, John Reynolds, Isham Mills, James Johnson,
Edward Lee, Andrew Galbreath, Thomas Cocke, Nathaniel Henderson, John
Shaugh, Robert Wright, John Mills and Robert Hamilton who being elected
tried and sworn upon their oath do say we find that the defendant is
Guilty in manner and form as charged in the Bill of Indictment.
On motion of the defendant by his attorney a Rule is allowed him to shew
cause why a new trial should be granted.

        STATE   )   This day came the State by the Attorney General and
         vs.   )   the defendant in his proper person and being charged
    GEORGE WOLF)   on the Bill of Indictment pleads Not Guilty and put
himself on the County and now on this day came a Jury to wit, John Mc--
Williams, Absalom Looney, Aaron Williams, Jacob B. Groves, Michael McCann,
Thomas Lee, Benjamin Thurman, Lewis Lawson, Thomas Stacey, William King,
Amis Grantham and Willie B. Kyle who being elected, tried and sworn & progress having been made in the trial of this suit by consent of the parties & with the assent of the Court the Jurors from rendering their verdict are respited until tomorrow.

A Deed of Conveyance (p 52) from Thomas Bray to James Forgey for one
hundred and sixty acres of land lying in Arkansas Territory Military boundary was proven in open Court by the oaths of William Elrod and Jacob
Hipshire and was ordered to be certified.

Court adjourned until tomorrow 9 O'clock A. M.
                    S. Powel

Thursday 10th October 1822.

Court met according to adjournment.
Present the Honorable Samuel Powel Judge.

        STATE   )   This day came the State by the Attorney General and
         vs.   )   the defendant in his proper person and by attorney
    GEORGE WOLFE)   and thereupon the Jury to wit, John McWilliams,
Absalom Looney, Aaron Williams, Jacob B. Groves, Michael McCann, Thomas
Lee, Benjamin Thurman, Lewis Lawson, Thomas Stacey, William King, Amis
Grantham and Willie B. Kyle the same Jury who were on yesterday respited
from rendering their verdict came now into open Court and upon their oaths
do say we find that the defendant is not Guilty in manner and form as
charged in the first and second Count of the Bill of Indictment and the
Jurors aforesaid (p 53) do further say that the defendant is Guilty in
manner and form as charged in the third Count of the Bill of Indictment.
Whereupon the Court fined him five dollars and imprisoned five days and
to remain in custody until fine and costs are paid.

    THOMAS MONAHON & wife)   It appearing to the satisfaction of the Court
         vs.   )   that the parties settled their difference a
    LARKIN WILLIS & wife)   and the plaintiff agrees to pay the Court
charges and his own witnesses. It is therefore ordered by Court this suit
be dismissed, agreeable to the agreement of the parties, - for which Execution may issue.

    STATE)   On affidavit of Gabrial McCraw prosecutor in behalf of the

vs.   )) State. It is ordered by the Court that this suit
WILLIAM PRYOR)   ) be continued until the next term of this Court.
Whereupon John A. McKinney and George Hale being bound in recognizance
for the appearance of William Pryor from day to day at the present term
of this Court surrenders the body of the said William Pryor in open Court
in discharge of themselves as Bail for the said William Pryor was ordered in Custody of the Sheriff.

STATE   ) The rule for (p 54) a new trial came on to be
    vs.   ) heard and after argument of Counsel as well on be-
ABSALOM HAWORTH) half of the State as of the defendant and the premises considered and fully understood. It is considered and adjudged by
the Court that the rule be discharged and that the defendant Absalom Haworth for this his offence be fined Twenty five dollars and be imprisoned
two hours and there to remain until fine and costs are paid.

CATHERINE HOWE) This day came the plaintiff by her attorney and
    vs.   ) dismisses her suit and the defendant assumes the
WILLIAM CLEPPER) costs. It is therefore considered by the Court
that the Plaintiff recover against the defendant her costs by her in this
behalf expended and the defendant in mercy.

JACOB HOWE   ) This day came the plaintiff by his attorney and
    vs.   ) dismisses his suit & the defendant assumes the
WILLIAM CLEPPER) costs. It is therefore considered by the Court
that the Plaintiff recover against the defendant his costs by him in this
behalf expended and the defendant in mercy & c.

JOHN DEN LESSEE of) On affidavit (p 55) of the Plaintiff this cause
WILLIAM BRADLEY) is continued until the next term of this Court
    vs.   ) and that Commission issue directed to any Jus-
THOMAS SPROUL   ) tice of the peace of Hawkins County to take
the deposition of John Burris which Deposition when taken to be read de
bene esse on the trial of this cause and that ten days notice of the time
and place of taking said depositions be given to the defendant.
And on affidavit of the defendant. It is ordered by the Court that a Commission issue directed to any Justice of the peace of Hawkins County to
take the deposition of Jacob Humble which deposition when taken to be read
de bene esse on the trial of this cause and that ten days notice of the
time and place of taking said deposition be given to the defendant.

E. EMBREE surviving) By consent of the parties by their attornies
partner E. EMBREE) this cause is continued until the next term
    vs.   ) of this Court and it agreed by the parties
AMIS GRANTHAM and) that the deposition of Luke Lea filed at the
others   ) present Term of this Court be read in Evidence on the trial of this cause.

GEORGE JOHNSON) This day came (p 56) the parties by their attor-
    vs.   ) nies and thereupon came a Jury, to wit, George Ro-
JOHN SHOUGH &   ) gers, John Reynolds, Isham Mills, John Burkheart,
JAMES Y. LONG   ) James Johnson, Edward Lee, Thomas Cocke, Moses Mc-
Ginnis, Jesse Patrick, Eppy Everett, John Sproul and Samuel U. Bradley who
being elected tried and sworn upon their oath do say we find that the note
in the plaintiffs declaration mentioned was executed by the defendants for
Gambling consideration as in their pleadings they have alledged. It is

therefore considered by the Court that the Plaintiff take nothing by his Writ but for his false clamor be in mercy and that the defendants go hence without day and recover against the Plaintiff their costs by them about their suit in this behalf expended and that Execution issue accordingly.

ARCHIBALD McCOY
?Admr & c of ROSEY
DAVIS
vs.
WILLIAM CLOUD

By consent of the parties It is ordered by the Court that this suit be refered to the arbitration of Charles McAnnally and Cleon Moore with leave to choose and umpire and their award returned under their hands and seals to be the Judgment of this Court and that the depositions taken heretofore be read as evidence on said arbitration.

SAMUEL REYNOLDS
and others
vs.
JOHN A. ROGERS

This day came (p 57) the parties by their attornies and thereupon came a Jury, to wit: George Rogers, John Reynolds, Isham Mills, John Burkheart, James Johnson, Edward Lee, Samuel Spiers, Francis Leeper, Lewis Sturgeon, George Moses, George Johnson, and Robert Brice who being elected tried and sworn, upon their oaths do say we find that the defendant did not assume and undertake in manner and form as the plaintiff hath complained as by pleadings he hath alledged. It is therefore considered by the Court that the plaintiffs take nothing by their Writ but for their false Clamor be in mercy and that the defendant go hence without day and recover against the plaintiffs his costs by him in this behalf expended and that Execution issue accordingly. Whereupon the Plaintiffs by their attorney moved for a rule to shew cause why a New Trial should be granted which is allowed by the Court.

WILLIAM CRUMLY
vs.
JOHNSON FRAZIER

By consent of the parties by their attornies this cause is continued until the next Term of this Court and it is agreed that this cause stand for trial on the Thursday of said Term.

E. EMBREE surviving
partner of E. & E.
EMBREE
vs.
AMIS GRANTHAM and
others

By consent (p 58) of the parties by their attornies. It is ordered by the Court that a commission issue directed to any Justice of the peace of Murray County Tennessee to take the deposition of John McKinney Junr and that a Commission issue directed to any Justice of the peace of White County Tennessee to take the deposition of William Roberts Junr that a Commission issue directed to any Justice of the peace of Lee County in the State of Virginia to take the depositions of William H. Carter, Thomas Roberts and Danswell Rogers and that a Commission issue directed to any Justice of the peace of Scott County in the State of Virginia to take the deposition of George George which depositions when taken to be read in Evidence on the trial of this cause on behalf of the defendants and that Thirty days notice of the time and places of taking said depositions be given.

A Deed of Conveyance from Ewel Moore to Sterling Cocke for Forty five acres of land was acknowledged in open Court and ordered to be registered.

THOMAS JOHNSON
vs.
JACOB HACKNEY

On affidavit (p 59) of the defendant. It is ordered by the Court that this cause be continued until the next Term of this Court and that the defendant pay all the costs up to the present time including the costs of this Term for which Execution may issue & c.

JOHN O. BRIAN Admr & c of JOHN CALDWELL Dec'd vs. JOHN H. DUNN & WILLIAM YOUNG	By consent of the parties this cause is continued until the next Term of this Court.

Court adjourned until tomorrow 9 O'clock A. M.
> S. Powel

Friday October 11th, 1822.

Court met according to adjournment.
Present the Honorable Samuel Powel-Judge.

A Deed of Conveyance from Gabriel McBran Sheriff of Hawkins County to Asabel Johnson for Four hundred acres of land was acknowledged in open Court and was ordered to be registered.

A Deed of Conveyance from (p 60) Charles McAnnally sheriff of Grainger County to John Cocke for one hundred and eighty eighty acres of land was acknowledged in open Court and was ordered to be registered.

JOHN COCKE & JOHN F. JACK vs. MOSES McGINNIS Admr of LAWRENCE STONE Dec'd	By consent of the parties this cause is continued until the next Term of this Court and by consent. It is ordered by the Court that a Commission issue directed to any Justice of the peace of Grainger or Claibourne County to take the depositions of George Evans, Sally Evans, Roda

Evans, George A. Bowen, Thomas Bowen, Bluford Woodall, Rachel Woodall, John Sanders, Henry Hipshire, Isaih Paine, John McPheeters and John Collins on behalf of the Plaintiffs which depositions when taken to be read in Evidence on the trial of this cause and that Five days notice of the time and place of taking said depositions be given to the adverse party. And by consent of the parties. It is ordered by the Court that a Commission issue directed to any Justice of the peace of Grainger County to take the depositions of Susannah Campbell on behalf of the defendant and that ten days notice of the time and place of taking said deposition be given to the Plaintiff and the depositions of Benjamin Craighead, John Bunch Senr, Coley Rucker, Wm. Rucker, George Coffee and Elender Malicote (p 61) and that five days notice of the time and place of taking said depositions be given to plaintiffs and that a Commission issue directed to any Justice of the peace of Claibourne County to take the deposition of John Neill and that ten days notice be given to the plaintiff of the time and place of taking said depositions a Commission issue directed to any Justice of the peace of Washington County Virginia to take the deposition of Peter J. Branch and Joseph C. Trigg and that he give the adverse party twenty days notice, also that a Commission issue to any Justice of the peace of Sullivan County to take the deposition of Daniel Rogan in behalf of the Defendant by giving the adverse party Ten days notice and that this cause be continued until next Term of this Court.

JOHN DEN LESSEE of EDWARD HOWEL	This day the Plaintiff by his attorney came into open Court and the rule allowed at a former day

vs.   ) of this Term for reinstating this cause and pra-
WILLIAM GRAHAM) ducing two afficavits and after hearing the argument of plaintiffs said attorney and it appearing to the Court that the
plaintiff was at the last Term regularly non suited. It was therefore
considered that the rule be discharged and that the Defendant recover of
the Plaintiff the costs of this Motion.

SAMUEL REYNOLDS &) This day came the parties by their attornies
others   ) and thereupon came a Jury, to wit. George Hale
vs.   ) Samuel Wilson, John McWilliams, Absalom Looney,
JAMES HAGAN   ) & the deposition of Charles Payne, Jonathon
Barnard, James Asbury and James Mullins which deposition when taken to
be read in Evidence on the trial of this cause on behalf of the defendant
and that Five days notice of the time and place of taking said depositions be given to the Plaintiffs.

STATE   ) Upon affidavit of Defendant this cause is continued
vs.   ) until the next Term of this Court.
EDWARD McCOY)

STATE   ) On motion of Thomas L. Williams attorney for Defts a
vs.   ) and for Reasons appearing to Court. It is ordered
GEORGE WOLFE) by the Court that the balance of time for which the
defendant was imprisoned be released and that he give security for the
fine and costs Whereupon Moses McGinnis came into open Court and enters
himself security for the fine and costs. It is therefore considered by
the Court that the State recover against George Wolfe and Moses McGinnis
his security the sum of Five dollars the fine before mentioned together
with the costs of this suit, and that Execution may issue.

ABSALOM B. TRIGGS) On motion (p63) of Plaintiff by his attorney.
vs.   ) It is ordered by the Court that Nicholas Long,
JOHN LYNN   ) Aaron Williams, John Cochram, Jacob B. Groves,
Thomas Lee, Joel Gillenwaters, John Moore and Willie B. Kyle who being
elected tried & sworn upon their oath do say we find that the Defendant
did assume and take upon himself in manner and form as the plaintiff against him has complained, and we assess the plaintiff damage by reason
of the non performance of said assumpsit to two hundred and ninety five
dollars and twenty nine cents, besides costs. Whereupon on motion of
the Defendant by his attorney A Rule is granted to shew cause why said
Verdict in this case should be set aside.

STATE   ) This day came the Defendant in his proper person
vs.   ) and being charged on the Bill of Indictment pleads
JACOB HIPSHIRE) Guilty and submits to the mercy of the Court.
Whereupon it is considered by the Court that the Defendant for this his
offence be fined three dollars and pay the costs in this behalf expended
& be held in custody until the fine and costs are paid or security given
therefor. Whereupon Henry Hipshire came into Court and offers himself as
Security for the fine and costs in this case and is accepted by the Court.
It is therefore considered by the Court that the State recover against
the Defendant and Henry Hipshire his security three dollars the fine a-
foresaid and also the costs in this behalf expended and that Execution
issue accordingly.

ROBERT NALL) Slander (p 64)

VS.   ) This day came the parties by their attornies and there
JOHN S. HILL)   upon came a Jury, to wit, Isham Mills, John Reynolds,
John Stokely, Robert Brice, George Myers, Isaac Laudeback, William Phipps,
Benjamin Thurman, James Johnson, Daniel Lipe, William Lyons and Jesse How-
ell who being elected, tried & sworn, well and truly to try the issues
Joined and progress having been made in the trial of this cause, the jur-
ors by the consent of the parties and with the assent, of the Court from
rendering their verdict are respited until tomorrow.

The Court adjourned until Tomorrow 9 O'clock.
                    S. Powel

Saturday 12th October 1822

Court met according to adjournment.
Present The Honorable Samuel Powel- Judge.

JOSEPH ROGERS)   By consent of the parties. It is ordered by the
    vs.   ) Court that a Commission issue directed to any Just-
JESSE HOWEL)   ice of the peace of this County to take the deposition of Thomas Barrat Junr on behalf of the defendant to be read de bene
esse on the trial of this cause and that he give the plaintiff Ten days
notice of the time and place of taking said deposition and that this cause
be continued until the next Term of this Court.

THOMAS JOHNSON)   By consent (p 65) of the parties - it is ordered
    vs.   ) by the Court that a commission issue directed to
JACOB HACKNEY)   any Justice of the peace of Augusta in the State of
Georgia to take the deposition of Polly Liggins on behalf of the defendant
and that Thirty days notice of the time and place of taking said deposition
be given and that a Commission issue directed to any Justice of the peace
of Greene County, Tennessee to take the depositions of Andrew Stephens and
William Kilgore on behalf of the defendant and that he give ten days notice of the time and place of taking said Depositions.

JOHN A. ROGERS   ) On motion of the Plaintiff by his Attorney
    vs.   ) to renew the order made at the last term of
SAMUEL WILSON Junr.) this Court to take the depositions of Fran-
) cis H. Gaines and John Morriset at St Ste-
JOHN A. ROGERS   ) phens Alabama and of William Henry Harrison
    vs.   ) at Cincinnati in the State of Ohio. It is
ELI BOYKIN   ) therefore considered by the Court that the
) said several orders in these suits be renew-
JOHN A. ROGERS   ) ed.
    vs.   )
WILLIAM COBB   )

JOHN A. ROGERS   ) On affidavit (p 66) of the defendant.
    vs.   ) It is ordered by the Court that a Commission
SAMUEL WILSON Junr.) issue, directed to any Justice of the peace
of McMinn County in the State of Tennessee to take the deposition of Robert Renfro to be read in Evidence on the trial of this cause and by consent of the Plaintiff it is ordered that he give ten days notice of the
time and place of taking said deposition.

ELIJAH C. GILLEMWATERS) This day came the Plaintiff by his attorney

Assr of MICHAEL) and the defendant in his proper person. And Jos-
McCANN   ) eph Bishop the defendant withdraws his certi va
  vs.) and confesses Judgment for the sum of Five hundred
JOSEPH BISHOP) and sixty three dollars and the costs of this suit.
It is therefore considered by the Court that the Plaintiffs recover against
the defendant Joseph Bishop and Samuel Wilson and Larkin Willis his securities the sum of Five hundred and Sixty three dollars and also the costs
in this behalf expended as above confessed and that execution issue accordingly.

  JOHN A. McKINNEY) This day came the plaintiff and dismissed his suit
   vs.   ) and the defendant in his proper (p67) person
  JOSEPH BISHOP) and confesses Judgment for the costs. It is therefore considered by the Court that the Plaintiff recover against the defendant his costs by him in this behalf expended and that execution issue accordingly.

  JOHN A. ROGERS) On affidavit of the defendant. It is ordered by
   vs.) the Court that a Commission issue directed to any
  ELI BOYKIN) Justice of the peace of McMinn County in the State
of Tennessee to take the deposition of Robert Renfroe to be read in Evidence on the trial of this cause, and by consent of Plaintiff it is ordered that ten days notice be given of the time and place of taking said deposition.

  JOHN A. ROGERS) On affidavit of the defendant. It is ordered by
   vs.) the Court that a Commission issue directed to any
  WILLIAM COBB) Justice of the peace of McMinn County in this State
to take the deposition of Robert Renfroe to be read in Evidence on the trial
of this cause and by consent of the Plaintiff it is ordered that ten days
notice be given of the time and place of taking said deposition.

  JOSEPH MORRISET) By consent of the parties. It is ordered by the
   vs.) Court that a Commission issue directed to any Jus-
  OLIVER JENKINS) tice of the peace of Hawkins County to take the
deposition (p 68) of John Callihan to be read de bene esse on the trial
of this cause on behalf of the defendant and that he give five days notice
of the time and place of taking said deposition.

  JOHN DEN LESSE) For reasons appearing to the Court it is or-
  of THOMAS BROOKE) dered by the Court that a Commission issue
   vs.   ) to any Justice of the peace to take the de-
  JACOB & THEAS FARRIS) positions of Thomas Johnston, Thomas Lopping-
ton and Hawsen Kenner to be read de bene esse in behalf of the defendant
and that the defendant give the Plaintiff Ten days notice of time and place
of taking said Depositions.

  MICHAEL McCANN) On motion of the Plaintiff by his attorney. It
   vs.) is ordered by the Court that a former order enters
  FRAZIER BRINDLEY) in this cause to take the deposition of William
Kirk be renewed and that a Commission issue accordingly.

  JOHN A. ROGERS) By consent of the parties. It is agreed by the par-
   vs.) ties That this suit be referred to the arbitration
  SAMUEL WILSON) of three men to be chosen by George Hale and William Lyons, and the award of those three men to be chosen by the said George

Hale and Wm/ Lyons returned into open Court at the next Term to be made the Judgment of the Court.

A Deed of Gift from John (p 69) Long to John Looney, Azariah Looney, Joseph M. Looney, Matilda Looney and Absalom Looney for a negro woman & four children was proven in open Court by the Oaths of James Y. Long and Nancy D. Long and was ordered to be registered.

BENJAMIN STUART ? By consent of the parties. It is order-
vs.) ed by the Court that a Commission issue
ROBERT W. GILLENWATERS) directed to Francis Dalzell esquire or
Hezekiah Hamblen to take the deposition of Thomas Lappington de bene esse the deposition to be taken at the house of said Francis Dalzell esquire, this evening.

JOHN PRYOR) By consent of the parties by their attornies. It
vs) is ordered by the Court that a Commission issue
PETER FRANKLIN) to any Justice of the peace for the County of
Hawkins to take the deposition of Duncan McCakl & Malcolm M. Phail de bene esse five days notice to the adverse Party shall be good and that a Commission to any Justice of the Peace for Sullivan County to take the deposition of Richard Netherland five days notice shall be good served on the adverse party.

JOHN A. ROGERS) On affidavit of the defendant. It is ordered
Vs.) that a Commission issue directed to any Jus-
SAMUEL WILSON Junr.) tice of the peace of Bledsoe County in this
State (p 70) to take the deposition of John Monahon to be read in Evid-ence on the Trial of this cause and that Twenty days notice of the time and place of taking said Deposition be given.

JOHN A. ROGERS) On motion of the defendants by their attornies
vs.) to renew the several orders made at the October
SAMUEL WILSON) Term 1821 and renewed at last Term for taking
*) depositions in these suits. It is therefore
JOHN A. ROGERS) considered by the Court that the said several
vs.) orders made at said Term of said Court be again
ELI BOYKINS) renewed and that Commissions issue accordingly.
) And that a Commission issue directed to any Jus-
JOHN A. ROGERS) tice of the peace of Warren County in this state
vs.) to take the deposition of John Hacket to be read
WILLIAM COKE) in Evidence on the Trial of this cause and that
Twenty days notice of the time and place of taking said deposition be given to tje Plaintiff.

MOSES McCONNEL &) The rule for a new trial came on this day to
the state of TENN-) be argued and after argument of Counsel as
ESSEE) well for as against the rule and the premises
vs.) fully (p 71) understood. It is therefore
C. ESKRIDGE KENNER) considered by the Court that the rule be made
absolute and a New Trial Granted. And on motion of the Defendant by his attorney. It is ordered by the Court that a Commission issue directed to any Justice of Hawkins County or to any Justice of the peace of Logan County Kentucky to take the deposition of James Bootman if taken in Hawkins County five days notice and if taken in Logan County Thirty days notice shall be deemed sufficient.

SAMUEL REYNOLDS) This day came the Rule for a new Trial to be heard
and others) and after argument of Counsel had thereon. It is
vs.) considered that the rule be discharged and that
JOHN A. ROGERS) the Defendant go hence without day and recover against the Plaintiff his costs by him in this behalf expended and that execution issue accordingly.

SAMUEL REYNOLDS) The rule for a new trial came on to be heard and
and others) argument had thereon and the plaintiff by his at-
vs.) torney comes into open Court and releases forty
JAMES HAGAN) four dollars eighty (p 72) eight cents of the
Verdict. It is therefore considered by the Court the rule be discharged
and that the plaintiff recover of the defendant the sum of Two hundred and
fifty dollars forty four cents being the balance of the damages found by
Jury together with the costs by them in this behalf expended and the defendant in mercy & c.

STATE) The rule for a new Trial this day came on to be
vs.) heard and after argument of Counsel had thereon
ABSALOM HAWORTH) as well for the rule as against it and the premises considered. It is ordered by the Court that the rule be discharged.
Whereupon the defendant by his attorney tenders his Bill of Exceptions &
prays the same may be signed and sealed which is done accordingly and made
part of the record and prays an appeal in the nature of a Writ of Error
to the Supreme Court of Errors and appeals to be held at the Court House
in Rogersville the first Monday of May next and entered into Recognizance
for his appearance & c and the appeal.

ROBERT NALL) Slander (p 73)
vs.) This day came the parties by their attornies and
JOHN S. HILL) thereupon came the Jury to wit, Isham Mills, John
Reynolds, John Stokeley, Robart Brice, George Myers, Isaac Lauderback, William Phipps, Benjamin Thurman, James Johnson, Daniel Carmichael, William
Lyons & Jesse Howel being the same Jury that were on Yesterday respited
from rendering their Verdict upon their oaths do say we find the defendant
guilty of speaking the words as the plaintiff against him hath complained
and we further find that the defendant was well Justified in speaking and
publishing the words charged in the declaration mentioned as by pleading
be both alledged. It is therefore considered by the Court that the Plaintiff take nothing by his Writ but for his false clamor be in mercy & c
and that (p 74) the defendant go hence without day and recover against
the plaintiff his costs by him about his suit in this behalf expended and
that Execution issue accordinglyl

JOHN A. ROGERS) On affidavit of the defendants. It is or-
vs.) dered by the Court that Commissions issue
SAMUEL WILSON Junr.) directed to any Justice of the peace of
) Shelby County in the State of Alabama to
JOHN A. ROGERS) take the depositions of Thomas Bailey for
vs.) each of the defendants in their suits to
ELI BOYKIN) be read in Evidence on the trial of these
) causes and that Forty days notice be given
JOHN A. ROGERS) of the time and place of taking said de-
vs.) positions.
WILLIAM COBB)

ISHAM REYNOLDS) This day came the plaintiff by his attorney and

& wife) filed his declaration and Caleb J. Parker one of
 vs.) the defendants in this suit being solemnly called
JOHN GRIGSBY &) to come into Court and defend the suit or Judg-
CALEB J. PARKER) ment would be entered against him by default came
not. It is therefore considered by the Court that the Plaintiff recover
against (p 75) the defendant the debt in the declaration mentioned to be
enquired of by a Jury at the next term of this Court.

JOHN DEN LESSEE of) The rule entered in this cause came on to be
JOSEPH RUSSELL) ~~argued~~ and after argument of Counsel thereon
 vs.) as well for as against said Rule and the pre-
ZACHARIAH STACEY) mises fully considered and understood. It is
ordered that said Rule be discharged. It is therefore considered by the
Court that the plaintiff recover of the defendant his term yet to come together with his damages by the Jury assessed and the costs in this behalf
expended and the defendant in mercy & c. Whereupon the defendant by his
attorney tenders a Bill of Exceptions which is signed and sealed and ordered to be made part of the record and prays an appeal in the nature of
a Writ of Error to the Supreme Court of Errors and appeals to be held at
the Court House in Rogersville on the first Monday of May next gave hand
& security and the appeal by the Court Granted all causes on the docket
are continued until the next Term of this Court.

Court adjourned until the Court in Course.
    S. Powel

Monday April 7th, 1823.

At a Circuit Court begun (p 76) and held for the County of Hawkins at the
Courthouse in Rogersville on the first Monday of April in the year of four
Lord One thousand eight hundred and twenty three and the forty seventh year
of American Independence.
Present the Honorable Edward Scott, Judge.

The Clerk of this County produced in open Court the Treasurers receipt for
the State Tax by him collected from the first day of October 1821 to this
30th day of September 1822 agreeably to an act of Assembly in such case
made and provided.

ARCHIBALD McCOY) By consent of the parties by their attornies.
admr of ROSEY) It is ordered by the Court that the rule of re-
DAVIS Dec'd) ference made at the last term of this Court be
 vs.) set aside.
WILLIAM CLOUD) The parties having entered into the following
agreement, to wit.
We Archibald McCoy & William Cloud – By a mutual agreement hath compromised
a suit pending in the Circuit Court of Hawkins County wherein Archibald Mc-
Coy administrator of Rosanna Davis Deceased was plaintiff and William Cloud
defendant By the said defendant paying to the said Plaintiff the estimation
of the wheat thirty Bushels and one half at Sixty-two and one half cts pr
Bushel and the defendant pay all lawful costs excepting the costs in case
(p 77) of the depositions from the Alabama State – the plaintiff McCoy
pays that costs. Given under our hands and seals this 4th day of April 1823.
        Archibald McCoy (seal)
Attest: Moses McGinnis Wm. Cloud (seal)
It is therefore considered by the Court that the plaintiff recover against
the defendant the sum of nineteen dollars six a fourth cents and also the

costs in this behalf expended except the costs that have accrued in taking the depositions in the State of Alabama. And it is further considered by the Court that the defendant recover against the plaintiff the costs that accrued as above stated agreeable to the aforesaid article of Agreement and that Executions issue accordingly.

Gabriel McCraw Sheriff of Hawkins County returns now here into Court one Writ of Venire Facias execution on the following persons to wit, Joseph McCullough Esq., Hezekiah Hamblen, John Johnson, Moses McGinnis, Orville Rice, John Reynolds, Samuel Wilson, Isaac Lauderback, Jacob Miller, Joel Gillenwaters, James Johnson, Jacob B. Groves, Robert D. Young, Michael McCann, William Nichols, Lewis Click, George Rogers, Larkin Willis, Joshua Smith, Thomas Stacey, Reuben Barnard, James Francisco, William Armstrong Esq., Samuel Chestnutt, William Smith & Arthur G. Armstrong from among whom the following persons were drawn as Grand Jurors for the present Term, to wit:

1. Moses McGinnis
2. John Johnson (p 78)
3. Joel Gillenwaters
4. Isaac Lauderback
5. George Rogers
6. Robert D. Young
7. Samuel Chestnut
8. Michael McCann
9. Jacob B. Groves
10 William Smith
11 John Reynolds
12 Jacob Miller &
13 William Nichols

Whereupon the Court appointed Jacob Miller Foreman of the Grand Jury who were severally sworn & being charged by the Judge withdrew from the Bar.

Robert W. Gillenwaters Constable was sworn as Officer to attend on the Grand Jury during the present term.

JANE WILLIAMS)	On motion of the plaintiff by her attorney
vs.) Certiorari)	a rule is allowed him to shew cause why the
WILLIAM THURMAN)	Certiorari should be dismissed.

THOMAS SIMS)	On motion of the plaintiff by his attorney a
vs.) Certiorari)	rule is granted to shew cause why the certior-
AMIS GRANTHAM)	ari should be dismissed.

A Deed of Trust from John Longmiller to William Hagood for a tract of land for the benefit of Francis Leeper was acknowledged in open Court and was ordered to be registered.

ARTHUR G. ARMSTRONG)?	This day (p 79) came the parties by their
vs.) Covt.)	attornies and thereupon came a Jury, to wit,
JOHN WRIGHT)	Samuel Wilson, Lewis Click, Larkin Willis,

Reuben Barnard, Joseph McCullough, James Johnson, James J. Wilson, Hiram Charles, Robert H. Jackson, James Breeden, John Gibbons and George Argenbright who being elected tried and sworn. Whereupon the said Plaintiff although solemnly demanded comes not nor doth he further prosecute his writ. Whereupon the said Jurors are Wholly discharged from giving any Verdict of and upon the premises aforesaid. Therefore it is considered

by the Court here that the said Plaintiff take nothing by his Writ aforesaid and for his false clamour by in mercy & c and that the defendant go
hence without day and recover of the plaintiff the costs in this behalf
expended and the plaintiff in mercy & c.
On motion of the plaintiff by his attorney a rule is granted to shew cause
why the non suit should be set aside.

JOHN DEN LESSEE of WILLIAM BRADLEY vs. THOMAS SPROUL	This cause is continued until the next Term of this Court.

JOHN DEN LESSEE of CONDRY & COCKE vs. JOEL DYER	By consent of the parties this cause is continued until the next Term of this Court.

ISHAM REYNOLDS & wife   By consent (p 80) of the parties by their
vs.   attornies. It is ordered by the Court that
JOHN GRIGSBY and   the Judgment by default entered at the last
CALEB J. PARKER   term of this Court against Caleb J. Parker
one of the defendants in this suit be set aside and that he have leave to
plead so as not to delay trial.

JOHN COCK admr of   This day came the parties by their attornies
HENRY HOWEL Dec'd   and the reasons in arrest of Judgment having
vs.   come on new to be argued and the Court having
GEORGE EVANS   heard argument of Counsel as well in behalf
as against it and being fully advised thereon do consider that said reasons in arrest of Judgment be over ruled. It is therefore considered by
the Court that the plaintiff recover against the defendant the sum of
Eight hundred and eighty two dollars Seventy three cents the damages by
the Jurors aforesaid at the April Term 1821 of this Court together with
the costs in this behalf expended and the defendant in Mercy & c. From
which Judgment the defendant by attorney prays an appeal in the nature of
a Writ of Error to the next Supreme Court of Errors and appeals to be held
at the Courthouse in Rogersville on the first Monday of May next.

ETHEL'D WILLIAMS &   On affidavit (p 81) of the defendant this
others   cause is continued until the next term of this
vs.   Court and by consent of the parties by their
DAVID PROFFIT   attornies. It is ordered by the Court that a
Commission issue directed to any Justice of the peace of Hawkins County
to take the deposition of Thomas Bunch to be read in Evidence on the trial
of this cause on behalf of the Plaintiff and it is agreed by the parties
that said Deposition may be taken at the office of the Clerk and Master
in Equity, this evening.

JOHN DEN LESSEE of WILLIAM WHITESIDES vs. DAVID PROFFIT	On affidavit of the defendant this cause is continued until the next term of this court.

JOHN A. ROGERS   On motion of the plaintiff by his attorney. It is
vs.   ordered by the Court that he have leave to amend
WILLIAM COBB   the replication to the second plea of the defendant.

The Court adjourned until tomorrow 8 O'clock A. M.
                                    Edw. Scott.

Tuesday 8th April 1823 (p 83)

Court met according to adjournment.
Present The Honorable Edward Scott Judge.

JOHN BLAIR'S Executors)   On afficavit of the defendant this cause
          vs.   )   is continued until the next term of this
THOMAS BLACKBURN   )   Court and it is ordered by the Court that
a Commission issue directed to any Justice of the peace of Monroe County
Tennessee to take the deposition of George C. Harris and that a Commission issue directed to any Justice of Greene County to take the deposition of Daniel Coffman and that a Commission issue directed to any Justice
of the peace of Blount County to take the depositions of Joshua Parsons
and Elijah Ellis to be read in Evidence on the trial of this cause on behalf of the defendant and that he give the Plaintiffs Ten days notice of
the time and place of taking said depositions.

MOSES McCONNELL and   )   Gregory Smith who had been heretofore sum-
    the STATE of TENNESSEE)   moned as a Witness on behalf of the plain-
          vs.   )   tiffs in this suit and being solemnly call-
E. ESKRIDGE KENNER   )   ed came not but made default. Therefore
on motion of the Plaintiffs by their attorney. It is considered by the
Court that the plaintiffs recover against the said Gregory Smith the sum
of one hundred and twenty five dollars agreeable to an act of Assembly in
such case mand and (p 83) provided unless sufficient cause of his disability to attend be shown at the next Term of this Court after notice of
this Judgment.

MOSES McCONNELL and   )   Christion Morell who had heretofore been
    the STATE of TENNESSEE)   summoned as a witness on behalf of the
          vs.   )   plaintiffs in this suit and being solemn-
B. ESKRIDGE KENNER   )   ly called came not but made default.
Therefore on motion of the plaintiffs by their attorney. It is considered by the Court that the plaintiffs recover against the said Christion
Morell the sum of one hundred and twenty five dollars, agreeable to an
act of Assembly in such case made and provided unless sufficient cause
of his disability to attend be shown at the next Term of this Court after
notice of this Judgment.

MOSES McCONNELL and   )   Hezekiah Hamblen who has heretofore been
    the STATE of TENNESSEE)   summoned as a Witness on behalf of the
          vs.   )   plaintiffs in this suit and being solemn-
C. Eskridge Kenner   )   ly callen came not but made default.
Therefore on motion of the plaintiffs by their attorney. It is considered by the Court that the plaintiffs recover against the said Hezekiah Hamblen the sum of One hundred and twenty five dollars agreeable to an Act
of Assembly in such case made and provided unless sufficient cause of his
disability (p 84) to attend be shown at the next Term of this Court
after the notice of this Judgment.

MOSES McCONNELL and   )   William Reynolds who had heretofore been
    the STATE of TENNESSEE)   summoned as a Witness on behalf of the

vs.   )   plaintiffs in this suit and being solemnly call-
C. ESKRIDGE KENNER)   ed came not but made default. Therefore on motion of the plaintiffs by their attorney. It is considered by the Court
that the plaintiffs recover against the said William Reynolds the sum of one
hundred and twenty five dollars agreeable to an act of Assembly in such case
made and provided unless sufficient cause of his disability to attend be
shown at the next Term of this Court after notice of this Judgment.

JOHN PRYOR   )   On affidavit of the Plaintiff, this cause is contin-
vs.   )   ued until the next Term of this Court and that a Com-
PETER FRANKLIN)   mission issue directed to any Justice of the peace
in the State of Georgia, Albama or in Tennessee to take the deposition of
Malcomb McPhail to be read in evidence on the trial of this cause on behalf
of the Plaintiff and that Thirty days notice of the time and place of taking
said deposition be given to the adverse party.

MICHAEL McCANN)   On afficavit (p 85) of the Plaintiff this cause
vs.   )   is continued until the next term of this Court and
FRAZIER BRINLEY)   it is ordered that the order entered in this cause
on a former term of this Court to take the deposition of William Kirk be
renewed and that a Commission issue accordingly.

THOMAS JOHNSON)   On affidavit of the Plaintiff this cause is contin-
vs.   )   ued until the next term of this Court and that a Com-
JACOB HACKNEY)   mission issue directed to any Justice of the peace
of Madison County in the State of Alabama to take the depositions of John
Johnson and William Burket to be read in evidence on the trial of this cause
on behalf of the Plaintiff and that Thirty days notice of the time and place
to taking said deposition be given to the defendant. And on motion of the
defendant by his attorney. It is ordered by the Court that the order entered at the last term of this Court in this cause to take the depositions of
Andrew Stephens and William Kilgore be renewed and that a Commission issue
accordingly.

A Deed of Conveyance from Thomas Johnson by Asabel Johnson his attorney in
fact to Lewis Milam for One hundred and fifty acres of land was acknowledged in open Court and was ordered to be registered.

JOHN DEN LESSEE of)   By consent (p 86) of the parties this cause is
FRANCIS DALZELL   )   continued until the next Term of the Court.
     vs.   )
GEORGE STIFE Senr &)
GEORGE STIFE Junr.)

MOSES MCCONNELL and   )   This day came the parties by their attornies
the STATE of TENNESSEE)   and thereupon came a Jury, to wit, Samuel
     vs.   )   Wilson, Larkin Willis, Lewis Click, William
C. ESKRIDGE KENNER   )   Armstrong, Peter Franklin, Jacob Wax, George
Argenbright, John Wills, Charles Stuart, Thomas Roberts, Elijah Gillenwaters,
& Fleming B. Evans who being elected tried and sworn and progress having been
made in the trial of this cause and the Jurors having retired from the box to
consult of their verdict returned now here into Court and by the consent of
the parties by their attornies and with the assent of the Court a Juror is
with drawn and the rest of the Jurors from rendering their verdict in this
case are discharged and this cause ordered to stand continued until the next
Term of this Court.

THOMAS HAMBLEN)   By consent of the parties by their attornies this

vs.) cause is continued until the next Term of this Court.
JOHN HAMBLEN)

JOHN DEN LESSEE of) This (p 87) day came the plaintiff in his pro-
THOMAS BROOKS) per person and dismisses his suit and assumes
  vs) Ejectment) the costs. It is therefore considered by the
JACOB FARRIS and) Court that the defendants go hence without
LENCAS FARRIS   ) day and recover against the Plaintiff their
costs by them in this behalf expended and that Execution issue accordingly.

STERLING COCKE) This day came the Plaintiff in his proper person
  vs.   ) and dismisses his suit and the defendant assumes
CHARLES STURAT) the costs. It is therefore considered by the Court
that the plaintiff recover against the defendant his costs by him about
his suit in this behalf expended and the defendant in mercy & c.

BENJAMIN STURRT) This day came the parties by their attor-
  vs.   ) nies and thereupon came a Jury, to wit,
ROBERT W. GILLENWATERS) Lewis Click, William Armstrong, Lencas
Farris, James J. Wilson, John Beal, Robert Crawford, Timothy D. Hunt,
John Stokeley, Jacob Crew, James M. Jackson, Robert Carden and Levi Painter who being elected tried and sworn and progress having been made in
the trial of this cause (p 88) the Jurors from rendering their verdict
are respited until tomorrow.

JACOB SEAVERS) This day came the parties by their attornies
 vs.) det issue) and thereupon came a Jury, to wit, Reuben Bar-
MARY CROWBARGER) nard, Joseph McCullough, James Johnson, Orville
Rice, Thomas Stacey, Daniel Carmichael, William Davis, John Reese, James
Breeden, Abraham Vernon, William McClure, and Willie B. Kyle who being
elected tried and sworn upon their oath do say we find that the defendant does detain from the plaintiff as he against her in his declaration
has complained a negro male Slave named Gilbert worth Five Hundred dollars, one negro male slave named Samuel worth Five Hundred dollars, one
negro female slave named Eliza worth Three Hundred dollars and one male
Slave named William worth Two hundred dollars amounting in the whole to
One thousand nine hundred dollars and we assess the plaintiffs damage by
reason of the detention thereof to Two hundred and fifty dollars besides
costs and we find that the negro woman named Dalsa has deceased since the
Commencement of this action and we further find that the right of action
did accrue within three years next before the suing out of the original
Writ. Whereupon on motion of the defendant by her attorney a rule is
allowed to (p 89) shewwcause why a new Trial should be granted.

Court adjourned until tomorrow 8 O'clock A. M.
       Edw. Scott

Wednesday 9th April 1823.

Court met according to adjournment.
Present The Honorable Edward Scott, Judge.

JOHN PRYOR) On affidavit of the Plaintiff. It is ordered by
  vs.   ) the Court that a Commission issue directed to any
PETER FRANKLIN) Justice of the peace of Sullivan County to take the
depositions of Philip S. Hale and Duncan McCall to be read de bone esse

on the trial of this cause and Ten days notice of the time and place of taking said depositions to be given to the adverse party.

This day appeared in open Court Robert L. Careathers and produced his License to practise as an attorney in the several Courts of Law and Equity of this State and took the oaths required by law and was admitted as an attorney of this Court.

This day appeared in open Court Aaron Finch and produced his License to practise as an attorney in the several Courts of Law and Equity of this State and took the oaths required by law and was admitted as an attorney of this Court.

BENJAMIN STUART) This day (90) came the parties by their
     vs.) attornies and thereupon came the same Jury
ROBERT W. GILLENWATERS) that was on yesterday respited from rendering their verdict, to wit, Lewis Click, William Armstrong, Leneas Farris, James J. Wilson, John Beal, Robert Crawford, Timothy D. Hunt, John Stokeley, Jacob Crew, James M. Jackson, Robert Carden, and Levi Painter who being elected tried and sworn upon their oath do say we find that the defendant is Guilty of the Trespass in manner and form as the plaintiff against him in his declaration has complained and further find that he was not Justified as in pleading he has alledged and assess the plaintiffs damage to One hundred and twenty nine dollars and sixty five cents besides costs. On motion of the defendant by his attorney a Rule is allowed him to shew cause why a New Trial should be granted.

JOHN A. ROGERS) By consent of the parties these suits are re-
     vs.) ferred to the arbitration of George Hale and
ELI BOYKIN) William Lyons and Robert L. Careathers and their
) award returned into Court under their hands
JOHN A ROGERS) and seals to be the Judgment of this Court.
     vs.)
SAMUEL WILSON Senr.)

STATE) Assault and Battery (p 91)
    vs.) appeal) This day came the state by the Attorney General and
THOMAS HALE) the defendant in his proper person and by attorney and being charged on the Bill of Indictment plead Guilty and submits to the Mercy of the Court. Whereupon the Court being fully advised thereon do consider that the defendant for such his offense be fined in the sum of Fifty dollars and to pay the costs in this behalf expended and held in custody until fine and costs are paid or Security given therefor. Whereupon Samuel Lee and Jonathon White came into open Court and offer themselves as Security for the fine and costs in this suit. It is therefore considered by the Court that the State recover against the said Thomas Hale and Jonathon White and Samuel Lee his securities the sum of Fifty dollars the Fine aforesaid and also the costs of this prosecution and that Execution issue accordingly.

ARCHIBALD McKINNEY) This day came the parties by their attorneys
     vs.) and thereupon came a Jury, to wit, Reuben Bar-
JOHN McCOY) nard, Joseph McCullough, James Johnson, Orville Rice, Thomas Stacey, James Steel, James Nugent, Joseph Bishop, William Giddens, Francis Leaper, Joseph Flora and Wright Bond who being elected, tried and sworn and progress having been (p 92) made in the trial of this

cause the Jurors from rendering their verdict are respited until tomorrow.

STATE	)	Forfeited Recognizance.
vs.	)	This day came the State by the Attorney General and
WILLIAM PRYOR	)	William Pryor being bound in recognizance in the sum

of Five hundred dollars for his personal appearance to the present term of this Court and being solemnly called to come into Court came not but made default and hath forfeited his recognizance. It is therefore considered by the Court that the State recover against the said William Pryor the sum of Five hundred dollars unless he appears at the next term of this Court and shews sufficient cause why this Judgment should not be made final and that Scire Facias issue against him.

The Court adjourn until Tomorrow 8 O'clock.
Edw. Scott

Thursday 10th April 1823.

Court met according to adjournment.
Present The Honorable Edward Scott Judge.

A Deed of relinquishment from John A. McKinney to Isham Mills for Four hundred acres of land was acknowledged in open Court and was ordered to be registered.

THOMAS HAMBLEN	)	On affidavit (p 93) of John A. McKinney attorney
vs.	)	for the defendant. It is ordered by the Court that
JOHN HAMBLEN	)	a Commission issue directed to any Justice of the

peace of Morgan County Alabama to take the deposition of Sarah Bishop and that a Commission issue directed to any Justice of the peace of Giles County Tennessee to take the deposition of James Ford to be read in evidence on the trial of this cause on behalf of the defendant and that Thirty days notice to Alabama and Twenty days in this state be given to the plaintiff of the time and place of taking said depositions.

The Sheriff returned Isham Mills summoned as a Juror and being solemnly called came not and for this his offence. It is ordered by the Court that he be fined Two dollars and fifty cents and that Execution issue for the same.

The Sheriff returned William Brice summoned as a Juror and being solemnly called to come into Court came not and for this his offence. It is ordered by the Court that he be fined Two dollars and fifty cents and that Execution issue for the same.

WILLIAM BURGESS &	)	This cause is continued until the next
REBECCA BURGESS his wife	)	term of this Court as on affidavit of
vs.	)	the Plaintiff.
ALEXANDER SEVIER	)	

ARCHIBALD McKINNEY	)	This day (p 94) came the parties by their
vs.) appeal	)	attornies and thereupon came the same Jury that
JOHN McCOY	)	was on yesterday respited from rendering their

verdict to wit, Reuben, Barnard, Joseph McCullough, James Johnson, Orville Rice, Thomas Stacey, James Steel, James Nugent, Joseph Bishop, William Giddens, Francis Leeper, Joseph Flora and Wright Bond came now into open Court and upon their oaths do say we find for the defendant. It is therefore considered by the Court that the defendant go hence without day and recover against the plaintiff & John A. McKinney his security his costs by him in this behalf expended and that Execution issue accordingly.

An assignment on a platt and certificate of Survey for Twelve acres of land from Gabriel McCrow to Abraham Vernon was acknowledged in ipen Court and was ordered to be certified.

An assignment on a platt and certificate of Survey from Gabriel McCrow to Absalom Kyle for Ten acres of land was acknowledged in open Court and was ordered to be certified.

An assignment on a plot and certificate of Survey from Richard Mitchell to William Davis for Thirty acres of land was acknowledged in open Court and ordered to be certified.

ABRAHAM B. TRIGG) This day (p 95) came the parties by their att-
vs.   )   ornies and thereupon came a Jury, to wit, Isaac
JOHN LYNN   )   Lauderback, Michael McCann, Moses McGinnis, Samuel Chestnut, Robert D. Young, William Smith, George Rogers, William Nic-
chols, John Reynolds, Joel Gillenwaters, John Johnson and Jacob B. Groves
who being elected tried and sworn upon their oaths do say we find that the
defendant did not expressly assume in manner and form as the plaintiff against him hath complained as by pleading he hath alledged. It is therefore considered by the Court that the Plaintiff take nothing by his Writ
but for his false clamor be in mercy and that the defendant go hence without day and recover against the plaintiff his costs by him in this behalf
expended & that Execution issue accordingly.

The Sheriff having returned William Carmack as being summoned on the Traverse Jury and being solemnly called to come into court came not. It is
therefore considered by the Court that the said William Carmack for this
his offenxe be fined Two dollars and fifty cents & that Execution issue
& c.

A Deed of Conveyance from Isham Mills to Lewis Mitchell for Four hundred
acres of land was acknowledged in open Court and was ordered to be registered.

JOHN BLAIRS Executors) This day (p 96) came the parties by their
vs.   )   attornies and thereupon came a Jury, to wit,
THOMAS BLACKBURN   )   Lewis Click, Larkin Willis, William Armstrong,
Jacob Crews, James Dodson, Robert Hamilton, Elijah C. Gillenwaters, William Patterson, Spencer Acuff, Lewis Mitchell, Jacob Wax and John Critze
who being elected tried and sworn upon their oath do say we find that the
defendant did pay and satisfy the amount of the Judgment and costs in the
Scire Facias mentioned to John Blair deceased in his lifetime and before
the issuing of the Scire facias in this cause as by pleading he hath alledged. It is therefore considered by the Court that the Defendant go hence
without day and recover against the Plaintiffs his costs by him in this behalf expended and that Execution issue accordingly.

LIJAH KINCHELOE) This day came the parties by their attornies and
vs.) No 1)   there upon came a Jury, to wit, Reuben Barnard,
JOHN A. ROGERS)   Joseph McCullough, James Johnson, Orville Rice,

Thomas Stacey, Joseph Lackey, James M. Jackson, James L. Etter, Michael Harrel, James J. Wilson, William Martin and James Murrel who being elected tried and sworn upon their oath do say we find that the defendant hath not kept and performed the condition of the obligation (p 97) in the declaration mentioned as by pleading he hath alledged and assess the Plaintiffs damage to seven hundred and fifty dollars besides costs. On motion of the defendant by his attorney a rule is allowed him to shew cause why a new trial should be granted.

HOUSEN KENNER) This day came the parties by their attornies and
vs.) appeal) thereupon came a Jury, to wit, Isaac Louderback,
LEWIS STURGEON) Moses McGinnis, Samuel Chestnut, William Smith, George Rogers, William Nichols, John Johnson, John Reynolds, Samuel Wilson, Lewis Click, Larkin Willis and William Armstrong who being elected, tried and sworn upon their oath do say, we find for the defendant. It is therefore considered by the Court that the defendant go hence without day and recover against the plaintiff & Peter Parsons his Security his costs by him in this behalf expended and that execution issue accordingly.

JOHN A. ROGERS) By consent of the parties and with leave of the
vs.) Court this suit is referred to the arbitration of
ELI BOYKIN) George Hale, William Lyons and Michael McCann and their award returned into Court under their hands and seals to be the Judgment of this Court and that the order of reference made in this suit on yesterday be set aside.

LIJAH KINCHELOE) Edward (p 98) Erwin Surgoine who had heretofore
vs.) been summoned as a Witness on behalf of the defen-
JOHN A. ROGERS) dant in this suit and being solemnly called to come into Court came not but made default therefore on motion of the defen- by his attorney. It is considered by the Court that the defendant recover against the said Edward E. Surgoine the sum of One hundred and twenty five dollars agreeable to an act of assembly in such case made and provided un- less sufficient cause of his disability to attend be shewn at the next Term of this Court after notice of this Judgment.

Robert D. Young a Grand Juror for the present term being solemnly called to come into Court and serve on the Traverse Jury came not. It is there- fore considered by the Court that the said Robert D. Young for this his offence be fined Two dollars and fifty cents and that Execution issue acc- ordingly.

JOHN A. ROGERS) This cause is continued until the next Term of this
vs.) Court as an affidavit of defendant.
WILLIAM COBB)

The Court adjourn until tomorrow 8 O'clock.
Edw. Scott.

Friday 11th April 1823 (p 99)

Court met according to adjournment.
Present The Honorable Edward Scott Judge.

LYDIA COOPER an infant) This day came the parties by their attor-
who sues by CHRISTOPHER) nies and thereupon came a Jury, to wit.

COOPER her Father)   Isaac Lauderback, Moses McGinnis, Samuel Chest-
& next friend   )   nut, William Smith, William Nichols, George Ro-
    vs.   )   gers, John Johnson, John Reynolds, Lewis Click
WILLIAM MALONEY)   Larkin Willis, Samuel Wilson and William Armstrong who being elected tried and sworn. Whereupon the Plaintiff by his
attorney says he will not further prosecute this suit. Therefore it is
considered by the Court that the plaintiff be non suited and that the defendant go hence without day and recover against the plaintiff his costs
in this behalf expended and that Execution issue accordingly.

WILLIAM HORD   )   Scire Facias.
    vs.   )   This day came the parties by their attornies and
JOHN WALLEN admr)   therefore came a Jury, to wit. Isaac Lauderback,
of ELISHA WALLEN)   Moses McGinnis, Samuel Chestnut, William Smith,
Dec'd   )   William Nichols, George Rogers, John Johnson,
John Reynolds, Lewis Click, Larkin Willis, Reuben Barnard and Joseph McCullough who being elected tried and sworn upon their oath do say we find that
the defendant has not paid (p 100) the debt in the Scire Facias mentioned
as in pleading he has alledged. Therefore It is considered by the Court
that the plaintiff have Execution against the proper goods and chattels
lands and tenements of John Wallen for the sum of Four hundred & forty
dollars and fifty cents the amount of the Judgment in the Scire Famias mentioned with One hundred and fifty dollars and forty five cents being the
amount of costs mentioned in the Scire Facias and also the costs on this
Scire Facias.

JOSEPH X? STAPLETON)   This day came the plaintiff by his attorney
    vs.   )   and dismisses his suit and thereupon the de-
JOHN A. ROGERS   )   fendant comes into open Court in his proper
person and confesses Judgment for the sum of Forty two dollars and Sixty
two and a half cents and costs. It is therefore considered by the Court
that the Plaintiff recover against the defendant the sum of Forty two dollars and Sixty two and a half cents as above confessed and also the costs
by him in this behalf expended and that execution issue accordingly.

JOSEPH ROGERS)   On affidavit of John A. McKinney defendants attorney
   vs.   )   this cause is continued until the next Term of this
JESSE HOWEL)   Court.

JOHN DEN LESSEE)   (p 101) On motion of the plaintiff by his att-
of ETHELDRED   )   orney. It is ordered by the Court that a Com-
WILLIAMS & others)   mission issue directed to any Justice of the
   vs.   )   peace of Grainger County to take the deposit-
DAVID PROFFIT   )   ion of Charles McAnnally to be read de bene
esse on the trial of this cause and that Five days notice of the time and
place of taking said deposition be given to the adverse party.

JAMES JONES CAVEATOR)   This day came the parties by their attornies
    vs.   )   and thereupon came on for argument the ques-
ANDREW PHID CAVEATEE)   tion of Law arising on the issues of fact found by the Jury in this case and argument of counsel having been heard as
well on the part of the Plaintiff as Defendant and the premises being by
the Court here fully considered and understood and it appearing to the satisfaction of the Court that No Grant ought to Issue on so much of the entry
and survey of the Caveatee in said proceeding set forth as is covered by
the Grant from the state of North Carolina to James Jones also the Grant

from the State of Tennessee to James Jones mentioned in the Caveat of the said Jones. It is therefore considered by the Court that no grant issued in so much of the entry and survey of Andrew Reid the Caveatee as is covered by said two Grants, to the said James Jones (p 102) the Caveator. And it is further considered by the Court that the plaintiff James Jones recover of the defendant and Joseph Hamilton and John Kennedy his Securities his costs by him in this behalf expended in this Court and the County Court for which Execution may issue.

On affidavit. It is ordered by the Court that the fine of Two dollars and fifty cents assessed against Robert D. Young on yesterday be set aside on the payment of costs for which Execution may issue.

FRANCIS SMITH) Scire Facias.
vs.) This cause having come on to be heard and
NIMROD PORTER Sheriff) finally determined and the Court having seen
of MANRY COUNTY) and inspected the Scire Facias of the plain-
tiff and demurer of the defendant thereto and argument of counsel being heatd on both sides because it appears that the Writ of Scire Facias is not suffiecient to enable the plaintiff to maintain his action. It is therefore considered by the Court that the demurrer of the defendant be sustained and it is further considered by the Court that the defendant go hence without day and recover of the plaintiff his costs in this and the County Court expended and that Execution issue accordingly.

JOHN A. ROGERS) By consent (p 103) of the parties and with the
vs.)) assent of the Court this cause is referred the Ar-
ELI BOYKIN) bitration of William Lyons, George Hale and Rob-
ert L. Careathers and their award returned into Court under their hands and seals to be the Judgment of this Court and that the order of Refer-ence made in this suit on Yesterday be set aside.

JOHN DEN LESSEE of) On affidavit of John A. McKinney the plaintiffs
WILLIAM BRADLEY) attorney. It is ordered by the Court that a
vs.) Commission issue directed to any Justice of the
THOMAS SPROUL) peace of Hawkins County to take the deposit-
ions of John Burris and John Marshall to be read de bene esse on the trial of this cause and that a commission issue directed to any Justice of the peace of McMinn County to take the deposition of Govr Joseph McMinn and that five days notice in Hawkins County and ten days notice in McMinn Co-unty be given to the defendant of the time and place of taking said de-positions.

MICHAEL PEARSON) On affidavit of Peter Elrod the plaintiffs agent
vs.) this cause is continued until the next Term of
THOMAS JOHNSON) this Court.

JOHN COCKE &) This day (p 104) came the parties by their
JOHN F. JACK) attornies and thereupon came a Jury to wit,
Vs.) Joseph McCullough, James Johnson, William
ROBERT McGINNIS) Nichols, John Reynold, George Rogers, Will-
admr of LAWRENCE STONE) iam Smith, Isaac Lauderback, Samuel Chest-
Dec'd) nut, Reuben Barnard, Lewis Click, Thomas
Stacey and Larkin Willis who being elected tried and sworn upon their oath do say we find on the first plea that the defendant di assume in manner and form as charged in the declaration and on the third plea find that the

defendant has not fully administered as in pleading he has alledged and that
he has not fully administered all the assests that have come to his hands
and that he has not right to retain said assets & that he has assets in his
hands to the amount of seven hundred and two dollars, and we assess the
plaintiffs damage to Seven hundred and two dollars besides costs. It is
therefore considered by the Court that the plaintiffs recover against the
defendant the sum of Seven hundred and two dollars the damages aforesaid
by Jurors aforesaid assessed and also the costs by them about this suit
in this behalf expended to be levied of the assests so found as foresaid
in the hands of the administrator for whidh execution may issue.

ARTHUR G. ARMSTRONG)   This day the (p 105) rule granted on a for-
       vs.   )   mer day of the present Term to set the non
   JOHN WRIGHT   )   suit entered in this case having come on to
be argued and the Court being fully advised thereon having maturely considered that said rule be discharged.

ABRAHAM B. TRIGG)   On motion of the plaintiff by his attorney a rule
      vs.   )   is allowed him to shew cause why a new trial sh-
   JOHN LYNN   )   ould be granted which after argument of Counsel
is discharged. In the progress of the trial of this cause a Bill of Exceptions having been tendered by the Plaintiffs attorney was signed sealed and ordered to be made a part of the record and an appeal in the nature of a Writ of Error and assigned errors to the Supreme Court of Errors
and appeals to be held for the first Judicial circuit at the Court House
in Rogersville on the first Monday in May next being now prayed by the
plaintiff was granted by the Court he having entered into bond with Security according to law.

JOSEPH MORRISET)   This cause is continued until the next Term of
     vs.   )   this Court as on affidavit of the defendant.
   OLIVER JENKINS)

WILLIAM WHITE)   Appeal (p 106)
     vs.   )   In this cause the Court having seen and inspected
   JOHN A ROGERS)   the records of the County Court in this behalf and
being fully advised thereon and on motion of the plaintiff by his attorney.
It is considered by the Court here that the Judgment of the County Court
in this behalf be affirmed. It is therefor considered by the Court here
that the appeal be dismissed and that the plaintiff recover of the defendant John A. Rogers and Peter Parsons his security the sum of Thirty five
dollars the amount of the Judgment before the Justice together with the
costs in this behalf expended and that Execution issue accordingly.

JOHN KING & others)   On motion of the plaintiff by his attorney.
      vs.   )   It is ordered by the Court that a Commission
   WILLIAM ALEXANDER)   issue directed to any Justice of the peace
of Henry County in the State of Virginia to take the depositions of John
Redd, Waller Bedd, John Waller and Lewis Franklin to be read in evidence
on the trial of this cause and that Thirty days notice of the time and
place of taking said depositions be given to the defendant. And on motion
of the defendant by his attorney It is ordered by the court that a Commission issue directed to any Justice of the peace of Henry County Virginia
(p 107) to take the deposition of Thomas Sterling on behalf of the defendant and that Thirty days notice of the time and place of taking said
deposition be given to the plaintiff.

On motion, it is ordered by the Court that the fines of Two dollars and fifty cents assessed against Isham Mills, William Brice and William Carmack be set aside on the payment of the costs for which executions may issue.

STATE) It appearing to the satisfaction of the Court on the
vs.) affidavit of George A. Bowen that he had proved at a
GEORGE WOLFE) former term of this Court his attendance as a witness in this suit and that the clerk had neglected to enter the same of record. It is therefore considered by the Court that the said George A. Bowens attendance be now entered of record and that the clerk tax the same in the Execution. Whereupon the said George A. Bowen proves Four days and Fifty six miles travelling to and from Court.

JOHN KING & others) This cause is continued until the next term
vs.) of this Court as an affidavit of the defend-
WILLIAM ALEXANDER) ant.

JAMES FORD and) (p 108) Demurrer
PHILIP SANDERS) This day came on to be heard the demurrer
vs.) in this cause and after argument of Counsel
RICHARD G. WATERHOUSE) had thereon,, and the premises considered
and others) and fully understood. It is ordered that
the demurrer be sustained and that the defendant have leave to answer over again.

Court adjourned until tomorrow 9 O'clock A. M.
                                        Edw. Scott

Saturday 12th April 1823.

Court met according to adjournment.
Present The Honorable Edward Scott, Judge.

This day appeared in open Court Michael McCann and produced his licence to practise as an attorney in the several Courts of law and Equity of this State and took the oaths required by law and was admitted as an attorney of this Court.

CONDRY and COOK) On affidavit of Richard Mitchell agent for defend-
vs.) ant. It is ordered by the Court that a Commission
JOEL DYER) issue directed to any Justice of the peace of
Grainger County to take the deposition of James Blair, Alexander Blair, and Joseph Cobb on behalf of the defendant and that ten days notice of the time and place of taking said depositions be given to the plaintiffs.

LIJAH KINCHELOE) On affidavit (p 109) of the defendant it is or-
vs.) dered by the Court that a Commission issue direct-
JOHN A. ROGERS) ed to any Justice of the peace of Shelby County in the State of Alabama to take the deposition of William Burket on behalf of the defendant and that Thirty days notice of the time and place of taking said Deposition be given to the plaintiff.

JAMES SUTTON) On motion of the Defendant by his attorney. It is
vs.) ordered by the Court that the plaintiff give Sec-
JOSEPH LACKEY) urity for the prosecution of this suit on the first

day of next Term or the same shall be dismissed.

JOHN A. ROGERS) On motion of the plaintiff by his attorney.
vs.) It is ordered that an order made at a former
WILLIAM COBB) Term of this Court for taking the depositions
) of Francis Faines and John Morriset in Alabama
and) and William H. Harrison of Cincinnati in Ohio
) be renewed and that Commissions issue accord-
JOHN A. ROGERS) ingly.
vs.)
SAMUEL WILSON Jr.)

ARCHIBALD McKINNEY) By consent of the parties by their attornies
vs.) this cause is continued until the next Term
LIJAH KINCHELOE) of this Court.

THOMAS SIMS) This day came (p 110) the parties by their attor-
vs.) nies and argument of Counsel on both sides being
AMIS GRANTHAM) heard and the Court having inspected the record of
the Judgment in this cause in the County Court and the premises being by
the Court fully considered and understood. It is considered by the Court
that the Judgment of the County Court be in all things affirmed and the
Writ of Certiorari be dismissed and that the plaintiff recover against
the defendant Amis Grantham and John A. Rogers and Gabriel McCraw his securities the sum of Twenty seven dollars and eighty four cents being the
amount of the Judgment of the Court and twelve and an half per cent on
said the amount of said Judgment together with his costs in this and the
County Court expended for which Execution may issue.

JOHN A. ROGERS) On motion of the plaintiff by his attorney.
vs.) It is ordered by the Court that a Commisssion
ALEXANDER FINLEY) issue directed to any Justice of the peace for
Washington County in the State of Virginia to take the deposition of Edward Campbell on behalf of the plaintiff and that Twenty days notice of
the time and place of taking said deposition be given to the adverse
party.

JOHN COCKE and) In this (p 111) cause the defendant prays an
JOHN F. JACK) appeal from the Judgment of the Court to the Su-
vs.) preme Court of Errors and Appeals to be held
ROBERT McGINNIS) for the first Judicial Circuit at the Courthouse
admr of LAWRENCE) in Rogersville on the first Monday of May next
STONE Dec'd) gave bond and security according to law and the
appeal by the Court granted.

LIJAH KINCHELOE) The rule for a new trial having come on to be
vs.) heard and after argument of Counsel as well for
JOHN A. ROGERS) as against said rule and the premises considered
and fully understood. It is ordered by the Court that the rule be made
absolute and a New trial Granted, and on motion of the plaintiff by his
attorney leave is given him to amend the replication which is amended and
filed accordingly.

NANCY A. BARKER) On affidavit of William Barker agent for the de-
vs.) fendant. It is ordered by the Court that a Com-
LANGLEY S. HALL) mission issue directed to any Justice of the peace

of St Clair County Alabama to take the deposition of Thomas M. Barker on behalf of the plaintiff and that Thirty days notice of the time and place of taking said deposition be given to the adverse party.

JAMES JONES)   In the progress (p 112) of this case the defendant
vs.) Caveat)   by his attorney Tendered a Bill of exceptions and
ANDREW REED)   prayed that it might be sealed and signed, and made
a part of the Record in this suit which was done. And thereupon the defendant by attorney comes into Court and prayed an appeal in the nature of a Writ of Error to the Supreme Court of errors and appeals to be held at Rogersville on the first Monday in May next and gave Bond and security for the prosecution thereof and the Appeal by the Court Granted.

JANE WILLIAMS)   This day came the parties by their attorneys and
vs.)   argument of Counsel on both sides being heard
WILLIAM THURMAN)   and the Court having inspected the record of the
Judgment in this cause in the County Court and the premises being by the Court fully understood it is considered by the Court that the Judgment of the County Court be in all things affirmed and the Writ Certiorari be dismissed and that the plaintiff recover against the said William Thurman and Charley P. Miller and Cornelius Carmack his security the sum of Twenty five dollars and four cents being the amount of the Judgment of the Court below and twelve and an half per cent on the amount of said Judgment together with his costs in this and the County Court expended for which execution may issue. In this cause the defendant read the affidavit of Elisha Thurman and David Long taken in this Court to support his petition.

JAMES WHITE)   This day (p 113) came the plaintiff by his
vs.)   attorney and filed his declaration and Absa-
ABSALOM LOONEY &)   lom Looney one of the defendants in this cause
JOHN LAUGHMILLER)   being solemnly called to come into Court and
admr of FRED'K)   defend the suit or Judgment would be entered
LAUGHMILLER Dec'd)   against him by default came not. It is there-
fore considered by the Court that the Plaintiff recover against the defendant according to his declaration and that a Jury come here at the next Term of this Court to enquire what damages the plaintiff hath sustained.

BENJAMIN STUART)   This day came on to heard the rule for a
vs.)   New Trial in this cause and after argu-
ROBERT W. GILLENWATERS)   ment of Counsel thereon as well for as
against the rule and the premises considered and fully understood. It is ordered that the rule be made absolute and a New Trial granted.

JACOB SEAVERS)   This day came on to be heard the rule for a new
vs.)   Trial in this cause and after argument of Coun-
MARY CROWBARGER)   sel as well for as against the rule and the pre-
misses considered and fully understood. It is ordered by the Court the rule be discharged. In the progress of the trial of this cause a Bill of exceptions was (p 114) signed and sealed by the Court and made part of the record in this cause and reasons in arrest of Judgment filed & overruled. And thereupon prayed an appeal in the nature of a Writ of Error to the Supreme Court of Errors and Appeals to be held at the Courthouse in Rogersville on the first Monday May next gave bond and security according to law and the appeal by the Court granted.

JOHN A. ROGERS) Demurrer

vs.) This day came the parties by their attornies
SAMUEL WILSON Junr.) and the demurrer of the plaintiff to the third
plea of the defendant came on for argument and argument of Counsel being
heard hath on the part of the plaintiff and defendant and the premises considered and fully understood. It is considered by the Court that the said
third plea of the defendat and the matters and things therein contained are
not good and sufficinet in law and the demurrer to said third of the defendnat be sustained.

COUNTY OF HAWKINS) This cause is côhtânued until the nest Term of
vs.) this Court for argument on the rule to dismiss
THOMAS JOHNSON) the Certiorari.

CALEB J. PARKER) This cause is continued until the next Term for
vs.) further argument.
SARAH LAWSON &)
others)

HENRY SHROEDER & Son) This day (p 115) Jacob Hackney comes into
for the use SCHLEY &) Court in his proper person and confesses
SHROEDER) Judgment for the sum of Four hundred and
vs.) Debt) twenty two dollars and seventy five cents
JACOB HACKNEY) and the costs. It is therefore considered
By the Court that Henry Shroeder and Son for the use of Schley and Shroeder recover of Jacob Hackney the sum of Four hundred and twenty two dollars and seventy five cents and the costs in this behalf expended as above
confessed and that execution issue accordingly.

JAMES W. HILL) This cause having come on to be heard and finally
vs.) determined and the Court having seen and inspect-
GEORGE JOHNSON) ed the record of the proceedings assignment of
& others) Errors and plea of the defendant and heard argument of Counsel as well on behalf of the plaintiff as defendant and it
appearing to the satisfaction of the Court that there is error in the record and proceedings of the County Court of Hawkins. It is therefore considered by the Court that the Judgment of said Court be reversed, annulled and for nothing held and that the cause be set down for Trial on this
Docket & that said Hill recover of the defendants his costs by him in this
Court expended and that Execution issue accordingly.

LIHAH KINCHELOE) On motion (p 116) of the plaintiff by his att-
vs.) orney leave is given him to amend the replication
in the JOHN A. ROGERS) in this suit upon payment of all the costs occ-
asioned there by.

JOHN A. ROGERS) This cause having come on to be heard and finally
vs.) determined & the Court having seen and inspected
PEGGY SURGOINE) the record of the proceeding and after argument
Admr of JAMES) thereon and the premises considered and fully un-
SURGOINE Dec'd) derstood. It is therefore considered by the Court
that the Judgment of Court below be in all things affirmed and it is further considered by the Court that the defendant go hence without day and
recover of the plaintiff and James Bradley and Peter Parsons his securities her costs by her in this behalf expended and that execution issue
accordingly.

JOHN COCKE Admr of) In this cause the plaintiff by his attorney moved

HENRY HOWEL, Dec'd)   the Court to strike out the prayer for an appeal
     vs.   )   made in this cause because no bond and security
GEORGE EVANS   )   was given to prosecute said appeal which the
Court refused to do.

JAMES FORD and   )   The plea (p 117) in abatement having been
PHILIP SANDERS   )   overruled on a former day of this term and
     vs.   )   on motion. It is ordered by the Court that
RICHARD G. WATERHOUSE)   the defendants pay all the costs up to this
& others   )   term including this Term for which Execution may issue & c.

JOHN WRIGHT   )   Scire Facias.
     vs.   )   In this cause a Demurrer to the Scire Facias of the
JOHN A. ROGERS)   plaintiff having been filed and said demurrer having come on to be argued and the Court having heard argument of Counsel
thereon and the premises considered and fully understood. It is considered by the Court that the Demurrer be overruled and that the plaintiff recover of the defendant the sum of Ten dollars and twenty five cents of the
amount of the costs of the suit James Livsey against John Wright according to the Scire Facias made known together with the costs in this behalf
expended for which Execution may issue.

JOHN SHOUGH   )   This cause is continued until the next term of this
     vs.   )   Court for argument.
JAMES SPENCER)

JACOB MEFFORD   )   This cause (p 118) having come on to be
Assee of WILLIE   )   heard and finally determined and the Court
B. KYLE for the   )   having seen and inspected the record and
use of ROBERT HAMILTON)   the matters being heard and fully under-
     vs.   )   stood.
GEORGE WHITE Consta-)   It is therefore considered by the Court
ble and JOHN G. WIN-)   that the plaintiff recover of the defend-
STON and ROBERT CARDEN)   ant and Jonathon Long their security the
his securities & JON-)   sum of Thirty eight dollars seventy two
ATHAN LONG Sect'y for)   and a fourth cents being twelve and a
appeal   )   half per cent thereon and also eight sev-
en and an half cents the costs before the Justice together with the costs
in this behalf expended and that execution issue accordingly.

Court adjourned till Court in Course.
           Rdw. Scott.

Monday 6th October 1823 (p 119)

At a Circuit Court begun and held for the County of Hawkins at the Courthouse in Rogersville on the first Monday being the 6th day of October in
the year of our Lord one thousand eight hundred and twenty three and the
forty eighth year of American Independence.
Present the Honorable Edward Scott - Judge.

Gabriel McCrow Sheriff of Hawkins County returns into Court one Writ of Venire Facias Executed upon the following persons to wit. Jacob B. Groves,
Jacob Groves, Lewis Click, Dickerson Thurman, Samuel Wilson, William Bradley, Isham Mills, Thomas Cocke, Absalom Kyle, Hezekiah Hamblen, David Mc-

Annally, Andrew Galbreath, Benjamin Davis, Jesse Cobb, Samuel Riggs, John Johnston, Isaac Lauderback, Daniel Carmichael, Willie B. Kyle, Orville Rice, Thomas Armstrong, James Francisco, John S. Wells, Robert McMinn, and John Mitchell from among whom the following persons were drawn as Grand Jurors for the present Term, to wit.

1. John Johnston - foreman
2. John S. Wells
3. Isaac Lauderback
4. Samuel Riggs
5. Thomas Armstrong
6. Daniel Carmichael
7. Lewis Click
8. Samuel Wilson
9. Jacob B. Groves
10 John Mitchell
11 Hezekiah Hamblen
12 David McAnnally
13 Jacob Groves

who were severally sworn and being charged by the Judge withdrew from the Bar.

Robert W. Gillenwaters (p 120) Constable was sworn as Officer to attend on the Grand Jury during the present Term.

This day appeared in open Court Thomas Emerson and produced his licence to practise as an attorney in the several Courts of law and Equity of this State and took the oaths required by law and was admitted as an attorney of this Court.

A Deed of Conveyance from Thomas Johnson, by ASAhel Johnson his Att'y in fact to John Davis for Thirty six and an half acres of land was acknowledged in open Court and ordered to be registered.

A Deed of Conveyance from Thomas Johnson by Asahel Johnson his attorney in fact to John David for Twenty six acres of land was acknowledged in open Court and ordered to be registered.

THOMAS HAMBLEN) This day came the Plaintiff by his attorney and
     vs.   ) with leave of the Court dismisses his suit.
JOHN HAMBLEN) It is therefore considered by the Court that the defendant go hence without day and recover of the plaintiff his costs by him in this behalf expended and that Execution issue accordingly.

JOHN M PRESTON   ) This day (p 122) came the Plaintiff by his
     vs.   ) attorney and dismisses his suit and confess-
STOCKLEY D. MITCHELL) es Judgment for all the Costs except the attorneys fee. It is therefore considered by the Court that the defendant recover of the plaintiff his costs in this behalf expended except the attorneys Tax fee for which Execution may issue.

MARY MORRISET) This day came the plaintiff in her proper person
     vs.   ) and dismisses her suit and confesses Judgment for
JOSEPH MORRISET) all the costs except the costs of defendant witnesses, and the defendant by his attorney comes and confesses Judgment for the costs of his Witnesses. It is therefore considered by the Court the defendant go hence and recover of the Plaintiff the costs as above confessed and that the Plaintiff recover of the defendant the costs of his own

witnesses for which Execution may issue.

JOHN DEN LESSEE of)   This day came the parties by their attornies
ETHELDRED WILLIAMS)   and thereupon came a Jury to wit, William
& others   )   Bradley, Robert McMinn, James Williams, Francis
      vs.   )   Leeper, (p 122) William Phipps, Joseph Huf-
DAVID PROFFIT   )   master, George Argenbright, William Brice,
Pleasant Johnson, William Martin, Philip Critz and James Dodson who being
elected tried and sworn and progress having been made in the trial of this
cause by the consent of the parties by their attornies and with the assent
of the Court the Jurors from rendering their verdict are respited until
tomorrow.

Court adjourned until tomorrow 9 O'clock A. M.
                Edw. Scott

Tuesday 7th October 1823.

Court met pursuant to adjournment.
Present The Honorable Edward Scott Judge.

JOHN DEN LESSEE)   By consent of the parties and with leave of the
of WILLIAM BRAD-)   Court this cause is refered to the arbitration
LEY   )   of Hezekiah Hamblen, Richard Mitchell, Jacob
     vs.   )   Miller, John Young, Cal William Ford and Will-
THOMAS SPROUL)   iam Alexander and their award returned into
open Court under the hands and seals to be the Judgment of this Court.

A Deed of Conveyance from Dicks Alexander to Jacob Fitzpatrict and Benjamin Hagwood for four tracts (p 123)   of land containing Two hundred
and fifty nine acres of land was acknowledged in open Court and ordered to be registered.

MATTHEW BANTON)   This day came the plaintiff in his proper person
    vs.   )   and dismisses his suit and confesses Judgment for
SOLOMON DAVIS)   one half of the costs and thereupon Solomon Davis
and Moses McGinnis comes into open Court in their proper persons and confesses Judgment for the other half expended. It is therefore considered
by the Court that the Plaintiff recover of the defendant and Moses McGinnis one half of the costs and that the defendant recover of the Plaintiff
the other half of the costs in this behalf expended and that Executions
issue accordingly.

A Deed of Conveyance from Jonathon White to Harvey Andrews for One acre
and ninety square poles of land lying in the town of Mount Sterling was
acknowledged in open Court and ordered to be registered.

JOHN DEN LESSEE of)   This day came the parties by their attornies
ETHELDRED WILLIAMS)   and thereupon came a Jury, to wit, William
and others   )   Bradley, Robert McMinn, James Williams, Fran-
     vs.   )   cis Leeper, William Phipps, Joseph Huffmaster,
DAVID PROFFIT)   George (p 124) Argenbright, William Brice,
Pleasant Johnson, William Martin, Philip Critz and James Dodson, the same
Jury that were on Yesterday respited from rendering the verdict and now
on this day having received their charge from the Judge retired from the

box to consult of their verdict returned into open Court and say they cannot agree. Whereupon the Court ordered them in Custody of the Sheriff.

Court adjourned until tomorrow 9 O'clock A. M.

Edw. Scott

Wednesday 8th October 1823.

Court met pursuant of adjournment.
Present The Honorable Edward Scott Judge.

JOHN DEN LESSEE
of ETHELDRED WILL-
IAMS and others
vs.
DAVID PROFFIT

This day came the parties by their attornies and thereupon came a Jury, to wit, William Bradley, Robert McMinn, James Williams, Francis Leeper, William Phipps, Joseph Huffmaster, George Argenbright, William Brice, Pleasent Johnson, William Martin, Philip Critz and James Dodson the same Jury as of yesterday who being elected tried and sworn upon their oaths do say we find that the defendant is Guilty of the Trespass and Ejectment in the Plaintiffs declaration mentioned and assess the Plaintiffs damage to (p125) Six cents besides costs. On motion of the defendant by his attorney a rule is allowed him to shew cause why a new trial should be granted.

STATE
vs.
HEZEKIAH EMBERSON

Forfeited Recognizance.
The defendant Hezekiah Emberson being bound in recognizance in the sum of three hundred dollars for his appearance at the present term of this Court and being solemnly called to come into Court came not but forfeited his recognizance. It is therefore considered by the Court that the State recover against the said Hezekiah Emberson the sum of Three hundred dollars unless he appears at the next Term of this Court and show sufficient cause why this Judgment should not be made final and that Scire Facias issue. And Peter Elrod being bound in recognizance in the sum of Two hundred and fifty dollars for the personal appearance of said Hezekiah Emberson at the present term of this Court and being solemnly called to bring into Court the body of the said Hezekiah Emberson as he was bound to do brought him not but wholly made default and forfeited his recognizance. It is therefore considered by the Court that the state recover against the said Peter Elrod the sum of Two hundred and fifty dollars unless he appears at the next term of this Court and shew sufficient cause why this Judgment should not be made final and that Scire Facias issue & c.

JOHN PRYOR
vs.
PETER FRANKLIN

By the consent of the (p 126) parties by their attornies this cause is continued until the next Term of this Court and on affidavit of the Plaintiff. It is ordered by the Court that a Commission issue directed to any Justice of the peace of Sullivan County to take the depositions of Philip S. Hale and that a Commission issue directed to any Justice of the peace of the Counties of McMinn, Roane, Hawkins or Sullivan to take the depositions of Malcolm McPhail & Duncan McCall, and Five days notice if taken in McMinn or Roane County be given to the adverse party of the time and place of taking said depositions. And by consent of the parties. It is ordered by the Court that a Commission issue directed to any Justice of the peace of Sullivan County to take the depositions of John Hicks Senr., John O'Brian, Joseph Everett & Jeremiah Cloud to be read in Evidence on the trial of this cause on behalf of the defendant and that ten days notice be given to the Plaintiff of the time and place of taking said depositions.

JOHN KING & others)
     vs.)
WILLIAM ALEXANDER)

By consent of the parties, this cause is continued until the next Term of this Court.

MOSES McCONNEL and)
the STATE of TENN-)
ESSEE)
    vs.)
C. ESKRIDGE KENNER)

This (p 127) day came the parties by their attornies and thereupon came a Jury, to wit, Dickerson Thurman, Isham Mills, Jesse Cobb, Willie B. Kyle, Moses McGinnis, William Messick, Jonathon Henderson, John M. Vaughan, John Beal, Amis Grantham, James Amis and Thomas Cox who being elected tried and sworn upon their oath do say we find for the defendant. It is therefore considered by the Court that the defendant go hence without day and recover of the Plaintiff Moses McConnel and John Nugent his Security the costs by him in this behalf expended and that Execution issue accordingly.

MOSES McCONNEL)
and the STATE)
of TENNESSEE)
    vs.)
GREGORY SMITH)

For reasons disclosed in the affidavit of the defendant it is ordered by the Court that the forfeiture entered against the said defendant be set aside.

JOHN BALCH)
    vs.)
ALEXANDER SEVIER)

By consent of the parties by their attornies this cause is continued until the next Term of this Court and on affidavit of the defendant. It is ordered (p 128) by the Court that a Commission issue directed to any Justice of the peace of Greene County to take the depositions of Valentine Sevier Christion Dyche and Pheneas Jones to be read in evidence on the trial of this cause on behalf of this defendant and that ten days notice of the time and place of taking said depositions be given to the Plaintiff.

WILLIAM BRANNEN)
    vs.)
ALEXANDER SEVIER)

By consent of the parties by their attornies this cause is continued until the next term of this Court, and on affidavit of the defendant. It is ordered by the Court that a Commission issue directed to any Justice of the peace of Harden County Tennessee to take the deposition of Lewis H. Brayles and that a Commission issue directed to any Justice of the peace of Greene County to take the depositions of Hugh Carver, Jacob McPherson, Elijah Russell & Joseph Brown Esquire and that ten days notice of the time and place of taking said Depositions be given to the Plaintiff.

JAMES SUTTEN)
    vs.)
JOSEPH LACKEY)

At a former Term of this Court a rule was made directing the plaintiff to give bond to prosecute this suit or that it should be dismissed and it appearing to the Court that no bond has been given. It is therefore ordered by the Court that this suit be dismissed (p 129) and that the defendant recover against the Plaintiff his costs by him in this behalf expended and that execution may issue for the same.

BENJAMIN STUART)
    vs.)
ROBERT W. GILLENWATERS)

John Sharp who was security for the Plaintiff for the prosecution of this cause comes here into Court and by consent of the Defend-

ant the said John Sharp is exonerated and discharged from being Security
for the prosecution of this suit and thereupon came into open Court,
Cregton Itson and enters himself Security for the prosecution of this
suit and agrees that if the Plaintiff should be cast in this action that
he shall pay all costs and damages that may be adjudged against him or
that he the said Cregton Itson will pay it for him.

STATE   ) this day came the States by the Solicetor Gen-
  vs,   ) eral and with leave of the Court enters a Nolle
JOHN B. BARKLEY) prosequi and it appearing that John Blair, Pryor
Lee, Robert L. Careethers, Orville Bradley, John Kennedy, William B. Reece
Stockley D. Mitchell, Peter Parsons, James P. Taylor, John A. McKinney,
Michael McCann, Langley S. Hall, Samuel U. Bradley, Lucas Kennedy, John A.
Aiken, James McCarty, Dicks Alexander and Robert H. Jackson, were his appearance bail who came into open Court by themselves and by attorney and
donfesses Judgment for the costs. It is therefore considered by the Court
that the State recover of the above named persons the costs in this behalf
expended and that Execution issue & c.

STATE   )? On affidavit of the (p 130) defendant this cause is
  vs.   ) continued until the next term of this Court.
JAMES SMITH)

The Court adjourn until Tomorrow 8 O'clock.
        Edw. Scott.

Thursday 9th October 1823.

Court met pursuant to adjournment.
Present The Honorable Edward Scott Judge.

JAMES MURRELL) Petition for Divorce.
  vs.   ) In this case the petitioner having heretofore filed
NANCY MURRELL) his petition praying for a Divorce from the bonds
of Matrimony subsisting between him and his wife Nancy Murrell and it appearing to the satisfaction of the Court that a copy of his said petition
had heretofore been served on the said Nancy Murrell and she had been regularly served with a subpoena calling on her to appear and answer the
said petition and the said Nancy having failed to appear and answer the
s ame and the Court having proceeded to the examination of testimony touching the facts charged in said petition and the Court being fully satisfied
from the testimony that the said Nancy has been guilty of wilful and malicious desertion and absence from the Bed and board of her said husband
for more than two full years before filing his said petition. (p 131)
The Court being satisfied that the petitioner was a citizen of the County
of Hawkins and State of Tennessee more than one whole year before the filing his petition. It is therefore considered ordered and adjudged and decreed by the Court that the Bonds of matrimony heretofore subsisting between the said James Murrell and his wife Nancy Murrell be and the same is
hereby decreed Void annulled and for nothing held and that the said James
Murrell from his said wife Nancy Murrell be and is hereby divorced from
the Bonds of Matrimony. It is further considered by the Court that the
defendant recover of the Plaintiff and Micajah Hammons his security the
costs in this behalf expended for which Execution may issue.

MARY CROWBARGER &) On affidavit of the Plaintiffs. It is ordered

JOHN CRITZ Exr & Exx) by the Court that a Commission issue directed
of GEORGE CROWBARGER) tp any Justice of the peace of Hawkins County
Dec'd) to take the deposition be bene esse of John
      vs.) Gibbon to be read on the trial of this cause
JACOB SEAVERS) and that ten days notice of the time and place
of taking said deposition be given to the defendant, and that A Commission
issue directed to any Justice of the peace of Scott County, Virginia to
take the depositions of Cal Andrew, W. Henry, John Wolfe, Esqr. Frederack
Akeard, Jacob Devalt, Isaac (p 132) Isham, William Bird, Zachariah Haynes and Susannah Haynes his wife and that Thirty days notice of the time
and place of takinggsaid depositions be given to the adverse party.

STATE) This day came the State by the attorney General
     vs.) and Richard Morriset the defendant being brought
RICHARD MORRISET) to the Bar present also his counsel and having
been charged on the Bill of Indictment plead Not Guilty and put himself
on the County and thereupon came a Jury to wit, James Williams, George R.
Smith, John McWilliams, Robert McMinn, Wright Bond, James L. Etter, Reuben
Lawson, William Bradley, Willie B. Kyle, Winder Kenner, Peter Elrod and
William Stuart who having been tried and elected by the Prisoner Richard
Morriset and sworn Well and truly to try the issue of traverse the State
against the said Richard Morriset do upon their oaths say that the defendant is not Guilty in manner and form as charged in the Bill of Indictment.
Whereupon on Motion of the attorney General a rule is allowed him to shew
cause why the defendant should be taxed with the costs, and after argument
of counsel as well for as against said rule and the premises considered
and fully understood. It is ordered by the Court the rule be discharged,
and it is (p 133) further considered by the Court that the defendant
Richard Morriset be discharged and that the County Trustee pay the costs
in this behalf expended and that the Clerk of this Court issue certificates to those persons entitled to the same.

JOHN A. ROGERS) The reasons disclosed in the affidavit of the
     vs.) defendant it is ordered by the Court that
EDWARD E. SURGOINE) the forfeiture entered against the defendant
at the last term of this Court be set aside. Whereupon the plaintiff by
his attorney tenders a Bill of Exeeptions which is signed sealed and ordered to be made part of the record.

MOSES McCOMNEL) For reasons disclosed in the affidavit of the
and the STATE of) defendant. It is ordered by the Court that the
TENNESSEE) forfeiture entered against the defendant at the
     vs.) last term of this Court be set aside.
WILLIAM REYNOLDS)

STATE) This day came the State by the attorney General
     vs.) and the defendant Claibourn Jones being brought
CLAIBOURN JONES) to the Bar was charged on the Bill of Indictment and pled Not Guilty. Whereupon the Court remanded him back to Jail;

ROBERT JOHNSON) By consent (p 134) of the parties and with the
     vs.) assent of the Court this cause is refered to the
LIJAH KINCHELOE) arbitration of Francis Leeper, William Lyons, Daniel Chambers, George White Esquire, Richard Mitchell and Joseph W. Carden
and their award returned into open Court under their hands and seals to be
the Judgment of this Court.

JOHN DEN LESSEE of)   This day came the parties by their attornies
FRANCIS DALZELL and)   and thereupon came a Jury, to wit, George
WILLIAM SIMPSON   )   R. South, John McWilliams, Robert McMinn,
       vs.)Ejectment)   Wright Bond, James L. Etter, Reuben Lawson,
GEORGE STIPE Senr   )   William Bradley, Winder Kenner, Peter El-
& GEORGE STIPE Junr)   rod, William Stuart, George Argenbright and
William Thurman who being elected tried and sworn upon their oaths do say
we find that the defendants are not Guilty of the Trespass and Ejectment
in the plaintiffs declaration mentioned. It is therefore considered by
the Court that the defendants go hence without day and recover of the
plaintiffs their costs by them in this behalf expended and that Execution
issue accordingly.

A Deed of Conveyance (p 135) from David Proffit to Asabel Johnson for
one hundred and eighty acres of land was proven in open Court by the oath
of William Alexander one of the subscribing witnesses and ordered to stand
for further proof.

STATE   )   This day came the State by Sterling Cocke Attorney
     vs.   )   General who prosecutes in behalf of the State and
ADDISON JONES)   the defendant being brought to the Bar by order of
the Court and being charged on the Bill of Indictment pleads Not Guilty
and thereupon files his affidavit and by his attorney moved the Court for
a change of Venue in this cause and for reasons appearing to the satisfaction of the Court supported by said affidavit of defendant that a fair
and impartial trial cannot be had in this cause in the County of Hawkins.
It is therefore considered by the Court that the Venue be changed to the
County of Greene being the nearest adjoining County free of like exceptions and that the clerk of this Court make out a Transcript of the record and proceedings and transmit the same to the clerk of the Circuit
Court of Greene County and that the cause be docketed in that Court for
trial and it is further considered by the Court that the Jail of Hawkins
County is insufficient and that the Sheriff of this County (p 136)
deliver over to the Sheriff or Jailor of Washington County the said Addison Jones for safe keeping.

The Court adjourn until tomorrow 9 O'clock.
                     Edw. Scott

Friday 10th October 1823.

Court met pursuant to adjournment.
Present The Honorable Edward Scott Judge.

MOSES McCONNELL and   )   For reasons disclosed in the affidavit of
THE STATE of TENNESSEE)   the defendant. It is ordered by the Court
       vs.   )   that the forfeiture entered against the
CHRISTION MORRELL   )   defendant at the last term of this Court
be set aside and that he pay the costs in this behalf expended for which
Execution may issue.

MOSES McCONNEL and   )   For reasons disclosed in the affadavit of
the STATE of TENNESSEE)   the defendant. It is ordered by the Court
       vs.   )   that the forfeiture entered against the de-
HEZEKIAH HAMBLEN   )   fendant at the last term of this court be
set aside.

A Deed of Conveyance from Elizabeth Sanders to Joseph Morriset for Sixteen and a half acres of land was acknowledged in open Court and ordered to be registered.

JUDITH SMITH by) Petition (p 137) for Divorce.
ASHBY GRIGGSBY her) It appearing to the satisfaction of the Court
next friend) that a Subpoena had been issued and returned
vs.) not Executed. It is ordered by the Court that
SAMUEL SMITH) publication be made in the Political Economist
printed in Greenville for four weeks successively calling on the said Samuel Smith to appear at the next Term of this Court and answer said Petition or that it would be taken as confessed and the Court proceed thereon exporte and decree accordingly and that this cause be set for hearing at the next Term of this Court.

JOHN DEN LESSEE of) This day came on to be heard the rule for a new
ETHELDRED WILLIAMS) trial in this cause and after argument of Coun-
& others) nsel thereon as well for as against said rule
vs.) and the premises considered and full under-
DAVID PROFFIT) stood. It is ordered by the Court that the r
rule be discharged. It is therefore considered by the Court that the plaintiffs recover of the defendant their term yet to come together with the damages by Jury assessed and the costs in this behalf expended and the Defendant in Mercy & c. From which Judgment the defendant prays an appeal in the nature of a Writ of Error to the Supreme (p 138) Court of Errors and Appeals to be held at the Courthouse in Rogersville on the first Monday of May next gave bond and security according to law and the appeal by the Court Granted.

JOHN A. ROGERS) On affidavit of Osbourne Boykin agent for the defen-
vs.) dant. It is ordered by the Court that a Commission
ELI BOYKIN) issue directed to any Justice of the peace of Haw-
kins County to take the deposition of James Bootman and by consent of the parties It is ordered that said deposition be taken this evening.

WILLIAM CRUMLEY) On affidavit of the Plaintiff. It is ordered
vs.) by the Court that a Commission issue directed to
JOHNSON FRAZIER) any Justice of the peace of Monroe County to take
the depositions of Aaron Parker and Jacob Smiley and that Ten days notice of the time and place of taking said depositions be given to the adverse party.

E. EMBREE surviving) On affidavit of Amis Grantham. It is order-
Partner of E & E .) ed by the Court that a Commission issue dir-
EMBREE) ected to any Justice of the peace (p 139)
vs.) of Grainger County to take the deposition of
AMIS GRANTHAM &) Richard Grantham and that ten days notice of
others) the time and place of taking said deposition
be given to the Plaintiff.

WILLIAM WALKER) On affidavit of Peter Elrod, agent for the Plain-
vs.) tiff, it is ordered by the Court that a Commission
ASABEL JOHNSON) issue directed to any Justice of the peace of Knox
County Kentucky to take the Deposition of Lewis Webb and that thirty days notice of the time and place of taking said deposition be given to the adverse party.

ROBERT CARDEN) On motion of the defendant by his attorney. It
   vs.) is ordered by the Court that the plaintiff app-
JAMES P. McCARTY) ear at the next term of this Court and shew
cause why he should not give additional security for the prosecution of
this suit.

ROBERT CARDEN) For reasons appearing to the satisfaction of the
   vs.)Q Court on the affidavit of the Plaintiff that a
JAMES P. McCARTY) fair and impartial trial of this cause cannot be
had in the County of Hawkins. It is therefore ordered by the Court that
the Venue be changed to the County of Greene (p 140) it being the nearest adjoining County free from the like exceptions and that the clerk of
this Court make out a transcript of the record and proceedings and transmit the same to the Clerk of the Circuit Court of Greene County & that the
said Robt. Carden appear at the next term of the Circuit Court of Greene
and shew cause why he should not give additional security for the prosecution of this suit.

STATE) This day came the State by the Attorney General and
 vs.) the defendant being brought to the Bar by order of the
JOHN JONES) Court and being charged on the Bill of Indictment pleads
Not Guilty and thereupon files his affidavit and by his attorney moved
the Court for a change of Venue in this cause and for reasons appearing
to the satisfaction of the Court supported by said affidavit of defendant that a fair and impartial trial cannot be had in this cause in the
County of Hawkins. It is considered by the Court that the Venue be changed to the County of Greene, it being the nearest adjoining County free of
the like exceptions and that the Clerk of this Court make out a Transcript
of the record and proceedings had in said prosecution and transmit the
same to the clerk of the Circuit Court of Greene County and that this cause
be docketed in that Court for trial and it is further considered by the
Court that the Jail of Hawkins County is insufficient and that the Sheriff
of this County deliver over to the Sheriff or Jailor of Washington (p 141)
County the said John Jones for safe keeping.

STATE   ) This day came the State by the Attorney General
 vs.   ) and Claibourn Jones the defendant being brought
CLAIBURN JONES) to the Bar-present also his counsel and having
been charged on the Bill of Indictment pleads Not Guilty and put himself
on the Country, and thereupon came a Jury to wit, Robert McMinn, Haynes
Amis, Christion Morell, Dickenson Thurman, John McWilliams, Willie B.
Kyle, Joel Gillenwaters, William Carmack, William Alexander, James L.
Etter, William Bradley and John C. Gillenwaters who being elected tried
and sworn well and truly to try this issue of traverse, upon their oath
do say, we find the Defendant not Guilty in manner and form as charged
in the first and second Counts in the Bill of Indictment and we further
find the Defendant Guilty in Manner and form as charged in the third and
last Count in the Bill of Indictment. Whereupon the Defendant by attorney
moves the Court to grant a New Trial in this case, which motion is overruled by the Court and thereupon the Defendant by attorney files reasons
in arrest of Judgment and after hearing arguments of Counsel as well on
behalf as against said reasons and the Court being fully advised thereon.
It is considered and ordered that said reasons in arrest of Judgment be
discharged and that the defendant Claibourn Jones for this his offence
be fined fifty dollars that he receive thirty lashes on his bare back to
be inflicted by the Sheriff of this County at the public whipping post on

tomorrow at (p 142) ten O'clock in the fore noon, and that he be imprisoned in the Jail of Washington County for the space of six calendar months, it being represented to the Court that the Common prison of this County is insecure and that here remain in prison until the fine and costs in this case are paid or good and sufficient security given therefore, and that the Sheriff of this County deliver the said Defendant Claibourn Jones into the Custody of the Sheriff of Washington County accordingly and said Defendant in mercy & c.

JAMES FORD and PHILIP SANDERS vs. RICHARD G. WATERHOUSE & others	This day came James Ford one of the Plaintiffs by his attorney and the defendants by their attornies and the death of Philip Sanders the other plaintiff in this cause being suggested. And thereupon came on the

demurrer for argument heretofore filed and after hearing Counsel thereon and the premises considered and fully understood. It is considered by the Court that the demurrer be overruled. But because it is unknown to the Court here what damaged the Plaintiff hath sustained by reason of the premises therefore let a Jury come at the next Term of this Court to inquire what damages the plaintiff hath sustained in this behalf.

The Court adjourn until tomorrow 7 O'clock.
                Edw. Scott.

Saturday 11th October 1823 (p 143)

Court met pursuant to adjournment.
Present The Honorable Edward Scott Judge.

JOHN DEN LESSEE of ETHELDRED WILLIAMS & others vs. DAVID PROFFIT	In the progress of the trial of this cause the defendant by his attorney tendered a Bill of Exceptions which is signed sealed and ordered to be made a part of the record.

STATE vs. CLAIBOURNE JONES	From the Judgment rendered in this cause the defendant prays an appeal in the nature of a Writ of Error to the Supreme Court of Errors and Appeals

to be held at the Court House in Rogersville on the first Monday of May next which is Granted by the Court and it is ordered that the Sheriff of this County deliver to the Sheriff or Jailor of Washington County the said Claibourn Jones for safe keeping according to a previous order made in this cause.

ISAIAH JONES vs.) Sci Fa HUGH MALONY	Scire Facias. In this cause the Scire Facias having been returned executed on the defendant Hugh Malony and the Sher-

iff8s return shewing that James Weems the other defendant is dead and the said Hugh Malony being (p 144) solemnly called to come into Court and defend the suit according to the Scire Facias to him made known came not but made default. It is therefore considered by the Court that the Plaintiff recover against the defendant Hugh Malony the sum of One hundred and twenty five dollars and fifty cents the costs of the suit in said Scire Facias mentioned together with the costs of this suit and that Execution issue accordingly.

STATE)   Forfeited Recognizance.

   vs.   ) This day came the State by the Attorney General
  JACOB HIPSHEAR) and Jacob Hipshire being bound in recognizance
in the sum of One hundred and twenty five dollars for his personal appearance to the present Term of this Court to prosecute and give evidence
on behalf of the State against David McCoy and being solemnly called came
not but made default. It is therefore considered by the Court that the
State recover against the said Jacob Hipshere the sum of One hundred
and twenty five dollars unless he appears at the next Term of this Court
and shew sufficient cause why this Judgment should not be made final and
that Scire Facias issue against him & c.

The Court adjourn until Court in Course.
     Edw. Scott.

Monday 28th March 1824 (p 145)

At a Circuit Court begun and held for the County of Hawkins at the Courthouse in Robersville on the fifth Monday being the twenty ninth day of
March in the year of our Lone One thousand eight hundred and Twenty four
pursuant to an act of the General Assembly passed at Murfreesborough the
3rd day of November A. D. 1823.
Present The Honorable Samuel Powel Judge.

The Court adjourned until tomorrow 3 O'clock P. M.
     S. Powel

Tuesday 30th March 1824.

Court met persuant to adjournment.
Present The Honorable Samuel Powel Judge.

The Clerk of this Court produced in open Court the Treasurers Receipt for
the State Tax by him collected from the 1st day of October 1822 to the
30th day of September 1823 and also a receipt from the Trustee of this
County for Funs collected by him in the year 1823 as required by law
the production of which is ordered to be entered of record.

The Court adjourned until tomorrow 3 O'clock P. M.
     S. Powel

Wednesday 31st March 1824.

Court met pursuant to adjournment.
Present The Honorable Samuel Powel Judge.

Court adjourned until tomorrow (p 146) 9 O'clock A. M.
     S. Powel

Thursday 1st April 1824.

Court met pursuant to adjournment.
Present The Honorable Samuel Powel Judge.

   BETSEY HENDERSON   ) Petition for Divorce.
     vs.   ) In this cause on Motion of the Plain-
  ROLLIN MOTTISON HENDERSON) tiff by her attorney. It is ordered

by the Court that process issue according to law and it being suggested in the Plaintiffs Petition that the defendant is not an Inhabitant of this State. It is ordered that publication be made in the American Economist printed in Greenville for four weeks successively calling on the said Rollin Mattison Henderson to appear at the next term of this Court and answer said Petition or that it will be taken as confessed, and the Court proceed thereon ex-parte and decree accordingly and that this cause be set for hearing at the next Term of this Court.

Court adjourned until tomorrow 9 O'clock A. M.
                    S. Powel

Friday 2nd April 1824.

Court met pursuant to adjournment.
Present The Honorable Samuel Powel Judge.

Court adjourned until tomorrow 9 O'clock A. M.
                    S. Powel

Saturday 3rd April 1824 (p 147)

Court met pursuant to adjournment.
Present The Honorable Samuel Powel Judge.

JUDITH SMITH by her)	Petition for Divorce.
next friend ASHBY)	This day came the plaintiff by her attorney
GRIGGSBY)	and the defendant Samuel Smith being solemn-
vs.)	nly called to come into Court and answer the
SAMUEL SMITH)	Petition of Judith Smith or the same would

be taken as confessed and heard ex-parte and the Court proceed to decree accordingly came not but made default.

Court adjourned until Monday 9 O'clock A. M.
                    S. Powel

Monday 5th April 1824.

Court met pursuant to adjournment.
Present The Honorable Samuel Powel Judge.

JUDITH SMITH by her)	Petition for Divorce.
next friend ASHBY)	This day came the plaintiff by her attorney
BRIGGSBY)	and the defendant being solemnly called to
vs.)	come into Court and answer the Petition of
SAMUEL SMITH)	Judith Smith or the same would be taken as

confessed and heard exparte and the Court proceed to decree accordingly came not but made default.

Gabriel McCrow Sheriff (p 148) of Hawkins County returns now into Court our Writ of Venire Facias Executed on the following persons to wit.
John Mitchell, Moses McGinnis, William Crumnly, Philip Critz, John Critz Jesse W. Hale, Reuben Barnard, William Lyons, Samuel Wilson, Esqr. Joel Gillenwaters, Esqr. Elijah Gillenwaters, Cleon Moore, John Reynolds, Nicholas Long, George Hays, Hezekiah Hamblen, Thomas Cocke, John Cockram, Jacob Miller, Thomas Caldwell, Arthur G. Young, Andrew Galbreath, John A.

Rogers, George Smith and Joseph McCullough Junr from among whom the following persons were drawn as Grand Jurors for the present Term, to wit.
1. Joel Gillenwaters Foreman.
2. John Reynolds.
3. Hezekiah Hamblen
4. Nicholas Long
5. Thomas Caldwell
6. Moses McGinnis
7. Jesse W. Hale
8. Joseph McCullough Jr
9. George Hays
10 John Mitchell
11 Elihah C. Gillenwaters
12 Samuel Wilson Esqr
13 John A. Rogers
who were severally sworn and being charged by the Judge withdrew from the Bar.

Robert W. Gillenwaters Constable was qualified in due form of law as officer to attend on the Grand Jury during the present Term.

The Sheriff returned Jesse Spiers Constable as summoned to attend on the Court during the present Term.

MICHAWL McCANN)   It is ordered (p 149) by the Court that this
        vs.   )   cause be continued until the next Term of this
FRAZIER BRINLEY)   Court and on motion of the Plaintiff by his attorney It is ordered that Commission issue directed to any Justice of the peace of Botetonat County in the State of Virginia to take the deposition of William Kirk to be read in Evidence on the trial of this cause on behalf of the Plaintiff and that Thirty days notice of the time and place of taking said deposition be given to the defendant.

CHARLES KING   )   By consent of the parties by their attornies this
        vs.   )   cause is continued until the next Term of this
SAMUEL CHESTNUT)   Court. And on motion of the Plaintiff by his attorney. It is ordered by the Court that a Commission issue directed to any Justice of the peace of McMinn County in this State to take the deposition of Henry Reynolds to be read in Evidence on the trial of this cause on behalf of the Plaintiff and Fifteen days notice of the time and place of taking said deposition be given to the adverse party.

JOHN DEN LESSEE of)   This cause is continued until the next Term
WILLIAM WHITESIDES)   of this Court.
        vs.   )
DAVID PROFFIT   )

Ordered by the Court that (p 150) it shall be the duty of the Clerk to Docket all causes whether instituted in this Court by Original Writ or brought by writ of Certiorani in the order in which such writs may have issued and all appeals from a Justice shall be docketed in the order in which such Writs may have issued and all appeals and Writs of Error from the County Court or Appeals, from a Justice shall be docketed in the order in which the same may be received by the Clerk of this Court.
It shall be the duty of the Clerk previous to each Term to make out three dockets one for the Court one for the Bar and one for the Clerk upon which

all the causes in Court shall be entered together with all the rules &
orders that may be taken therein. The causes at issue or those put at
issue one week before the Commencement of the Court shall be entered in
their proper order on the first part of the docket and be called the issue Docket, and all argument causes & causes not at issue shall be entered
in the same order on the after part of the docket and be called the reference docket.

The causes on the issue Docket shall be first called and disposed of.
The causes on the Reference Docket shall then be called and if at issue
shall be disposed of in the same manner as if they had been on the issue
docket.

A Deed of Conveyance from Jacob Mefford to Harvey Andrews for Twenty acres
of land was acknowledged in open Court and ordered to be registered.

ALBERT G. RICE By   )   This day (p 151) came the plaintiff by
LYMAN RICE his father)   his attorney and with leave of the Court
& C   )   dismisses his suit and thereupon Thomas
        vs.   )   Hale the defendant comes into Court and
THOMAS RICE   )   confesses Judgment for the costs in this

behalf expended. It is therefore considered by the Court that the plaintiff recover of the defendant the costs that have acrued in this behalf
and that execution issue accordingly.

CREIGHTON EIDSON)   By consent of the parties and with leave of
        vs.   )   the Court this cause is refered to the arbit-
RICHARD M. STARNES)   ration fo Hacob Miller, Jacob B. Groves and
Daniel Chambers and their award returned into Court under their hands and
seals to be the Judgment of this Court.

A Deed of Conveyance from Henry Crowley to Joel Coffee for Sixteen acres
was acknowledged in open Court and ordered to be registered.

A Deed of Conveyance from Henry Crowley to Benjamin Coffee for Seventy
five acres of land was acknowledged in open Court and ordered to be registered.

ELEANOR HARMON by)   This day (p 152) came the plaintiff by
her father and next) her attorney and with leave of the Court
freind   )   dismisses her suit and thereupon William
DAVID HARMON   )   Johnston the defendant comes into open Court
        vs.   )   in his proper person and confesses Judgment
WILLIAM JOHNSTON   )   for the costs. It is therefore considered
by the Court that the plaintiff recover of the defendant the costs in
this behalf expended and that Execution issue accordingly.

JAMES FORD and   )   This day came the parties by their attor-
PHILIP SANDERS   )   nies and thereupon came a Jury, to wit.
        vs.   )   George Smith, Jacob Miller, John M. Vaughan,
RICHARD G. WATERHOUSE)   James Jones, Thomas Taylor, Richard Starnes,
& others   )   Abraham Vernon, William Davis, John Beel,
David Rowan, Jacob Myers and George Francisco who being elected tried and
sworn upon their oath do say we find for the plaintiff James Ford and assess his damage to Thirteen dollars and ninety five and a half cents besides
costs. On motion of the plaintiff by his attorney a rule is allowed him
to shew cause why a new trial should be granted.

THOMAS JOHNSON)　　On affidavit of the　(p 153)　plaintiff this cause
　　vs.　　　　))　is continued until the next Term of this Court.
JACOB HACKNEY)

BENJAMIN STUART　　　　)　　This day came the parties by their attornies
　　vs.　　　　　)　　and thereupon came a Jury, to wit.　Reuben
ROBERT W. GILLENWATERS)　　Barnard, Philip Oritz, Andrew Galbreath,
John M. Vaughan, James Jones, Thomas Taylor, Abraham Vernon, George Francisco, Stonmix Hord, Joseph McMinn, Thomas Hale & Dickerson Thurman who being tried elected and sworn and progress having been made in the trial of
this cause by consent of thepparties by their attornies and with the assent of the Court the Jurors from rendering their Verdict are respited until tomorrow.

Court adjourned until tomorrow 9 O'clock A. M.
　　　　　　　　　S. Powel

Tuesday 6th April 1824.

Court met pursuant to adjournment.
Present The Honorable Samuel Powel Judge.

JUDITH SMITH by)　Petition for Divorce.
her next friend)　This day came the plaintiff by her attorney and
ASHBY GRIGGSBY)　Samuel Smith the defendant being solemnly called
　　vs.　　　)　to come into Court and answer the petition of
SAMUEL SMITH　)　Judith Smith or the same would be takine as confessed and heard exparte and the Court proceed to decree accordingly came
not but made default.　And it appearing to the satisfaction of the Court
that publication had been regularly made according to an order made at
the last term of this Court.　It is ordered that this cause be continued
until the next term of this Court.

JOHN DEN LESSEE of)　By consent of the parties and with the assent
WILLIAM BRADLEY　)　of the Court this cause is refered to the ar-
　　vs.　　　)　bitration of Hezekiah Hamblen, Richard Mit-
THOMAS SPROUL　　)　chell, Jacob Miller, John Young, Cal William,
Hord and William Alexander and their award returned into open Court under
their hands and seals to be the Judgment of this Court.

A Bill of Sale from Jacob Mefford to Micajah Lee for his Right to five negroes was acknowledged in open Court and ordered to be registered.

WILLIAM BRONNON)?　By consent of the parties this cause is contin-
　　vs.　　)　ued until the next Term of this Court.
ALEXANDER SEVIER)

WILLIAM R. WRIGHT)　In this　(p 155)　cause the parties having en-
　　vs.　　　)　tered into a Conference and the defendant hav-
ROBERT YOUNG Senr.)　ing agreed to pay the Complainant his costs
upon dismissing his Bill.　Whereupon on motion of the Complainant by his
attorney.　It is ordered adjudged　and decreed by the Court that said
Bill be and the same is hereby dismissed and said costs are accordingly
paid into the office of this Court.

WILLIAM BURGESS &)　By consent of the parties by their attornies

REBECCA BURGESS) It is ordered by the Court that a Commission
  his wife   ) issue directed to any Justice of the peace of
    vs.   ) Hawkins County to take the deposition of Will-
ALEXANDER SEVIER) iam Bronnon to be read in Evidence on the trial
of this cause on behalf of the defendant and by consent of the parties
to be taken at Jacob Hackney's. this evening

WILLIAM CRUMLEY) By consent of the parties by their attornies
    vs.   ) this cause is continued until the next term of
JOHNSON FRAZIER) this Court.

MARKHAM KENNER) By consent of the parties this cause is contin-
    vs.   ) ued until the next Term of this Court.
PETER ELROD)

BENJAMIN STEWART   ) This day came (p 156) the parties by
    vs.   ) their attornies and thereupon came a
ROBERT W. GILLENWATERS) Jury to wit, Reuben Barnard, Philip Critz,
Andrew Galbreath, John M. Vaughan, James Jones, Thomas Taylor, Abraham
Vernon, George Francisco, Stommis Hord, Joseph McMinn, Thomas Hale, and
Dickerson Thurman, the same Jury that were on yesterday respited form
rendering their verdict and being elected tried and sworn upon their
oaths do say we find that the defendant is Guilty of the Trespass in manner and form as the plaintiff against him in his declaration has complained and further find that he was not justified as in pleading he hath
alledged and assess the plaintiffs damage to One hundred and twelve dollA
ars and sixty cents besides costs. It is therefore considered by the
Court that the Plaintiff recover of the defendant the sum of one hundred
and twelve dollars and sixty cents the damages aforesaid by the Jurors
aforesaid assessed together with the costs by him about his suit in this
behalf expended and the defendant in mercy & c.

Court adjourned until tomorrow 9 O' clock A. M.
                  S. Powel

Wednesday 7th April 1824.
Court met pursuant to adjournment.
Present The Honorable Samuel Powel Judge.

WILLIAM BRANNON) On affidavit of the (p 157) defendant. It is
    vs.   ) ordered by the Court that a Commission issue
ALEXANDER SEVIER) directed to any Justice of the peace of Greene
County to take the depositions of Hugh Cavner, James McPherson, Elijah
Russell, Joseph Brown Esqr, John M. Kilgore Esqr, Valentine Sevier and
John Rhea to be read in Evidence on the trial of this cause on behalf of
the defendant and that Ten days notice of the time and place of taking
said depositions be given to the Plaintiff.

STATE   ) Forfeited Recognizance.
  vs.   ) The defendant Jacob Hipshere being bound in Rec-
JACOB HIPSHERE) ognizance for his personal appearance at the last
Term of this Court and having solemnly called to come into Court, came not
and forfeited his recognizance and now on this day personally appeared in
open Court and prays that the forfeiture entered against may be set aside.
And for reasons appearing to the satisfaction of the Court. It is ordered
that the forfeiture entered against Jacob Hipshire at the last Term of this
Court be set aside on the payment of costs.

STATE) On affidavit of the defendant this cause is contin-
vs.) ued until the next Term of this Court.
ABSALOM HAWORTH)

WILLIAM CRUMLY) On affidavit (p 158) of the plaintiff It is
vs.) ordered by the Court that a Commission issue
JOHNSON FRAZIER) directed to any two Justices of the peace of
Monroe County to take the depositions of Aaron Parker and Jacob Smiley
and that Ten days notice of the time and place of taking said depositions be given to the adverse party.

STATE) This day came the State by the attorney General
vs.) and the defendant in his proper person and by at-
ISHAM GIDDENS) torney and being charged on the Bill of Indictment
plead not Guilty and put himself on the County and thereupon came a Jury,
to wit, John Cockram, Philip Crits, Jacob Miller, Andrew Galbreath, Thomas McCurgon, Reuben Lawson, Stephen Arnold, Howel Brewer, John Beal,
Davis S. Rogers, Peter Franklin and Stephen Weare who being elected, tried
and sworn upon their oaths do say we find that the defendant is Guilty in
manner and form as charged in the Bill of Indictment. It is therefore
considered by the Court that the defendant Isham Giddens for this his offence be fined Twenty five dollars and to pay the costs in this behalf expended and held in custody until fine and costs are paid or Security given
therefor.

JOHN LONG) By consent (p 159) of the parties by their attor-
vs.) nies this cause is continued until the next Term of
JACOB BURRIS) this Court.

JOHN A. ROGERS) By consent of the parties It is ordered that
vs.) this cause stand for trial on next Friday if
SAMUEL WILSON Jr.) reached before that time.

JOHN PRYOR) By consent of the parties by their attornies this
vs.) cause is continued until the next Term of this
PETER FRANKLIN) Court.

A Power of Attorney from Micajah Lee to Jacob Mefford was proven in open-
Court by the oath of Joseph McCullough a subscribing witness thereto and
ordered to be certified.

A Deed of Conveyance from Samuel Powel to William E. Cocke for two lots
in the Town of Rogersville was proven in open Court by the oaths of James
P. Taylor and Orville Bradley and was ordered to be registered.

A Power of Attorney from Martin Beaty to Wilkins Taumhill Caskin of Nashville Bank was proven in open Court by the oath of James Forgey and ordered to be certified.

STATE) This day came (p 160) the State by the Attorney
vs.) General and the defendant in his proper person and
JAMES SMITH) by Attorney and having been charged on the Bill of
Indictment plead Not Guilty and put himself on the Country and thereupon
came a Jury, to wit, George R. Smith, William Giddens, Isham Giddens, James Jones, John Denny, Jonathon Henderson, William Johnson, Thomas Monahon, Alexander W. Williams, Matthew Bonton, Francis Bambill and John Day,
who being elected tried and sworn upon their oaths do say we find that
the defendant is not Guilty in manner and form as charged in the Bill of
Indictment.

Whereupon on motion of the Attorney General a Rule is allowed him to shew cause why the defendant should be taxed with the costs and after argument of Counsel thereon as well for as against said rule and the premises condidered and fully understood. It is ordered by the Court that the rule be discharged and it is further considered by the Court that the defendant James Smith be discharged and that the County Trustee pay the cost in this behalf expended and that the Clerk of this Court issue certificates to those persons entitled to the same.

Court adjourned until tomorrow 9 O'clock A. M.
                        S. Powel

Thursday 8th April 1824   (p 161)

Court met pursuant to adjournment.
Present The Honorable Samuel Powel Judge.

JOHN PRYOR) On motion of the Plaintiff by his attorney. It
    vs.) is ordered by the Court that a Commission issue
PETER FRANKLIN) directed to any Justice of the peace of Roan or
McMinn County to take the deposition of Malcolm McPhail and that Ten days notice of the time and place of taking said deposition be given to the adverse party.

JOHN DEN LESSEE of) On motion and affidavit it is ordered by the
JAMES MOORE) Court that Thomas Hopkins have leave to de-
    vs.) fend this suit with Walter Beaty the Tenant
WALTER BAITY) in possession on entering into the Common
rule and giving security for the costs. And thereupon John M. Vaughan came into open Court and undertook that if the said Thomas Hopkins should be cost in this action he shall pay the costs and charges or that he will pay it for him.

STATE) This day came the State by the Attorney General
    vs.) and with leave of the Court enters a Nollie Pros-
ALLEN CHUMLY) equi in this suit.

STATE) Forfeited Recognizance (p 162)
    vs.) The defendant David Chumly having been bound in
DAVID CHUMLEY) Recognizance at a former Term of this Court for
the personal appearance of Allen Chumly and having been solemnly called to bring to Court the body of the said Allen Chumly brought him not and forfeited his recognizance and now on this day the said David Chumly appeared in open Court and prays that the forfeiture entered against him may be set aside and for reasons disclosed in the affidavit of the defendant. It is ordered that the forfeiture entered against him be set aside on the payment of costs, and it is further considered by the Court that the said David Chumly pay all the costs in the prosecution against Allen Chumley for which Execution may issue & c.

JOHN G. ROBERTS) On affidavit of John A. McKinney Plaintiffs att-
    vs.) orney. It is ordered by the Court that a Comm-
ROBERT NALL) ission issue directed to any Justice of the peace
of the City of Richmond in Virginia to take the deposition of Henry Gibson and that a Commission issue directed to any Justice of the peace of Powbotton County in Virginia to take the deposition of John H. Randolph which depositions when taken to be read in evidence on the trial of this

cause on behalf of the Plaintiff and that (p 163) Forty days notice of the time and place of taking said depositions be given to the adverse party.

JOHN BLEVINS) By consent of the parties by their attornies this
vs.) cause is continued the next term of this Court.
ROBERT GAMBILL &)
JOHN BEALL)

CREIGHTON EIDSON) The parties having refered this cause to ar-
vs.) bitrators and they having returned their a-
RICHARD M. STARNES) ward into open Court in the words and figures
following, to wit.

CROTON ITSON) fals imprisonment & c.
vs.) WB Daniel Chambers, Jacob B. Groves & Jacob
RICHARD M. STARNES) Miller being chosen to arbitrate & settle sd
suit having heard the Evidence & considered the premises do consider that
the Def't Starnes pay all costs of suit and to pay five dollars damage.
Given under our hands this 8th day of April 1824.
                                    Daniel Chambers
                                    Jacob B. Groves
                                    Jacob Miller
It is therefore considered by the Court that the Plaintiff recover of the
defendant the sum of five dollars the damages awarded by the arbitrators
and also the costs in this behalf expended and that Execution issue acc-
ordingby.

A Deed of Conveyance (p 164) from David Proffit to Asabel Johnson for
one hundred and eighty acres of land was further proven in open Court
by the oath of Jacob Peck and ordered to be registered.

JOSEPH ROGERS) By consent of the parties by their attornies this
vs.) cause is continued until the next Term of this
JESSE HOWEL v) Court.

STATE) This day came the State by the attorney General
vs.) and Jonathon Tipton the defendant being brought
JONATHON TIPTON) to the Bar present also his Counsel and having
been charged on the Bill of Indictment plead not Guilty and put himself
on the Country and thereupon came a Jury, to wit, Reuben Barnard, George
R. Smith, Philip Critz, Willie B. Kyle, Robert Nell, John Day, Henry
Crowley, William Johnson, John Cockram, Joseph Flora, John Denny and
Henry Province who being elected tried and sworn well and truly to try
this issue of traverse upon their oath, do say, we find the Defendant not
Guilty in manner and form as charged in the first county of the Bill of Indictment and we further find that the Defendant is Guilty in manner and
form as charged in the second County of the Bill of Indictment.
Whereupon on motion of the defendant by his attorney a Rule is allowed
(p 165) him to shew cause why a new Trial should be granted.

Court adjourn until Tomorrow 9 O'clock.
                                    S. Powel

Friday 9th April 1824.

Court met according to adjournment.
Present The Honorable Samuel Powel Judge.

A Deed of Conveyance from Caleb J. Parker to Richard White for 200 acres of land was proven in open Court by the oaths of Nicholas Long & George Long two of the subscribing witnesses thereto and was ordered to be Registered.

A Deed of Conveyance from William E. Cocke to Stockley D. Mitchell, William Simpson, Nicholas Fain and John A. McKinney Trustees & c for a lot in the Town of Rogersville was proven in open Court by the oaths of Orville Bradley and Moses Rice and was ordered to be registered.

A Deed of Conveyance from William E. Cocke to William Simpson, Nicholas Fain and John A. McKinney for a Lot in the Town of Rogersville was proven in open Court By the oaths of Orville Bradley and Moses Rice and ordered to be registered.

STATE)
vs.)
Negro JOE a slave)
the property of ROB'T)
NALL)

The record in this cause having been inspected by the Court and Counsel heard and the matters (p 166) fully understood. It is considered by the Court that the Sentence ought not to have been pronounced on said defendant by the Special Court and that the Judgment of the said Special Court be quashed and for noting held, and it is further ordered by the Court that the Sheriff of this County be directed to convene a Special Court according to act of Assembly to give such Judgment as the law will authorise them and that the Clerk of this Court deliver to the Court so convened the papers brought up by Certiorari and A Copy of this Judgment and that they proceed in the case.

STATE)
vs.)
JONATHON TIPTON)

Assault and Battery
This day came the State by the Attorney General and the defendant Jonathon Tipton being brought to the Bar present also his counsel and being charged on the Bill of Indictment plead not Guilty and put himself on the Country and thereupon came a Jury, to wit, Andrew Galbreath, George R. Smith, Reuben Barnard, Philip Critz, Jacob Miller, John Shaugh, James Jones, John W. Williams, John Day, Stephen Weare, Joseph Huffmaster and James Byrd who being elected tried and sworn well and truly to try this issue of traverse upon their oath do say we find that the defendant is Guilty in manner (p 167) and form as charged in the Bill of Indictment. It is therefore considered by the Court that the defendant Jonathon Tipton for this his offence be fined twenty five cents and pay the costs in this behalf expended and to be held in custody until fine and costs are paid or Security given therefor.

JOHN A. ROGERS)
vs.)
WILLIAM COBB)

This day came the defendant and with leave of the Court withdraws his pleas and the Plaintiff dismisses his suit and thereupon the defendant in his proper person confesses Judgment for the costs. It is therefore considered by the Court that the plaintiff recover of the defendant his costs by him in this behalf expended and that execution issue accordingly.

ISHAM REYNOLDS &)
wife)
vs.)
JOHN A. ROGERS)

On afficavit of the defendant. It is ordered by the Court that this cause be continued until the next Term of this Court and that a Commission issue directed to any Justice of the peace of Monroe County to take the deposition of Henry Chestnut & Sarah Lawson and that Ten days notice of the time and place of taking said deposition be given to the Plaintiffs.

JAMES WHITE)	For reasons (p 168) appearing to the satis-
vs.)	faction of the Court. It is ordered that this
ABSALOM LOONEY &)	cause be continued until the next Term of this
JOHN LAUGHMILLER)	Court.
Adm & c.)	

A Deed of Conveyance from Preston Lawson to Caleb J. Parker for his share of Two hundred acres of land was proven in open Court by the oaths of Michael Harrel and James Sanders and ordered to be registered.

JOHN KING & others)	On affidavit of the defendant this cause is
vs.)	continued until the Next Term of this Court
WILLIAM ALEXANDER)	and on motion of defendant by his attorney

It is ordered that a Commission issue directed to any Justice of the peace of Harlon County Kentucky to take the deposition of John Bailey Senr and that a commission issue directed to any Justice of the peace of Henry County in Virginia (p 169) to take the depositions of Thomas Sterling, Henry Clark and William F. Mills and that Forty days notice served on Robert King shall be sufficient. And on motion of the Plaintiffs by their attorney. It is ordered by the Court that a Commission issue directed to any Justice of the peace of Henry County in Virginia to take the depositions of George Horston, Mary Red and John C. Taylor which depositions when taken to be read in evidence on the trial of this cause on behalf of the Plaintiffs and that Forty days notice of the time and place of taking the same be given to the adverse party.

NANCY A. BARKER)	This cause is continued as an affidavit of defen-
vs.)	dant until the next Term of this Court.
LANGLEY S. HALL)	

STATE)	This day came the State by the attorney General
vs.)riot)	& the defendants in their proper persons and with
ISHAM GIDDENS)	leave of the Court withdraws their plea of not
SIMON MILLS &)	Guilty and plead Guilty and submit to the mercy
JOHN MILLS Jr.)	of the Court. Whereupon it is considered by the

Court that Isham Giddens and Simon Mills for this their offense Be fined Ten dollars each and John Mills Jr. Five dollars and pay the costs in this behalf expended and held in custody until fine & costs are paid or Security given therefor.

LIJAH KINCHELOE)	On affidavit of the defendant this cause is con-
vs.)	tinued until the next Term of this Court.
JOHN A. ROGERS)	

E. EMBREE surviving)	On affidavit (p 170) of Amis Grantham
partner & c.)	this cause is continued until the next Term
vs.)	of this Court and on motion of the Defend-
AMIS GRANTHAM & others)	ants by their attorney. It is ordered by

the Court that a Commission issue directed to any Justice of the peace of Grainger County to take the deposition of Richard Grantham and that Ten days notice of the time and place of taking said deposition be given to the Plaintiff.

STATE)	For passing counterfeit money & c.
vs.)	Rule for a New Trial.
JONATHON TIPTON)	This day came on to be heard the Rule for a new

Trial and after argument of Counsel theron as well for as against the rule and the premises considered and fully understood. It is ordered by the Court that said rule be discharged. And it is considered by the Court that the Defendant Jonathon Tipton for this his offense be fined Fifty dollars and that he receive Ten lashes on his bare back with a whip or cowskin between the hours of one and Four O'clock P. M. on tomorrow to be inflicted by the Sheriff of this County at the public whipping post and that he be imprisoned in the Jail of this County for the space of one month and that he pay the costs in this behalf expended and that he remain in prison until fine and costs are paid or Security given therefore.

STATE) Forfeited Recognizance (p 171)
vs.) This day came the State by the Attorney General and
JESSE WALKER) the defendant Jesse Walker being bound in recognizance
in the sum of Six hundred dollars for his personal appearance to the present Term of this Court to answer a charge of the State exhibited against him and being solemnly called to come into Court came not but made default. It is therefore considered by the Court that the State recover against the said Jesse Walker the sum of Six hundred dollars unless he appear at the next Term of this Court and shew sufficient cause why the Judgment should not be made final and that Scire Facias issue against him & c.

STATE) Forfeited recognizance.
vs.) This day came the State by the Attorney General
ELIZABETH WALKER) and the defendants being bound Jointly and sever-
JACOB RUSH) ally in Recognizance in the sum of Six hundred o
JESSE CREECH and) dollars for the personal appearance at the pres-
JOHN ROBINSON) ent Term of this Court of Jesse Walker and be-
ing solemnly called to bring into Court the said Jesse Walker brought him not and forfeited their recognizance. It is therefore considered by the Court that the State recover against the Defendants the sum (p 172) of Six hundred dollars unless they appear at the next Term of this Court and shew sufficient cause why this Judgment should not be made final and that Scire Facias issue against them & c.

ZACHARIAS STACEY) This day came the parties by their attornies and
vs.) thereupon came a Jury to wit George R. Smith,
HIRAM CHARLES) Andrew Galbraith, Reuben Barnard, Philip Crity,
John Cockram, John Shough, John McWilliams, James Jones, James Byrd, John Denny and Thomas Monahon who being elected tried and sworn upon their oaths do say that the defendnat is not Guilyt of Trespass in the declaration mentioned as by his pleadings he hath alledged. It is therefore considered by the Court that the plaintiff take nothing by his Writ but for his false clamor be in mercy and that the defendant go hence without day and recover of the plaintiff the costs in this behalf expended and that Execution issue accordingly.

ZACHARIAH STACEY) Joseph Russell who had heretofore been summoned
vs.) as Witness on behalf of the Plaintiff in this
HIRAM CHARLES) suit and being solemnly called to come into
Court came not but made default. Therefore (p 173) on motion of the Plaintiff by his attorney. It is considered that the Plaintiff recover against the said Joseph Russell the sum of One hundred and twenty five dollars agreeable to an Act of Assembly in such case made and provided unless sufficient cause of disability to attend be shewn at the next Term of this Court after notice of this Judgment.

WILLIAM WALKER) On affidavit of the Defendant this cause is con-

vs.   )   tinued until the next Term of this Court.   And
JONATHON HENDERSON)   on motion of the defendant by his attorney.
It is ordered by the Court that a Commission issue directed to any Justice of the peace of Grainger County to take the deposition of James
Allen and a Commission issue directed to any Justice of the peace of Claibourn County to take the depositions of Gree Bunden and James Mitchell and
that a Commission issue directed to any Justice of the peace of Washington County to take the deposition of David Thompson and that Ten days
notice of the time and place of said depositions be given to the Plaintiff.

JOHN A. ROGERS   )   On affidavit of the Plaintiff this cause is con-
      vs.   )   tinued until the next Term of this Court.
ALEXANDER FINLEY)

JAMES W. HILL)   This day (p 174) came the Plaintiff by his attor-
      vs.   )   ney and dismisses this suit and thereupon the de-
GEORGE JOHNSON)   fendants George Johnson & Thomas L. Williams by
& others   )   their attorney confess Judgment for the costs.
It is therefore considered by the Court that Plaintiff recover of the defendant George Johnson the costs in this behalf expended as above confessed and that Execution issue accordingly.

JOHN A. ROGERS   )   On affidavit of the Plaintiff this cause is con-
      vs.   )   tinued until the next Term of this Court.
SAMUEL WILSON Jr.)

JOHN A. ROGERS)   On affidavit of the Plaintiff this cause is con-
      vs.   )   tinued until the next Term of this Court.
ELI BOYKIN   )

JOHN A. ROGERS)   On affidavit of Osbourn Boykin agent for defend-
      vs.   )   ant. It is ordered by the Court that a Commiss-
ELI BOYKIN   )   ion issue directed to any Justice of the peace
of Hawkins County to take the deposition de bene esse of John D. Hill
and that Ten days notice of the time and place be given to the Plaintiff.

MICHAEL PEARSON)   On affidavit of Peter Elrod agent for the Plain-
      vs.   )   tiff this cause is continued until the next Term
THOMAS JOHNSON)   of this Court.

ARCHIBALD McKINNEY)   By consent (p 175) of the parties this cause
      vs.   )   is refered to the arbitration of John Miller,
LIJAH KINCHELOE   )   William Lyons, Peter Parsons & George White
with leave to choose an umpire and their award returned into open Court
under their hands and seals to be the Judgment of the Court.

ROBERT JOHNSON)   The parties having refered this cause to arbit-
      vs.   )   rators and they having returned their award into
LIJAH KINCHELOE)   open Court inn the following words and figures
to wit.
We the undersigned being appointed by Court to arbitrate and settle a mat-
ter of difference between Doctor Robert Johnson and Lijah Kincheloe depending in the Circuit Court of Hawkins County met in the town of Surgoinsville
and after being duly sworn and hearing of Testimony as well for Plaintiff
as defendant and considering the premises do unanimously agree that the

plaintiff hath not any legal cause of action against the said Elijah Kincheloe therefore do award that the amount now produced before us be balanced and that the suit be dismissed and the plaintiff pay the costs. Given under our hands and seals this 20th day (p 176) of October 1823.

Richard Mitchell   (seal)
J. W. Carden   (seal)
George White   (seal)
Daniel Chambers   (seal)
Francis Leeper   (seal)

It is therefore considered by the Court that the defendant go hence without day and recover of the Plaintiff the costs in behalf expended and that execution issue accordingly.

LIJAH KINCHELOE)   This day came the parties by their attornies and
    vs)   No 2   )   thereupon came a Jury to wit, Andrew Galbreath,
JOHN A. ROGERS)   George Smith, Reuben Barnard, Philip Critz, James Jones, John W. Williams, Joseph Huffmaster, James Byrd, John Denny Preston Blevins, Thomas Monahon and John Walker who being elected tried and sworn and it appearing to the satisfaction of the Court that this cause is not at issue. It is considered and ordered by the Court that the Jurors aforesaid from rendering their Verdict in this cause be discharged.

Court adjourned until tomorrow 9 O'clock A. M.
                    S. Powel

Saturday 10th April 1824 (p 177)

Court met pursuant to adjournment.
Present The Honorable Samuel Powel - Judge.

ZACHARIAH STACEY)   Polly Bussel who had heretofore been summoned
    vs.   )   as a Witness on behalf of the Plaintiff in this
HIRAM CHARLES   )   cause and on yesterday after the Jurors were
sworn was solemnly called to come into Court came not but made default and it appearing to the Court that the same was omitted to be entered. It is considered by the Court that the Plaintiff recover against the said Polly Bussel the sum of One hundred and twenty five dollars agreeable to an act of Assembly in such case made and provided unless sufficient cause of her disability to attend be shown at the next Term of this Court after notice of this Judgment.

ZACHARIAH STACEY)   John Manis Jr who had heretofore been summoned
    vs.   )   as a witness on behalf of the plaintiff in this
HIRAM CHARLES   )   cause and on Yesterday after the Jurors were
sworn being solemnly called to come into Court came not but made default and it appearing to the Court that the same was omitted to be entered. It is considered by the Court that the Plaintiff recover against the said (p 178) John Manis Junr the sum of One hundred and twenty five dollars agreeable to an act of Assembly in such case made and provided, unless sufficinet cause of his disability to attend be shown at the next Term of this Court after notice of this Judgment.

CROWBARGERS Executors)   On affidavit of Philip Critz agent for the
    vs.   )   Plaintiffs. It is ordered by the Court
JACOB SEAVERS   )   that a Commission issue directed to any
Justice of the peace of Scott County in the State of Virginia to take the

depositions of Horaon Epperson, William Haynes, Thomas Foster & Michael Dickson, Robert McCulloch and that Ten days notice of the time and place of taking said deposition be given to the adverse party.

SPOTSWOOD LIPSCOMB)   On affidavit of the Plaintiff this cause is
  vs.   )   continued until the next Term of this Court.
JONATHON JONES   )

PATRICK CAREY)   On motion of the Plaintiff by his attorney. It is
  vs.   )   ordered by the Court that a Commission issue dir-
JOHN S. HILL)   ected to any Justice of the peace of Washington
County to take the depositio of Jacob Howard and that Ten days notice of the time and place be given to the adverse party.

CROWBARGERS Executors)   On affidavit (p 179) of Greenbury B. Mc-
  vs.   )   Kinney The agent for defendant. It is or-
JACOB SEAVERS   )   dered by the Court that this cause be continued until the next term of this Court and that a Commission issue directed to any Justice of the peace of Scott County Virginia to take the
deposition of Maj Walter, H. Fisher, James Fulton esqr, Jonathon Morrison
and that a Commission issue directed to any Justice of the peace of Sullivan County Tennessee to take the depositions of Walter H. Fisher, Jonathon Morrison, Richard Netherland and John Brown and that a Commission
issue directed to any Justice of the peace of Hawkins County to take the
deposition de bene esse of John Mills and that Ten days notice of the time
and place of taking said deposition be given to the Plaintiff. And on
motion of the Plaintiff by this attorney. It is ordered by the Court
that a Commission issue directed to any Justice of the peace of Hawkins
County Tennessee to take the deposition of David Kincaid de bene esse
and that Ten days notice of the time and place of taking said deposition
be given to the adverse party.

JOHN BEAL Jr.)   David Stuart who was Security for the Plaintiff
  vs.   )   for the prosecution of this cause came here into
DAVID EVERHEART)   open Court and by consent of the defendant the
(p 180) said David Stuart is exonerated and discharge from being Security for the prosecution of this suit. And thereupon came into open
Court John Beal Senr and enters himself Security for the prosecution
of this suit and agrees that if the plaintiff should be cost in this
action that he shall pay the costs and damages that may be adjudged against him or that he the said John Beal Senr will pay it for him.

BRYANT RUDD)   Petition for Divorce.
  vs.   )   The Plaintiff by his attorney comes into open Court
LEWIS RUDD)   and dismisses his petition. It is therefore considered by the Court that Lewis Rudd Recover against Bryant Rudd her costs
in this behalf expended and that Execution may issue for the same.

JAMES HAGAN   )   By consent of the parties this suit is refered
  vs.   )   to the Arbitration of George White, William Sim-
JOHN A. ROGERS)   pson and George Hale and their award returned to
next Court shall be the Judgment of this Court.

JOSEPH M. SICK)   On affidavit of the plaintiff. It is ordered by
  vs.   )   the Court that a Commission issue to any Justice
MARY SICK   )   of the peace of Scott County Virginia to take the
depositions of Adam Winager, Andrew Dean, Christopher Lark and that Ten

days notice be given of the time and place of Taking the same and that a Commission (p 181) issue in Hawkins County to take the Deposition of Catherine Winager de bene esse and that 10 days notice be given to the adverse party of the time and place of taking the same.

JOHN BALCH)
vs.)
ALEXANDER SEVIER)

This day came the parties by their attornies and thereupon came a Jury to wit, John Reynolds Hezekiah Hamblen, Nicholas Long, Thomas Caldwell, Moses McGinnis, Jesse W. Hale, Joseph McCullough, George Haynes, John Mitchell, Elijah Gillenwaters, Samuel Wilson and John A. Rogers who being elected tried and sworn and the Plaintiff by his attorney suffers a non suit and on motion of the Plaintiff by attorney a Rule is Granted him to shew cause why the non suit should be set aside and thereupon filed his affidavit and the rule considered and understood. It is ordered by the Court that the non suit be set aside and that the Plaintiff pay the costs of this Term for which Execution may issue therefor.

JOHN MILLER)
vs.)
ELIJAH JONES)

This cause is continued until the next Term of this Court as upon the affidavit of the Plaintiff.

LIJAH KINCHELOE)
vs.)
JOHN A. ROGERS)

In this cause the parties agree that three months be allowed the defendant to mae up the pleadings and that the cause stand for trial at the next Term.

ZACHARIAH STACEY)
vs.)
HIRAM CHARLES)

In this cause (p 182) the parties agree that a New Trial be granted and that The forfeitture entered against Joseph Russell a Witness in this cause be set aside on the payment of costs.

STATE)
vs)Scire Facias)
HEZEKIAH EMBERSON)

This day came the State by the attorney General and it appearing to the Court that a Scire Facias has been returned to this Court made known to the said Defendant to appear and shew cause if any he has why the Judgment entered against him at the last Term of this Court for the sum of three hundred dollars and the said Hezekiah Emberson being called came not & c. It is therefore considered by the Court that the Judgment be made final and that the State of Tennessee recover against Hezekiah Emberson the sum of three hundred dollars together with the costs in this behalf expended and the defendant in mercy & c.

JAMES FORD)
vs.)
RICHARD G. WATERHOUSE)

The Rule for a new trial having come on for argument and argument of Counsel being heard on both sides and the Court having fully considered and understood the premises. It is ordered that the rule for a new trial be discharged and thereupon it is ordered by the Court that the plaintiff recover of the defendant the sum of thirteen dollars (p 183) and ninety five & one half cents the damages by the Jury aforesaid assessed together with the costs by them in this behalf expended to be levied of the proper goods & chattels lands & tenaments of the said Robert Nall & Richard Mitchell and of the goods & chattels of the said William Paine in the hands of the defendants Richard G. Waterhouse and Orville Paine Executor to be administered and the defendants in mercy & c.

JOHN A. ROGERS)
vs.)
ALEXANDER FINLEY)

The Demurrer of the Plaintiff to the plea of the defendant having come on for argument and argument of Counsel on both sides being heard and the premises being by the Court fully considered and understood and it appearing to the satisfaction of the Court that the plea of the defendant and the matters and things therein contained are good and sufficient in law to abate the plaintiffs action. It is therefore considered that said suit of the plaintiff be abated and that the defendant go hence without day and recover against the plaintiff the costs in this behalf expended and that Execution issue accordingly.

LANGLEY S. HALL) This day came the plaintiff by his attorney and
vs.) the defendant (p 184) in his proper person
PETER PARSONS) and with leave of the Court confesses Judgment
for the sum of Fifty two dollars and fifty cents and the costs. It is therefore considered by the Court that the plaintiff recover of the defendant Peter Parsons the sum of Fifty two dollars and fifty cents and also the costs in this behalf expended as above confessed for which execution may issue.

STATE) In the progress of the trial of this cause the
vs.) defendant by his attorney tendered a Bill of
JONATHON TIPTON) Exceptions and prayed that the same may be signed sealed & made a part of the record in this cause which is done and thereupon the defendant by his attorney prays an appeal in the nature of a Writ of Error to the Supreme Court of Errors and appeal to be held for the first Judicial Circuit at the Courthouse in Rogersville on the first Monday of May next which is granted by the Court.

SAMUEL REYNOLDS) This day came the parties by their attornies
& others) and the demurrer of the plaintiff to the third
vs.) plea of the defendant came on for argument and
JAMES HAGAN) (p 185) argument of Counsel being heard both on the part of the plaintiff and defendant & the premises considered and fully understood. It is considered by the Court that the said third plea of the defendant and the matters and things therein contained and not good and sufficient in law and the demurrer be sustained and on motion leave is given the defendant to amend the said plea and that he pay the costs of the amendment & c.

JOHN G. WINSTON) In this cause on motion of the plaintiff by
vs.) his attorney and it appearing to the satisfact-
GOERGE WHITE) ion of the Court that the plaintiff was compelled to pay as one of the Securities of the defendant the sum of Twenty two dollars and thirty five cents on a Judgment rendered in the Circuit of Hawkins County against the defendant John G. Winston, Robert Carden and Jonathon Long. It is therefore considered by the Court that Plaintiffs recover of the defendant the sum of Twenty Two dollars and thirty five cents and also the costs of this motion and that Execution issue accordingly.

All causes on this docket not otherwise disposed of are continued until next Court.

Court adjourned until Court in Course.
S. Powel

Monday 4th October 1824 (p 186)

At a Circuit Court begun and held for the County of Hawkins at the Courthouse in Rogersville on the first Monday being the Fourth day of October in the year of our Lord One thousand eight hundred and twenty four and the Forty ninth of American Independence.

Present the Honorable Edward Scott - Judge.

Gabriel McCrow Sheriff of Hawkins County returns now here into Court one Writ of Venire Facias returnable to the present Term of this Court executed on the following persons being good and lawful men of Hawkins County appointed by the County Court of Hawkins County - viz.

James Francisco
Philip Critz
Joseph McCullough Jr.
John Johnston
Thomas Stacey
John A. Rogers
Clinton Armstrong
Absalom Kyle
Larkin Willis
James Williams
Abraham Hawk
Jacob Miller
Joseph W. Carden
Howel Brewer
Willie B. Kyle
Thomas Anderson
John Miller
William Smith
John Mitchell
John Reynolds
Shadrach Epperson
Hezekiah Hamblen

from among whom the following persons being drawn in due form of law and compose the Grand Jury for the present Term of this Court, to wit,

1.   Jacob Miller
2.   Thomas Stacey
3.   John Johnston
4.   Thomas Anderson
5.   Hezekiah Hamblen
6.   Howel Brewer (p 187)
7.   James Williams
8.   Larkin Willis
9.   Philip Critz
10   John Mitchell
11   John A. Rogers
12. Absalom Kyle
13   Joseph W. Carden

Whereupon the Court appointed Jacob Miller Foreman of the Grand Jury who were empanneled and sworn received their charge and withdrew from the Bar of the Court.

William Cloud Constable was appointed by the Court officer to attend on the Grand Jury for the present Term and was qualified in due form of Law.

JOHN DEN LESSEE of) This day came the parties by their attor-
GEORGE EVANS) nies and thereupon came a Jury to wit, Will-
vs.)Ejectment) iam Smith, Abraham Hawk, Elijah Jones, Will-
JESSE CHEEK) iam Molsby, Samuel Wilson, James Williford,
James Walker, Thomas Hale, Thomas Cox, Haynes Amis, Charles King and Jos-
uha Smith who being elected tried and sworn upon their oath do say we
find that the defendant is not Guilty of the Trespass and Ejectment as in
the Plaintiffs declaration mentioned. It is therefore considered by the
Court that the Plaintiff take nothing by his Writ but for his falxe clamour be in Mercy & c and that the defendant go hence without day and recover of the Plaintiff his costs by him in this behalf expended and that
execution issue accordingly.

JOHN DEN LESSEE of) This day came (p 188) the parties by their
WILLIAM WHITESIDES) attornies and thereupon came a Jury, to wit.
vs.) William Smith, Abraham Hawk, Elijah Jones, Will-
DAVID PROFFIT) iam Molsby, Samuel Wilson, James Williford,
James Walker, Thomas Hale, Thomas Cox, Haynes Amis, Charles King and Joshua Smith who being elected tried and sworn by consent of the parties and
with the assent of the Court a Juror is withdrawn and the rest of Jurors
from rendering their Verdict in this cause are discharged. And that this
cause be continued until the next Term of this Court.

JOHN DEN LESSEE of) This day came the parties by their attornies
CONDRY & COCKE) & thereupon came a Jury to wit, William Smith
vs.) Abraham Hawk, Elijah Jones, William Molsby,
JOEL DYER) Samuel Wilson, James Williford, James Walker,
Thomas Hale, Thomas Hale, Thomas Cox, Haynes Amis, Charles King and Joshua Smith who being elected tried and sworn upon their oath do say we find
that the defendant is not Guilty of the Trespass and Ejectment as in the
Plaintiffs declaration mentioned. It is therefore considered by the Court
that the defendant go hence and recover of the Plaintiffs his costs in
this behalf expended and that Execution issue accordingly.

Ordered by the Court (p 189) that the Clerk shall keep a roll containing
the names of all the practising attornies of this Court beginning with the
Youngest & so on in regular orders to the oldest. As soon as the minutes
are signed the Clerk shall call the roll and if any attorney has any motion to make to the Court he shall make the same when his mane is called
and motions will not be heard at any other time except on extraordinary
occasions to be adjudged of by the Court. Affidavits for continuance
in civil causes must be ready and offered when the cause is called and
no arguments will be heard thereon.

A Title Bond from Charles Dodson to Reuben Dodson for lands lying in
Greene County Tennessee was proven in open Court by the oaths of Nicholas Long and James Williford and ordered to be certified.

E. EMBREE surviving) This day came the parties by their attornies
partner & c.) and thereupon came a Jury to wit, William
vs.) Smith, Abraham Hawke, Elijah Jones, William
LINCOLN AMIS nad) Molsby, Samuel Wilson, James Williford, James
JAMES W. REYNOLDS) Walker, Thomas Hale, Joseph Russell, Lewis
Click, Charles King and Joshua Smith who being elected tried and sworn upon their oath do say we find for the Plaintiff and assess his (p 190)
damages to Fifteen hundred and eighteen dollars and foxn cents besides
costs. It is therefore considered by the Court that the plaintiff recover

of the defendants the sum of Fifteen hundred and eighteen dollars and four cents the damages aforesaid by the Jurors aforesaid assessed and also the costs in this behalf expended for which execution may issue.

JOHN DEN LESSEE of) WILLIAM BRADLEY) vs.) THOMAS SPROUL)	On motion of the defendant by his attorney. It is ordered by the Court that a Commission issue directed to any Justice of the peace of Rutherford County in this State to take

the deposition of John Bowman to be read in evidence on the trial of this cause on behalf of the defendant and that Thirty days notice of the time and place of taking said deposition be given to the Plaintiff.

JOHN A. ROGERS) vs.) SAMUEL WILSON Junr.)	On affidavit of the Plaintiff this cause is continued until the next Term of this Court.

JOHN A. ROGERS ✓) vs.) SAMUEL WILSON Junr.)	Nancy Larkins, William Y. Larkins ✓ and Elijah C. Gillenwaters who had (p 191) heretofore been summoned as witnesses on behalf of the

Plaintiff in this cause and being now solemnly called to come into Court came not but made default. It is therefore considered by the Court that the Plaintiff recover against the said Nancy Larkins, William Y. Larkins and Elijah C. Gillenwaters the sum of One hundred and Twenty five dollars each agreeable to act of Assembly in such case made and provided unless sufficient cause of their disability to attend be shewn at the next Term of this Court after notice of this Judgment.

JOHN A. ROGERS) vs.) ELI BOYKIN)	Bronnum Hill, Benjamin Moreland, Matthew Hill and William Reynolds who had heretofore been summoned as witnesses on behalf of the Plaintiff in this

cause and being now solemnly called to come into Court came not but made default. It is therefore considered by the Court that the Plaintiff recover against the said Brennum Hill, Benjamin Morelandm Matthew Hill and William Reynolds the sum of One hundred and Twenty five dollars each agreeable to an act of Assembly in such case made and provided unless sufficient cause of their disability to attend be shewn at the next Term of this Court after notice of this Judgment.

WILLIAM CRUMLEY) vs.) JOHNSON FRAZIER)	On motion of the Plaintiff this cause is continued until the next (p 192) Term of this Court and it is ordered that a Commission issue direct-

ed to any Justice of the peace of Monroe County to take the depositions of Aaron Parker and Jacob Smiley to be read in evidence on the trial of this cause on behalf of the Plaintiff and that ten days notice of the time and place of taking said depositions be given to the adverse party.

JOHN A. ROGERS) vs.) ELI BOYKIN)	Peter Bare and George Elkins who had heretofore been legally summoned as Witnesses on behalf of the defendant in this cause and being now solemnly call-

ed to come into Court came not but made default. It is therefore considered by the Court that the defendant Eli Boykin recover against the said Peter Bare and George Elkins the sum of One hundred and twenty five dollars each agreeable to an act of Assembly in such case made and provided unless sufficient cause of their disability to attend be shewn at the next Term of this Court after notice of this Judgment.

JOHN A. ROGERS)   This day came the parties by their attorneys and

vs.
ELI BOYKIN)   thereupon came a Jury to wit, William Smith, Abraham Hawk, William Molsby, James Williford, James Walker, Lewis Click, John Miller, James Francisco (p 193) Arthur G. Young, Reuben Barnard, Shadrock Epperson and Joshua Smith who being elected tried and sworn upon their oaths do say we find that the defendants is Guilty of speaking and publishing the words as the Plaintiff hath complained in the first count of his declaration and assess the plaintiffs by occasions thereof to Two hundred and thirty five dollars besides costs and as th the speaking proclaiming publishing and pronouncing the residue of the English words in the declaration mentioned the Jurors aforesaid on their oath aforesaid do further say that the defendant is not thereof Guilty as by pleading he hath alledged.

Whereupon on motion of the defendant by his attorney a rule is allowed him to shew cause why a new trial should be granted in this cause.

JOHN DEN LESSEE of)   Thomas Cocke who claims title to the land
ALEXANDER PORTER)   mentioned in the Declaration of Eject-
      vs.   )   ment in
RICHARD FEN with notice)
to CHARLES LITTLETON)

JOHN DEN LESSEE of)   these suits comes into Court and is admit-
ALEXANDER PORTER)   ted to defend in the room and stead of Ric-
      vs.   )   hard Fen and thereupon agrees that on the
RICHARD FEN with notice)   Trials he will confess lease Entry and
to WILLIAM S. HAYWOOD)   ouster and insist on his title only.

And thereupon Sterling Cocke comes into open Court and undertook that if the said Thomas (p 194) Cocke should be cost in this action he shall pay the costs and charges or that he the said Sterling Cocke will pay if for him.

Court adjourned until tomorrow 8 O'clock A. M.
                       Edw. Scott

Tuesday 5th October 1824.

Court met pursuant to adjournment.

Present The Honorable Edward Scott - Judge.

JOHN DEN LESSEE of)   On motion It is ordered by the Court that the
WILLIAM BRADLEY)   Rule of reference made at the last Term of
      vs.   )   this Court be set aside and that this cause be
THOMAS SPROUL)   continued until next Court.

JOHN A. ROGERS)   By consent of the Plaintiff by his attorney.
      vs.   )   It is ordered by the Court that the forfeit-
ELIJAH C. GILLENWATERS)   ture entered against the defendant on Yes-
terday for his non attendance as a Witness be set aside on the payment of costs for which Execution may issue.

WILLIAM BRONNON)   On affidavit of the Plaintiff this cause is con-
      vs.   )   tinued until the next Term of this Court and that
ALEXANDER SEVIER)   (p 195) a Commission issue directed to any Jus-
tice of the peace of Greene County in this State to take the deposition of Joseph Brown to be read in Evidence on behalf of the Plaintiff and that Five days notice of the time and place of taking said Deposition be given to the adverse party.

JOHN A. ROGERS)   By consent of the Plaintiff by his attorney
       vs.   )   It is ordered by the Court that the forfeit-
SAMUEL WILSON Jr.) ure entered against William Y. Larkins and
Nancy Larkins witnesses in this suit be set aside on the payment of costs
for which Executions may issue.

WILLIAM BURGESS &)   This day came the Parties by their attornies
REBECCA BURGESS his) and thereupon came a Jury, to wit, William
wife   ) Smith, Abraham Hawk, Shadrock Epperson, Jos-
       vs.) Slander) eph McCullough Senr. Reuben Barnard, George
ALEXANDER SEVIER   ) Rogers, John Armstrong, Joseph McCullough
Jr., Elijah Jones, Thomas Taylor, James Walker and John McWilliams who
being elected tried and sworn upon their oath do say we find that the Defendant is Guilty of Speaking publishing, proclaiming and pronouncing
the same English words in manner and form as the plaintiffs against
him hath complained and within six months next before suing out the original Writ (p 196) in this cause and assess the Plaintiffs damage by
occasion thereof to Five dollars besides costs. It is therefore considered by the Court that the Plaintiffs recover of the defendant the sum
of Five dollars the damages aforesaid by Jurors aforesaid assessed together with the costs in this behalf expended and that Execution issue
accordingly.

STATE   )   Vardy Collins and Benjamin Bunch who were bound in
   vs.   )   recognizance for the personal appearance of John Bunch
JOHN BUNCH)   at the present Term of this Court surrender the body
of the said John Bunch in Open Court in discharge of themselves as appearance Bail. Whereupon the Court ordered the said John Bunch in custody of the Sheriff.

A Deed of Conveyance from Thomas Roddy to David A. Deaderick for Sixty
four acres of land was acknowledged in open Court and ordered to be registered.

LIJAH KINCHELOE)   This day came the parties by their attornies
     vs.   )   and thereupon came a Jury, to wit (p 197)
JOHN A. ROGERS)   James Francisco, John Miller, Arthur G. Young,
Willie B. Kyle, Samuel Armstrong, John Kyle, Markham Kenner, Levy Painter, Cornelius Carmack, James Sanders, Richard Cole and Isaac Leuder-
back who being elected tried and sworn by consent of the parties by their
attornies and with the assent of the Court the Jurors aforesaid form rendering their verdict are respited until tomorrow.

The Court adjourned until tomorrow 9 O'clock A. M.
                                      Edw. Scott

Wednesday 6th October 1824.

Court met pursuant to adjournment.

Present The Honorable Edward Scott - Judge.

JOHN DEN LESSEE of)   On motion of the Plaintiffs by their attorney
CONDRY & COOKE   )   a rule is allowed them to shew cause why a new
     vs.   )   Trial should be granted in this cause.
JOEL DYER   )

STATE   )   This day came the State by the Attorney General
    vs.   )   and with leave of the Court enters a Nolli Pro-
ABSALOM HAWORTH)   sequi in this cause. It is therefore considered
by the Court that the defendant be discharged and that the Clerk of this
Court transmit a Bill of costs to the County Court of Greene for allowance.

LIJAH KINCHELOE)   This day came (p 198) the parties by their
   vs.) No 1   )   attornies and thereupon came a Jury to wit,
JOHN A. ROGERS)   the same Jury that were on Yesterday respited
from rendering their Verdict who were elected tried and sworn and progress having been made in the trial of this cause the Plaintiff by his
attornye with leave of the Court suffers a Non suit. Whereupon on motion of the Plaintiff by attorney a rule is allowed him to shew cause why
the non suit should be set aside.

STATE   )   Forfeited Recognizance
    vs.   )   This day came the State by the attorney General and
 ISAIAH JONES)   the defendant Isaiah Jones being bound in recognizance in the sum of Five hundred dollars for his personal appearance to the
present Term of this Court to answer a charge of the State exhibited against
him for Barratry and being now solemnly called to come into Court came not
but made default. It is therefore considered by the Court that the State
recover against the said Isaiah Jones the sum of Five hundred dollars, unless he appears at the next Term of this Court and shew sufficient cause
if any he can why this Judgment should not be made final and that Scire Facias issue against him & c.

STATE OF TENNESSEE)   Forfeited (p 199) Recognizance
      vs.   )   This day came the State by the Attorney Gener-
JAMES JONES   )   al & the defendant being bound in Recognizance
in the sum of Five hundred dollars for the personal appearance of Isaiah
Jones at the present Term of this Court and being now solemnly called to
bring into Court the body of the said Isaiah Jones brought him not but
made default and thereby forfeited his recognizance. It is therefore considered by the Court that the State recover of James Jones the sum of
Five hundred dollars unless he appears at the next Term of this Court and
shew sufficient cause why this Judgment should not be made final and that
Scire Facias issue & c.

STATE   )   Forfeited recognizance.
    vs.   )   This day came the State by the Attorney General and
 ISAIAH JONES)   the defendant appearing in open Court in his proper
person. It is considered by the Court that forfeitures entered against
the Plaintiff and his security be set aside.

A Deed of Conveyance from Gabriel McOrow Sheriff to Cleon Moore for One
hundred and Sixty acres of land was acknowledged in open Court and ordered
to be registered.

STATE OF TENNESSEE)   On motion (p 200) and for reasons appearing
   vs.) Sci Fa   )   to the satisfaction of the Court. It is or-
ELIZABETH WALKER)   dered that this cause be continued until the
JACOB RUSH   )   next Term of this Court.
JESSE CREEK and   )
JOHN ROGINSON   )

STATE OF TENNESSEE)   This day came the State by the Attorney
vs.) Riot as't & Battery)   General and the defendant in his proper
HEZEKIAH EMBERSON)   person and being charged on the Bill of
Indictment plead Guilty and submits to the mercy of the Court. Whereupon
on motion and for reasons appearing to the satisfaction of the Court It
is ordered that this cause be continued until the next Term of this Court
on giving security for his appearance at said Term.

MICHAEL McCANN)   This day came the parties by their attornies and
& Co.)   thereupon came a Jury, to wit, James Francisco,
   vs.)   John Miller, Arthur G. Young, Willie B. Kyle,
FRAZIER BRINLEY)   Samuel Armstrong, John Kyle Abraham Hawk, Leroy
Painter, Cornelius Carmack, James Sanders, Richard Cole and Isaac Lauderback who being elected tried and sworn and progress having been made in
the trial of this cause. The Plaintiffs by their attorney with leave of
the Court suffers a Non suit. Whereupon on motion (p 201) of the Plaintiffs by their attorney a rule is allowed them to shew cause why the Non
suit should be set aside.

JOHN DEN LESSEE of)   By consent of the parties by their attornies.
ALEXANDER PORTER)   It is ordered by the Court that these suits
   vs.)   be consolidated.
THOMAS COCKE)
)
JOHN DEN LESSEE of)
ALEXANDER PORTER)
   vs.)
THOMAS COCKE)
)
JOHN DEN LESSEE of)
ALEXANDER PORTER)
   vs.)
THOMAS COCKE)

STATE of TENNESSEE)   This day came the State by the Attorney Gen-
   vs.)   eral and with leave of the Court enters a
JOHN BUNCH)   Nolli prosequi in this cause.

STATE of TENNESSEE)   This day came the State by the Attorney Gen-
   vs.)   eral and with leave of the Court enters a
LITTLETON BROOKS)   Nolli Prosequi in this suit.
JOSEPH BROOKS)
THOMAS BROOKS)
and)
ANDREW COKER)

An assignment on a Plot and certificate of Survey from John Beal to David
Rowan for Twenty five acres of land was acknowledged in open Court and ordered to be certified.

STATE of TENNESSEE)   Personally (p 202) appeared in open Court
   vs.) Riot)   Littleton Brooks, Joseph Brooks, Thomas Bro-
LITTLETON BROOKS)   oks and Andrew Coker and James P. McCarty
JOSEPH BROOKS)   and Joseph Baker and acknowledged themselves
THOMAS BROOKS)   Jointly and severally indebted to the State
and)   of Tennessee in the sum of Five hundred doll-
ANDREW COKER)   ars to be levied of their proper goods and

chattels lands and Tenements to the use of the State but to be void on
condition that the said defendants make their personal appearance before
the Honorable Judge of the Circuit Court at the Courthouse in Rogersville
from day to day and answer a charge of the State exhibited against them
for a Riot and not depart without leave of the Court.

STATE of TENNESSEE)   This day personally appeared in open Court
    vs.   )   Hezekiah Emberson and William Alexander and
HEZEKIAH EMBERSON)   acknowledged themselves indebted to the State
of Tennessee that is to say Hezekiah Emberson in the sum of Two hundred
dollars and William Alexander in the sum of One hundred dollars to be levied of their proper goods and chattels lands and Tenements to the use of
the State but to be void on condition that the said Hezekiah Emberson
(p 203) make his personal appearance before the Honorable Judge of the
Circuit Court at the Courthouse in Rogersville on the Wednesday of the
next Term of this Court & answer a charge of the State exhibited against
him and not depart without leave of the Court.

STATE of TENNESSEE)   This day personally appeared in open Court
    vs.   )   Peter Elrod and acknowledged himself indebt-
HEZEKIAH EMBERSON)   ed to the State of Tennessee in the penal
sum of One hundred dollars to be levied of his proper goods and chattels
lands and Tenements to the use of the State but to be void on condition
that the make his personal appearance before the Honorable Judge of the
Circuit Court at the Courthouse in Rogersville on Wednesday of the next
Term of this Court and prosecute and give evidence on behalf of the State
against Hezekiah Emberson and not depart without leave of the Court.

CHARLES KING   )   By consent of the parties this cause is contin-
    vs.   )   ued until the next Term of this Court.
SAMUEL CHESTNUT)

STATE of TENNESSEE)   This day came the State by the Attorney Gen-
    vs.   )   eral and the defendant (p 204) John Bunch
JOHN BUNCH   )   being brought to the Bar present also his
Counsel and having been charged on the Bill of Indictment plead not Guilty and put himself on the Country and thereupon came a Jury to wit, William Smith, Shadrock Epperson, James Francisco, Joseph McCullough Senr.,
Arthur G. Young, George Johnson, Thomas Taylor, James Willis, Richard
Cole, Cornelius Carmack and Joseph Mooney and Haynes Amis who being elected
tried and sworn well and truly to try this issue of Traverse upon their
oaths do say we find that the defendant is Guilty in manner and form as
charged in the first Count of the Bill of Indictment and we further find
that he is not Guilty in manner and form as charged in the second count
of the Bill of Indictment. Thereupon the Court remanded the said John
Bunch into the custody of the Sheriff.

Court adjourned until tomorrow 8 O'clock A. M.
               Edw. Scott

Thursday 7th October 1824.

Court met pursuant to adjournment.

Present The Honorable Edward Scott - Judge.

STATE of TENNESSEE)   This day came the State by the Attorney
       vs.   )   General & the defendant John Bunch being broh-
JOHN BUNCH   )   ght (p 205) to the Bar in pursuance of the
order of the Court and being asked by the Court if he had anything to say
why the Judgment and sentence of the law should not be pronounced upon
him according to the verdict of the Jury rendered against him on Yesterday
and he saying nothing further than as heretofore. Whereupon all and singular the premises being seen and by the Court considered and fully understood. It is by the Court now here considered and adjudged that the said
John Bunch for such his offence be fined in the sum of Twenty five dollars and that the he be imprisoned in the Jail of Greene County for the
space of Three Calendar months. It being represented to the Court that
the Common prison of this County is insecure and that he there remain in
prison until the fine and costs in this case are paid or good and sufficinet security given therefor and that the Sheriff of this County deliver the said John Bunch into the Custody of the Sheriff of Greene County
accordingly.

STATE of TENNESSEE)   On affidavit of Alexander Sevier the Prosecut-
       vs.   )   or this cause is continued until the next Term
ISAIAH JONES   )   of this Court. And thereupon personally appeared in open Court Isaiah Jones, Michael Bright and James Jones and acknowledged themselves indebted to the State of Tennessee in the sum of Five
hundred (p 206) dollars each to be levied of their proper goods and
chattels lands and tenements to the use of the State but to be void on
condition that the said Isaiah Jones make his personal appearance before
the Honorable Judge of the Circuit Court at the Courthouse in Rogersville
on the Wednesday of the next Term of this Court and answer a charge of the
State exhibited against him for Barretny and not depart without leave of
the Court.

STATE of TENNESSEE)   Personally appeared in open Court Alexander
       vs.   )   Sevier and acknowledged himself indebted to the
ISAIAH JONES   )   State of Tennessee in the sum of Two hundred
and fifty dollars to be levied of his proper goods and chattels lands and
tenements to the use of the State but to be void on condition that he
make his personal appearance before the Honorable Judge of the Circuit
Court at the Courthouse in Rogersville on the Wednesday of the next Term
of this Court and give evidence on behalf of the State against the said
Isaiah Jones and not depart without leave of the Court.

STATE of TENNESSEE)   This day came the State by the Attorney Gen-
       vs.   )   eral & with leave of the Court enters a Nolli
SARAH HICKS   )   Prosequi in this case. And thereupon Anderson (p 207) Hicks comes into open Court and assumes the costs. It is
therefore considered by the Court that the State recover against the said
Anderson Hicks the costs in this behalf expended for which execution may
issue.

JOHN DEN LESSEE of   )   Etheldred Williams who claims title to
JAMES McBEE   )   the land mentioned in the declaration
       vs.   )   of Ejectment in this suit comes into open
RICHARD FEN with notice)   Court and on motion is admitted to defend
   to JAMES DODSON   )   in the room and stead of Richard Fen and
thereupon agrees that on the trial he will confess lease Entry and ouster
and insist on his title only.
And thereupon John Williams comes into open Court and undertook that if the
said Etheldred Williams should be cost in this action he shall pay the

costs and charges or that he the said John Williams will pay if for him.

JAMES HOGAN)   This day came the plaintiff by his attorney and
   vs.   )   with leave of the Court dismisses his suit and
JOHN SLAUGHTER)   thereupon James Bradley comes into open Court and
confesses Judgment for the costs. It is therefore considered by the Court
that the Plaintiff take nothing by his wit and that the defendnat go hence without day & recover of James Bradley the costs in this behalf expan-
ded & that Execution issue & c.

JOHN DEN LESSEE of)   On affidavit (p 208) of the defendant. It
JAMES McBEE   )   is ordered by the Court that a Commission iss-
   vs.   )   ue directed to any Justice of the peace of
ETHELDRED WILLIAMS)   Hawkins County to take the depositions De bene
esse of Jacob Miller Senr, Jamima Moffitt and Jacob Frizzle to be read on
the trial of this cause on behalf of the defendant and Ten days notice of
the time and place of taking said deposition be given to the plaintiffs.

JOHN BEAL   )   By consent of the parties this cause is referred
   vs.   )   to the arbitration of Joseph Bishop, John G. Win-
DAVID EVERHEART)   ston, Isham Reynolds, Thomas Cox, Henry Lauderback and Abraham Varnon and their award or a majority of them returned
into Court under their hands and seals to be the Judgment of the Court.

NANCY A. BARKER)   By consent of the parties this cause is refer-
   vs.   )   red to the arbitration of Joseph Russell, James
LANGLEY S. HALL)   Amis, Jacob Miller, John Stokeley and John Reynolds and their award or a majority of them returned into Court under
their hands and seals to be the Judgment of the Court.

STATE of TENNESSEE)   This day (p 209) came the State by the At-
   vs.) Riot   )   torney General and the Defendant in his proper
LITTLETON BROOKS)   person and having been charged on the Bill of
Indictment plead not Guilty and put himself on the Country and thereupon
came a Jury, to wit, William Smith, Abraham Hawk, Shadrach Epperson, James
Francisco, John Miller, Arthur G. Young, John W. Williams, Jacob Crews,
Lemmel Adkinson, Thomas Taylor , Thomas Monahon and Reuben Barnard who
being elected tried and sworn well and truly to try this issue of Traverse upon their oath do say we find that the defendant is Guilty in manner and form as charged in the Bill of Indictment.

STATE of TENNESSEE)   This day came the State by the Attorney Gen-
   vs.)Riot   )   eral and the defendants in their proper per-
JOSEPH BROOKS   )   sons and being charged on the Bill of Indict-
THOMAS BROOKS   )   ment plead Not Guilty and put himself on the
& ANDREW COKER))   Country and thereupon came a Jury, to wit.,
William Giddens, James Brine, William Hohnson, Benjamin Thurman, William
Davis, Joseph Mooney, Benjamin L. Bussell, Isham Reynold, James Chestnut,
John Rork, Peter Elrod and John Swain who being elected tried and sworn
upon their oaths do say we find that the defendants are Guilty in manner
and form (p 210) as charged in the Bill of Indictment.
And on motion of the Defendants by their attorney a rule is allowed them
to shew cause why a new trial should be granted in this cause.

Court adjourned until tomorrow 9 O'clock A. M.
                    Edw. Scott.

Friday 8th October 1824.

Court met pursuant to adjournment.

Present the Honorable Edward Scott - Judge.

ZACHARIAH STACEY)   On motion and for reasons appearing to the satis-
vs.) Sci Fa   )   faction of the Court. It is ordered that the
POLLY RUSSELL   )   forfeiture entered against the defendant at the
last Term of this Court be set aside and that she pay Clerk's costs in this
behalf expended for which execution may issue.

JOHN DEN LESSEE of)   This day came on to be heard the rule for a
CONDRY and COCKE)   new trial and after argument of Counsel there-
vs.   )   on as well for as against the rule and the pre-
JOEL DYER   )   mises seen and fully understood. It is considered by the Court that the rule be made absolute and a New trial granted
And it is agreed by the parties that the defendant is in possession of the
land in the Plaintiffs declaration mentioned (p 211) and that no proof
is required to show that fact.

AGNES RICE Assee & c)   On motion Arthur G. Young has permission to
vs.   )   prove his attendance as Witness in this suit
WILLIAM YOUNG   )   in the County Court subject however to any
objection that may be made hereafter by the paties. Whereupon he prove
4 days attendance in said Court.

ROBERT NALL)   On motion of the defendant by his attorney, It is o
vs.)   ordered by the Court he have leave to amend his plea
JOHN S. HILL)   on paying the whole of the costs, up to this Term
for which Execution may issue.

MICHAEL McCANN & Co.)   This day came on to be heard and determined
vs.   )   the rule granted at a former day of this
FRAZIER BRINLEY   )   Term to set aside the Non Suit and after
argument of Counsel thereon as well for as against the rule and the premises seen and fully understood. It is considered by the Court that the
rule be made absolute and that the defendant recover of the Plaintiffs
the costs expended at the present Term for which Execution may issue.

MICHAEL McCANN & Co.)   On motion of the Plaintiffs by their att-
vs.   )   orney. It is ordered by the Court that a
FRAZIER BRINLEY   )   Commission issue directed to any Justice of
the peace of Bottitonat County in the State of Virginia to take the deposition of William Kirk to be read in evidence on the trial of this cause
on behalf of the Plaintiff and that Thirty days notice of the time and
place of taking said deposition be given to the adverse party.

JOHN A. ROGERS)   By consent of the Plaintiff by his attorney
vs.   )   It is ordered by the Court that the forfeiture
SAMUEL WILSON Jr.)   entered against Benjamin Moreland a Witness in
this suit for his non attendance be set aside on payment of the costs for
which Execution may issue.

JOHN PRYOR)   On motion of the defendant by his attorney. It
vs.)   is ordered by the Court that a Commission issue
PETER FRANKLIN)   directed to any Justice of the Peace of Hawkins

County to take the deposition of Oliver Wheeler to be read de bene esse
on the trial of this cause on behalf of the defendant and that Ten days
notice of the time and place of taking said deposition be given to the
Plaintiff.

NANCY A. BARKER)   The parties (p 213) having referred this cause
    vs.   )   on a former day of this Term to Arbitrators and
LANGLEY S. HALL)   they having returned their award into open Court
in the words and figures following, to wit.

NANCY A. BARKER)   This suit being referred to James Amis, Joseph
    vs.   )   Russell, John Stokeley, John Reynolds and Jacob
LANGLEY S. HALL)   Miller and having heard the Evidence and fully
examined the premises and fully considered the same are unanimously of
opinion that the Plaintiff recover of the defendant for damages sustained
Twenty three dollars twelve and one half cents besides the costs of suit.
Given under our hands and seals this 8th day of October 1824.

                    James Amis
                    Joseph Russell
                    John Stokeley
                    John Reynolds
                    JoC Miller

It is considered by the Court that the plaintiff recover of the defendant
the sum of Twenty three dollars the damages awarded by the Arbitrators
aforesaid and also the costs in this behalf expended and that Execution
issue accordingly.

JAMES WHITE   )   This cause is continued until the next
    vs.   )   term of this Court as on affidavit of the
ABSALOM LOONEY and)   Plaintiff.
JOHN LOUGHMILLER   )
Admr & c   )
FREDERICK LOUGHMILLER)
dec'd   )

JOHN KING & others)   On affidavit (p 214) of the defendant this
    vs.   )   cause is continued until the next Term of this
WILLIAM ALEXANDER)   Court and that a Commission issue directed to
any Justice of the Peace of Henry County Virginia to take the depositions
of Thomas Sterling, William F. Mills, P. H. Fontaine, John Pane, Benjamin
Jones, Henry Clark and John C. Tyler and that thirty days notice of the
time and place be given and that a Commission issue directed to any Justice of the peace of Kentucky to take the deposition of John Bailey Senr
& that thirty days notice be given of time and place and that a Commission issue to any Justice of the peace of the State of Missourii to take
the deposition of Zachariah Woods and that Forty days notice of the time
and place of taking said deposition And that a Commission issue directed
to any Justice of the peace of Hawkins County to take the deposition of
James Cooper de bene esse, to be read on the trial of this cause on behalf of the defendant and that ten days notice of the time and place of
taking said deposition be given to Plaintiffs.

WILLIAM WALKER   )   On motion of the defendant by his attorney.
    vs.   )   It is ordered by the Court that a Commission
JONATHON HENDERSON)   (p 215) issue directed to any Justice of the

peace of Washington County in this State to take the deposition of David Thompson to be read in evidence on the trial of this cause on behalf of the Defendant and that Ten days notice of the time and place of taking said deposition be given to the Plaintiff.

JOHN A. ROGERS) On motion and by the consent of the parties. It
    vs.) is ordered by the Court that the forfeiture enter-
ELI BOYKIN) ed on a former day of this term against George
Elkins a Witness in this suit on behalf of Eli Boykin be set aside on the payment of the costs for which Execution may issue.

ACNES RICE Assee & c) On affidavit of Aeneas S. Galbreath agent
    vs.) for the Plaintiff. It is ordered by the
WILLIAM YOUNG) Court that a Commission issue directed to
any Justice of the peace of Marion County in this State to take the depositions of Susannah Rice and Anne McCoy and that ten days notice of the time and place of taking said depostions be given to the adverse party.

JAMES BRADLEY) On affidavit of the defendant. It is ordered by
    vs.) the Court that (p 216) a Commission issue dir-
JOSEPH McMINN) ected to any Justice of the peace of Monroe County
in this State to take the deposition of James Kirkpatrick and that Ten days notice of the time and place of taking said depostion be given to the Plaintiff.

JOHN CRITZ &) On affidavit of the defendant's agent. It
MARY CROWBARGER) is ordered by the Court that a Commission
Executors of GEORGE) issue directed to any Justice of the peace
CROWBARGER Dec'd) of Hawkins County to take the depositions
    vs.) of Absalom Looney and George Norton de bene
JACOB SEAVERS) esse and that Ten days notice of the time
and place of taking said deposition be given to the Plaintiff And on mo-
tion of the Plaintiffs by their attorney. It is ordered by the Court that a Commission issue directed to any Justice of the peace of Scott County Virginia to take the deposition of Richard Foster and that Thirty days notice of the time and place of taking said deposition be given to Greenbury G. McKinney defendants agent and that a Commission issue dir-
ected to any Justice of the Peace of Sullivan County in this State to take the depositions of Jonathon Bockman, John Peoples Esqr and David Bragg and that a Commission issue directed to any Justice of the Peace of Hawkins County to take the depositions of David Kincaid and Robert McMinn (p 217) de bene esse which depositions to be read in Evidence on the trial of this cause on behalf of the Plaintiffs and that Ten days notice of the time and place of taking said depositions given to Greenbury G. McKinney the defendants agent shall be deemed sufficinet.

JOHN BALCH) On affidavit of the defendant. It is ordered
    vs.) by the Court that a Commission issue direct-
ALEXANDER SEVIER) ed to any Justice of the Peace of Greene County
to take the depositions of Valentine Sevier, Alfred Hunter and Isaac Harmon and that five days notice of the time and place of taking said depositions be given to the Plaintiff.

ALEXANDER RICE by) In this cause on motion of the defendant
WILLIAM RICE his father) by his attorney leave is given him to file
& c) a Plea since the last continuance without

vs.) costs to which opinion of the Court in permitting

 OLIVER MILLER) ing said plea to be filed the plaintiff tendered

a bill of Exceptions which is signed sealed and ordered to be made a part of the record.

  JOSEPH ROGERS) This day (p 218) came the parties by their att-

   vs.) ornies and thereupon came a Jury to wit, Joseph

  JESSE HOWEL) McCullough, Arthur G. Young, John Reynolds, Thomas Monahon, John Swain, James Tucker, Henry Crowley, John G. Winston, William Davis, John Walker, Cornelius Carmack and Samuel Henderson who being elected tried and sworn upon their oath do say we find that the defendant did not assume in manner and form as the Plaintiff in his declaration hath complained as by pleading he hath alledged. It is therefore considered by the Court that the Plaintiff take nothing by his Writ but for his false clamor be in mercy and that the defendant go hence without day and recover of the Plaintiff his costs in this behalf expended and that Execution issue accordingly.

  JOHN O'BRIAN) This day came the Parties by their attornies

  Admr & c of) and thereupon came a Jury, to wit, William Smi-

  JOHN CALDWELL Dec'd) th, Shadroch Epperson, James Francisco, Reuben,

   vs.) Barnard, Willie B. Kyle, John McWilliams, Jess-

  JOHN H. DUNN &) e Howel, Thomas Harmon, Lewis Sturgeon, Jos-

  WILLIAM YOUNG & c) eph McMinn, George Morriset and Thomas Cox

who being elected tried and sworn upon their oaths (p 219) do say we find for the Plaintiff & assess his damage to Twenty nine dollars besides costs. Whereupon on motion of the defendant by his attorney a rule is allowed him to shew cause why a new trial should be granted .

  THOMAS JOHNSON) This day came the parties by their attornies and

   vs.) thereupon came a Jury, to wit, William Smith, Shad-

  JACOB HACKNEY) roch Epperson, James Francisco, John Miller, Reu-

ben Barnard, Willie B. Kyle, John McWilliams, William Bradley, Jesse Howel, Thomas Harmon, John Loughmiller and Lewis Sturgeon who being elected tried and sworn upon their oath do say we find for the Plaintiff and assess his damage to One hundred and Sixty dollars besides costs. It is therefore considered by the Court that the Plaintiff recover of the defendant One hundred and Sixty dollars the damages aforesaid assessed by Jurors aforesaid and also the costs in this behalf expended and that Execution issue accordingly.

Court adjourned until tomorrow 8 O'clock A. M.
     Edw. Scott

Saturday 9th October 1834.

Court met pursuant to adjournment.

Present The Honorable Edward Scott - Judge.

  JOHN BEAL) This suit (p 220) being referred by consent

   vs.) of the parties on a former day of this Term to

  DAVID EVERHEART) Arbitrators and they having returned their award

into open Court in the words and figures following to wit.
We the arbitrators do agree that David Everheart shall pay all the costs except John Beals Loan.

John G. Winston
Isham Reynolds
Henry Lauderback
Joseph Bishop
Abraham Varnon
Thomas Cox

By consent of the parties. It is considered by the Court that the plaintiff recover of the defendant the costs in this behalf expended except
the Attorney Tax fee as awarded by the arbitrators aforesaid and that Execution issue accordingly.

STATE of TENNESSEE)	This day came the State by the Attorney Gen-
vs.)	eral and the defendants in their proper per-
JOSEPH BROOKS)	sons and the rule for a new trial having come
THOMAS BROOKS &)	on to be heard and after argument of Counsel
ANDREW COCKER)	thereon and the premises seen and fully under-

stood. It is considered by the Court that the rule (p 221) be made ab-
solute a New trial granted. Whereupon the attorney General comes into
Court and by permission of the Court enters a Nolli Prosequi. And there-
upon the said defendants and Littleton Brooks, James Willis & James P Mc-
Carty confess Judgment for the costs. It is therefore considered by the
Court that the State recover of the defendants and Littleton Brooks, James
Willis and James P. McCarty their Securities the costs in this behalf ex-
pended and that Execution issue accordingly.

STATE OF TENNESSEE)	This day came the State by the attorney Gen-
vs.) Riot)	eral and the defendant in his proper person
LITTLETON BROOKS)	and a Verdict of Guilty having been found by

the Jurors on a former day of this Term. It is considered by the Court
now here that the defendant for this his offence be fined Five dollars
and pay the costs of this prosecution and held in custody until fine &
costs are paid or Security given therefor. Whereupon James P. McCarty
came into open Court and offers himself as Security for the fine and costs
It is therefore considered by the Court that the State recover of the defendant and James P. McCarty his security the sum of Five dollars the fine
aforesaid and also the costs of this prosecution for which Execution may
issue.

LIJAH KINCHELOE)	This day came (p 222) on to be heard and deter-
vs.) No 1)	mined the rule granted at a former day of this
JOHN A. ROGERS)	Term to set aside the Non suit and after argu-

ment of Counsel thereon as well for as against the rule and the premises
seen and fully understood. It is considered by the Court that the Non
suit be set aside & that the Plaintiff have leave to amend his declaration and pleadings and paying all the costs up to this Term for which Execution may issue.

THOMAS JOHNSON)	This day came the Plaintiff by his attorney and
vs.)	releases Thirty dollars of the Judgment. Where-
JACOB HACKNEY)	upon on motion of the defendant by his attorney

a rule is allowed him to shew cause why a New trial should be granted.

SPOTSWOOD LIPSCOMB)	On affidavit of the Plaintiffs attorney.
vs.)	It is ordered by the Court that a Commission
JONATHON JONES)	issue directed to any Justice of the peace

of Knox County in the State of Kentucky to take the depositions of Larkin Johnson (p 223) and that Thirty days notice of the time and place of taking said deposition be given to the adverse party.

JOHN O'BRION) This day came on for argument the rule for a new
Adm & c) trial and after argument thereon as well for as
vs.) against the rule and the premises seen and fully
JOHN H. DUNN) understood. It is considered by the Court that
& WM YOUNG) the rule be discharged and that the Plaintiff recover of the defendants and Peter Parsons their Security the sum of Twenty Nine dollars the damages assessed by the Jurors together with the costs in this behalf expended and that Execution issue accordingly.

WILLIAM WALKER) On motion of the Defendant by his attorney. It
vs.) is ordered by the Court that the Plaintiff give
JAMES WILLIS) additional security for the Costs in this suit
on the first day of next Term or shew sufficient cause to the contrary.

WILLIAM WALKER) On affidavit of the defendant. It is ordered by
vs.) the Court that a Commission issue directed to any
ASABEL JOHNSON) Justice of the Peace of Hawkins County (p 224)
in this State to take the deposition of William Johnson de bene esse and that Ten days notice of the time and place of taking said depositions be given to the Plaintiff.

JOHN A. ROGERS) This day came on to be heard and determined the
vs.) rule for a New Trial granted on a former day of
ELI BOYKIN) this Term and after argument of counsel thereon
as well for as against said rule and the premises seen and fully understood. It is considered by the Court that the rule be made absolute and a New Trial granted and that this cause be continued until the next Term of this Court.

STATE of TENNESSEE) This day came the State by the attorney Gen-
vs.) eral and with leave of the Court enters a
JONATHON TIPTON) Nolli prosequi in this cause and that the
Clerk of this Court make out a Bill of the Costs and present it to the County Court for allowance.

A Deed of Mortgage from George Hale to Nancy Dalzell for Two hundred and forty acres of land was proven in open Court by the oaths of William Simpson & Dicks Alexander and ordered to be registered.

ISHAM REYNOLDS) On motion (p 225) of the defendant by his att-
& wife) orney. It is ordered by the Court that a Comm-
vs.) ission issue directed to any Justice of the peace
JOHN A. ROGERS) of Monroe County in this State to take the depos-
itions of Sarah Lawson and Henry Chestnut and that Ten days notice of the time and place of taking said depsoitons be given to the Plaintiffs.

ROBERT NALL) For reasons appearing to the satisfaction of the
vs.) Slander) Court on the affidavit of the Plaintiff that a
JOHN S. HILL) fair and impartial trial of this cause cannot be
had in the County of Hawkins. It is ordered by the Court that the Venue be changed to the County of Greene it being the nearest adjoining County free from the like exceptions and that the Clerk of this Court

make out a Transcript of the record and proceedings and transmit the same to the clerk of the Circuit Court of Greene County.

ROBERT NALL) For reasons appearing to the satisfaction of
vs.) the Court on the affidavit of the Plaintiff
DAVID HAUNDSHELL) that a fair and impartial trial of this cause
cannot be had in the County of Hawkins. It is ordered by the Court that the Venue be changed to the (p 226) County of Greene it being the nearest adjoining County free from the like exceptions and that the Clerk of this Court make out a Transcript of the record and proceedings and transmit the same to the clerk of the Circuit Court of Greene County.

JOHN G. ROBERTS) On motion of the Plaintiff by his attorney. It
vs.) is ordered by the Court that a Commission issue
ROBERT NALL) directed to any Justice of the peace of the
City of Richmond Virginia to take the deposition of Henry Gibson and that Thirty days notice of the time and place of taking said deposition be given to the adverse party.

THOMAS JOHNSON) In this cause the rule for a new trial having
vs.) come on for determination and argument of Cou-
JACOB HACKNEY) nsel thereon being heard as well for as against
the rule and the premises seen and fully understood. It is considered by the Court that the rule be discharged.

JOHN DEN LESSEE of) On affidavit of John Kennedy attorney for the
ALEXANDER PORTER) Plaintiff. It is ordered by the Court that
vs.) a Commission issue directed (p 227) to any
THOMAS COOKE) Justice of the peace of Washington County to
take the depositions of James Aiken and James W. Anderson and that Ten days notice be given of the time and place of taking said deposition and that a Commission issue directed to any Justice of the peace of Warren County in this State to take the deposition of Thomas Hopkins and that Fifteen days notice of the time and place of taking said deposition be given to adverse party.

JOHN ROLLER) On motion of the plaintiff by his attorney. It
vs.) is ordered by the Court that a Commission issue
JOSEPH ROBERTS) directed to any Justice of the peace of Scott
County Virginia to take the depositions of Philip Roller, William Williams and Thomas Mitchell and that thirty days notice of the time and place of taking said deposition be given to the adverse party.

A Deed of Conveyance from James Vaughan to Richard Mitchell for One hundred and Sixty acres of land lying in the State of Illinois was proven in open Court by the oaths of Michael McCann and Willie B. Mitchell and was ordered by the Court to be certified.

E. EMBREE surviving) This (p 228) day came the defendants by
Partner & c) their attorney & on motion a rule is all-
vs.) owed them to shew cause why a New Trial
LINCOLN AMIS & JAS.) should be granted and after argument of
McREYNOLDS) counsel thereon as well for as against said
rule and premises seen and fully understood. It is considered by the Court that the rule be made absolute and a new trial granted. And on affidavit of Lincoln Amis. It is ordered by the Court that a Commission

issue directed to any Justice of the peace of Scott County Virginia to take the deposition of Danswell Roger and that Thirty days notice be given of the time and place of taking said deposition and that a Commission issue directed to any Justice of the peace of Grainger County in this State to take the deposition of Richard Grantham and that Ten days notice of the time and place of taking said deposition be given to the plaintiff.

PETER ELROD)   This day came the defendant by his attorney and the
    vs.   )   Plaintiff being solemnly called to come into Court
ISHAM MILLS)   and prosecute his suit came not but made default.
It is therefore considered by the Court that the defendant go hence without day and recover of the plaintiff his costs by him in (p 229) this behalf expended and that execution issue accordingly.

PETER ELROD   )   This day came the defendants by their attor-
    vs.   )   ney and the Plaintiff being solemnly called to
HEZEKIAH EMBERSON)   come into Court and prosecute his suit came
ISHAM MILLS   )   not but made default. It is therefore consid-
SIMON MILLS   )   ered by the Court that the defendants go hence
WILLIAM TAYLOR   )   without day and recover of the Plaintiff their
and JOHN MILLS   )   costs in this behalf expended and that Execut-
ion issue accordingly.

E. EMBREE surviving)   By consent of the parties. It is ordered
Partner & c   )   by the Court that the Plaintiff have leave
        vs.   )   to amend his Writ and declaration by rein-
LINCOLN AMIS & JAMES)   stating Amis Grantham.
McREYNOLDS   )

The Court adjourned until the Court in Course.
                              Edw. Scott

Monday 4th April 1825 (p 230)

At a Circuit Court begun and held for the County of Hawkins at the Courthouse in Rogersville on the first Monday being the fourth day of April in the year of Our Lord One thousand eight hundred and twenty five and the forty ninth of American Independence.

Present - The Honorable Edward Scott Judge.

Gabriel McCrow Sheriff returns now into open Court one Writ of Venire Facias returned to the present Term of this Court Executed on the following persons being good and lawful men of Hawkins County and appointed by the Court of pleas and quarter Sessions of said County - Viz -
John M. Vaughan
Joseph McMinn Jr.
Samuel Curry
Daniel Chambers
Samuel McPheeters
Thomas Armstrong
William Phipps
Clinton Armstrong
James Johnson Esqr
James Young

Samuel Wilson Esqr.
William Martin
Larkin Willis
Lewis Click
John A. Rogers
John Mitchell
Cleon Moore
Willie B. Kyle
Edward Lee
Andrew Galbreath Senr.
John Reynolds Esqr
Joseph McCullough
Joseph Huffmaster
from among whom the following persons being drawn in due form of law and
dompose the Grand Jury for the present Term of this Court to wit.
1.   Andrew Galbreath Senr
2.   John A. Rogers
3.   James Johnson (p 231)
4.   Samuel Wilson
5.   John M. Vaughan
6.   John Mitchell
7.   Lewis Click
8.   Clinton Armstrong
9.   Joseph Huffmaster
10 Larkin Willis
11 William Phipps
12 Thomas Armstrong
13 John Reynolds
Whereupon the Court appointed Andrew Galbreath Jr. Foreman of the Grand
Jury who were empanneled & sworn received their charge and withdrew from
the Bar of the Court.

Robert D. Young Constable was appointed by the Court officer to attend on
the Grand Jury for the present Term and was qualified in due form of law.

JOHN DEN LESSEE of)   This cause is continued until the next Term
WILLIAM BRADLEY   )   mof this Court as en affidavit of the defend-
          vs.   )   ant. And on motion of the defendant by his
THOMAS SPROUL   )   attorney It is ordered by the Court that a
commission issue directed to any Justice of the peace of Hawkins County to
take the depositions de bene esse of John Sproul and William Young and
that One days notice if seved on Orville Bradley and Twenty days notice
of the time and place of taking said depositions if served on William
Bradley shall be sufficient.
And on motion of the Plaintiff by his attorney. (p 232) It is ordered
by the Court that a Commission issue directed to any Justice of the peace
of Hawkins County to take the depositions of John Burriss Senr de bene
esse and that Ten days notice of the time and place of taking said depositions be given to the adverse party.

A Deed of Conveyance from Nathon Williams to Uriah Parks for One hundred
and Sixty acres of land lying in Arkansas Territory Military boundary
was proven in open Court by the oaths of Dicks Alexander and Samuel Powel and ordered to be certified.

JOHN ROLLER   )   This cause is continued until the next Term of
     vs.   )   this Court as on affidavit of the Defendant.
JOSEPH ROBERTS)   And on motion of the defendant by his attorney.

It is ordered by the Court that a Commission issue directed to any Justice of the peace of Lee County Virginia to take the depositions of Stockley Lawson and David Lawson to be read in evidence on the trial of this cause on behalf of the Defendant and that Thirty days notice of the time and place of taking said depositions be given to the Plaintiff.

The Clerk of this Court (p 233) produced in open Court the necessary receipt from the Treasurer of East Tennessee as required by law which was inspected by the Court and the production of said receipt was ordered to be entered of Record.

WILLIAM CRUMLY) On affidavit of the defendant this cause is con-
vs.   ) tinued until the next Term of this Court and on
JOHNSON FRAZIER) motion of the Plaintiff by his attorney. It is
ordered by the Court that a Commission issue directed to any Justice of the peace of Monroe County to take the deposition of Aaron Parker and that Twenty days notice of the time and place of taking said deposition be given to the adverse party.

This day personally appeared in open Court Nathaniel Kelsey and produced his license to practise as attorney in the Several Courts of law and Equity in this State and take the oaths required by law and was admitted to practise as an attorney of this Court.

MICHAEL McCANN) This day came the parties by their attornies and
vs.   ) thereupon came a Jury, to wit, Joseph McCullough
FRAZIER BRINLEY) Jr., Joseph Roberts, John Norman, Cornelius Car-
mack, James (p 234) Young, Daniel Chambers, Thomas Monahon, Henry Price, Benajamin Morlan, William Y. Larkin, Nicholas Long and Markham Kenner who being elected tried and sworn upon their oaths do say we find that the defendant did assume in manner and form as the plaintiff in his declaration hath complained and that he did assume within three years next before the serving out of the original Writ in this case and that the defendant has a set off for all except the sum of Fifty eight dollars fourteen cents & they assess the plaintiffs damage to Fifty eight dollars fourteen cents. It is therefore considered by the Court that the Plaintiff recover of the defendant the sum of Fifty eight dollars, fourteen cents the damages aforesaid by the Jurors aforesaid assessed together with the costs in this behalf expended and that Execution issue accordingly.

Court adjourned until tomorrow 8 O'clock A. M.
                    Edw. Scott

Tuesday 5th April 1825

Court met pursuant to adjournment.

Present The Honorable Edward Scott - Judge.

Personally appeared in open Court Tighlmon Howard and produced his license to practise as attorney in the several courts of law and Equity in this State and took the oaths required by law and was admitted to practise as an attorney of this Court.

A Deed of Conveyance (p 235) from Peter Franklin to Frederick A. Ross for One hundred acres of land was acknowledged in open Court and ordered to be registered.

A Deed of Conveyance from Frederick A. Ross to Jacob Burris for Two hundred and Ten acres of land was proven in open Court by the oaths of James Francisco and Philip Critz and ordered to be registered.

A Deed of Conveyance from James Francisco to George Francisco for One hundred and Ninety acres of land was acknowledged in open Court and ordered to be registered.

A Deed of Conveyance from Frederick A. Ross to Wiley Daniel for One hundred and thirty six acres of land lying in Bedford County was proven in open Court by the oaths of James Francisco and Jacob Burris and ordered to be certified.

A Deed of Conveyance from Frederick A. Ross to Peter Carpenter for Two hundred and ninety seven acres & one hundred & twelve poles of land lying in Bedford County was proven in open Court by the oaths of James Francisco and Jacob Burris and ordered to be certified.

A Deed of Conveyance from Frederick A. Ross to William Neese for Three hundred and (p 235) thirty two acres of land lying in Bedford County was proven in open Court by the oaths of James Francisco and Jacob Burris and ordered to be certified.

A Deed of Conveyance from Frederick A. Ross to Asabel Cross for One hundred and forty acres of land lying in Bedford County was proven in open Court by the oaths of James Francisco and Jacob Burris and was ordered to be certified.

A Deed of Conveyance from Frederick A. Ross to Kibble Terry for One hundred and sixty four acres of land lying in Bedford County was proven in open Court by the oath of James Francisco and Jacob Burris and was ordered to be certified.

A Deed of Conveyance from Frederick A. Ross to Jesse Rogers for Two hundred and eighty eight acres of land lying in Bedford County was proven in open Court by the oaths of James Francisco and Jacob Burris and was ordered to be certified.

A Deed of Conveyance from Frederick A. Ross to Moses Worldly for Two hundred and ninety seven acres and one hundred and twelve poles lying in Bedford County was proven in open Court by the oaths of James Francisco and Jacob Burris and ordered to be certified.

A Deed of Conveyance (p 237) from Frederick A. Ross to Thomas Hopkins for One hundred and thirty three acres of land lying in Rhea County was proven in open Court by the oaths of James Francisco and Jacob Burris and ordered to be certified.

JOHN DEN LESSEE of)   This day came the parties by their attornies
COWDRY & COCKE   )   and thereupon came a Jury, to wit, William
vs.) Ejectment   )   Martin, George Argenbright, Joseph McCullough
JOEL DYER   )   James, Young, John Shough, Philip Critz, Peter
Franklin, William Alexander, Andrew Derrick, Samuel Wilson Jr, Thomas Mon-

ahon and Jesse Manis who being elected tried and sworn upon their oath do say we find that the defendant is not Guilty of the Trespass and Eject- ment as in the Plaintiffs Declaration mentioned. It is therefore consid- ered by the Court that the defendant go hence without day and recover of the Plaintiffs his costs in this behalf expended and that Execution issue accordingly.

JOHN A. ROGERS)   This day came the Plaintiff by his attorney and
vs.) Slander)   with leave of the Court dismisses this suit and
ELI BOYKIN)   thereupon the defendant by his attorney comes
into Court and confesses Judgment for the costs. It is therefore consid- ered by the Court that the Plaintiff recover of the defendant the (p 238) costs by him about his suit in this behalf expended for which Execution may issue.

ARCHIBALD McKINNEY)   On motion It is ordered by the Court that the
vs.)   rule of Reference made at a former Term of
LIJAH KINCHELOE)   this Court be set aside.

E. EMBREE surviving)   In this cause the plaintiff by his Attorney
partner & c)   ,comes into Court and with leave enters a Nol-
vs.)   li Prosequi as to Amis Grantham and Lincoln
AMIS GRANTHAM)   Amis.
LINCOLN AMIS and)
JAMES McREYNOLDS)

E. EMBREE surviving)   This day came the parties by their attornies
partner & c.)   and thereupon came a Jury to wit, William Mar-
vs.)   tin, George Argenbright, Joseph McCullough,
JAMES McREYNOLDS)   James Young, John Shough, Philip Critz, Peter
Franklin, William Alexander, Andrew Derrick, Samuel Wilson Jr., Thomas Mon- ahon and Jesse Manis who being elected tried (p 239) and sworn upon their oaths do say we find that the defendant did assume and undertake in manner and form as the plaintiff in his declaration hath alledged and we further find that the promissory note mentioned in the declaration was not given to accomadate the plaintiff who wanted to borrow money from the Bank of the State of Tennessee but the same was given to secure the payment of the sum of money therein mentioned due to the plaintiff and assess his damage to Fifteen hundred and forty four dollars fifteen cents besides co- sts. It is therefore considered by the Court that the Plaintiff recover of the defendant the sum of Fifteen hundred and forty four dollars fifteen cents together with the costs in this behalf expended and that Execution issue accordingly.

JOHN A. ROGERS)   The parties having at a former Term of this
vs.)   Court referred this cause to arbitrators and
SAMUEL WILSON Senr.)   they having returned their award into open
Court in the words and figures following Viz-

STATE of TENNESSEE)   We George Hale, William Lyons and Robert L.
HAWKINS COUNTY)   Coreathers having been chosen under an order
JOHN A. ROGERS)   of the Honorable Circuit Court of Hawkins Co-
vs.)   unty April Term 1823 as Arbitrators to settle
SAMUEL WILSON)   (p 240) and determine the controversy between
said parties in a suit of slander instituted in said Court after examina- tion of such witnesses as were brought before us by the said litigants and

upon due deliberation do declare the following to be our award viz. That
the said John A. Rogers not having produced any evidence that Sam'l Wilson the def't used or uttered the words charged against him the 3rd Wilson by the said Rogers pay all the costs that have accrued in such action of Slander. Given under our hands & seals at Rogersville this 10th of April 1823.

George Hale (seal)
William Lyons (seal)
Robt. L. Coreathers (seal)

It is considered by the Court that the Plaintiff take nothing by his Writ but for his false clamor be in mercy and that the defendant go hence without day and recover of the plaintiff the costs in this behalf expended and that Execution issue accordingly.

JESSE HUMBLE) This day came the plaintiff into open Court and with
    vs.   ) leave of the Court dismisses his suit! It is there-
JOHN SHOUGH) fore considered by the Court that the defendant go
hence without day and recover of the Plaintiff his costs by him in this behalf expended (p 241) and that Execution issue accordingly.

JAMES WHITE) This day came the parties by their attor-
    vs.) nies and thereupon came a Jury, to wit,
ABSALOM LOONEY) William Martin, Joseph McCullough, James
and) Young, Hezekiah Hamblen, Dickerson Thur-
JOHN LAUGHMILLER) man, Cornelius Carmack, Peter Elrod, Geo-
Adm & c of) rge Johnson, Walter Allen, George Elkins,
FREDERICK LAUGHMILLER) William McClure and Mathias Shaver who
Dec'd) being elected tried and sworn upon their
oath do say that the defendant Absalom Looney and Frederick Laughmiller the intestate of the defendant John Laughmiller did assume as the Plaintiff in his declaration hath alledged and assess the Plaintiffs damage to one hundred and eight dollars and ninety Six cents and we further find that the defendant John Laughmiller had well and truly administered all and singular the goods and chattels which were of Frederick Laughmiller Dec'd which had come to the hands of the said John to be administered. Therefore it is considered by the Court that the plaintiff recover of the defendant Absalom Looney the said sum of One hundred and eight dollars and ninety Six cents and the costs in this behalf expended and that the said John Laughmiller go hence without day (p 242) and if any assets shall hereafter come to the hands of the said John as administrator of said Fred'k Laughmiller sufficient to satisfy said damages that then the Plaintiff shall have said damages satisfied out of said assets when they shall come to the hands of said administrator.

A Deed of Conveyance from Henry Crowley to William King for Fifty acres of land was acknowledged in open Court and ordered to be registered.

JOHN PRYOR) This day came the parties by their attornies and
    vs.) thereupon came a Jury, to wit, William Martin,
PETER FRANKLIN) Joseph McCullough, James Young, Hezekiah Hamblen,
Dickerson Thurman, Cornelius Carmack, Peter Elrod, George Johnson, Walter Allen, George Elkins, William McClure and Mathias Shover who being elected tried & sworn upon their oaths do say we find that the defendant is not Guilty in manner and form as the plaintiff against him hath complained. It is therefore considered by the Court that the Plaintiff take nothing by his Writ but for his false clamor be in mercy and that

the defendant go hence without (p 243) day and recover of the plaintiff the costs in this behalf expended and that Execution issue accordingly

JOHN DEN LESSEE of) By consent of the parties this cause is con-
JAMES McBEE & others) tinued until the next Term of this Court.
       vs.)
ETHELDRED WILLIAMS)

JOHN A. ROGERS) Robert Johnson who had been legally summoned
    vs.   ) as a Witness on behalf of the defendant in
SAMUEL WILSON Jr.) this cause and being now solemnly called to
come into Court came not but made default. It is therefore considered by the Court that the defendant Samuel Wilson Jr recover of the said Robert Johnson the sum of One hundred and twenty five dollars agreeable to act of Assembly in such case made and provided unless sufficient cause of his disability to attend be shewn at the next Term of this Court after notice of this Judgment.

CHARLES KING) By consent of the parties this cause is contin-
   vs.   ) ued until the next Term of this Court.
SAMUEL CHESTNUT)

JOHN A. ROGERS) This day (p 244) came the parties by their
vs.) Slander) attornies and thereupon came a Jury, to wit,
SAMUEL WILSON Jr.) Daniel Chambers, Joseph McMinn, George R. Smith,
Samuel McPheeters, Charles King, Benjamin Morland, Bennoni Harris, James Williams, Thomas Taylor, Francis Leeper, Moses McGinnis and Howel Brewer who being elected tried and sworn upon their oaths do say we find that the defendant is Guilty & that he is Guilty within six months next before serving out the obligation of speaking and publishing the words as the plaintiff hath complainted in the Third Count of his declaration & that he has no justification and assess the plaintiffs damage by occasion thereof to One hundred and twenty five dollars besides costs and as th the Speaking proclaiming and publishing the residue of the English words in the declaration mentioned the Jurors aforesaid on their oaths aforesaid do further say that the defendant is not thereof Guilty as by pleading he hath alledged.
Whereupon It is considered by the court that the plaintiff recover of the defendant the sum of One hundred and twenty five dollars the damages aforesaid by the Jurors aforesaid assessed together with the costs in this behalf expended and that Execution issue accordingly.

Court adjourned until (p 245) tomorrow 9 O'clock A. M.
                        Edw. Scott

Wednesday 6th April 1825.

Court met pursuant to adjournment.

Present The Honorable Edward Scott Judge.

ROBERT McGINNIS) By consent of the parties by their attornies. It
Admr of LAWREN) is ordered by the Court that Commissions issue
CE STONE Dec'd)√ directed to any Justice of the peace to take the
   vs.   ) depositions of such witnesses as either party
JOHN COCKE &) may think proper by giving the opposite party
JOHN F. JACK) five days notice of the time and place of taking

any depositions that they may cause to be taken in the counties of Grainger and Claibourne and if out of said Counties Ten days notice to be given.

STATE of TENNESSEE)   Assault & c.
        vs.   )   This day came the State by the Attorney Gen-
DAVID McCOY   )   eral and with leave of the Court enters a
Nolli prosequi in this cause. It is therefore considered by the Court that the Clerk of this Court make out a Bill of Costs and present it to the County Court for allowance.

STATE of TENNESSEE)   Riot
        vs.   )   This day came the State by the Attorney Gener-
WILLIAM TAYLOR   )   al and with leave of the (p 246) Court en-
ters a Nolli prosequi in this cause. It is therefore considered by the Court that the Clerk of this Court make out a Bill of the costs and present it to the County Court for allowance.

BETSEY HENDERSON   )   Petition for Divorce.
        vs.   )   This day came the plaintiff by his attorney
ROLLIN M. HENDERSON)   and the defendant being solemnly called to
come into Court and answer the Petition of Betsey Henderson or the same would be taken as confessed and heard exparte and the Court proceed to decree accordingly came not but made default.

JOHN PRYOR   )   On motion of the Plaintiff by his attorney a rule
    vs.   )   is allowed him to shew cause why a new trial gran-
PETER FRANKLIN)   ted and after argument of Counsel thereon as well
for as against the rule & the premises and fully understood. It is considered by the Court that the rule be discharged.

STATE of TENNESSEE)   Martin Sanders and Enoch Howel who were bound
        vs.   )   in recognizance for the personal appearance of
MARTIN WOODS   )   the defendant Martin Woods at the present Term
of this Court surrenders (p 247) the body of this said Martin Woods in open Court in discharge of themselves as appearance Bail. Whereupon the Court ordered the said defendant in custody of the Sheriff. And thereupon personally appeared in open Court Martin Woods, William Phipps and Thomas Barrot Senr and jointly and severally acknowledged themselves indebted to the State of Tennessee in the penal sum of One thousand dollars to be levied of their proper goods and chattels lands and tenements to the use of the State but to be void on condition that the said Martin Woods make his personal appearance before the Honorable Judge of the Circuit Court from day to day and answer a charge of the State exhibited against him and not depart without leave of the Court.

STATE of TENNESSEE)   Riot
        vs.   )   This day came the State by the Attorney Gen-
HEZEKIAH EMBERSON)   eral and the defendant in his proper person
and being charged on the Bill of Indictment plead Guilty and submit to the mercy of the Court. Whereupon the premises being seen and fully understood. It is considered by the Court that the defendant Hezekiah Emberson for this his offense be fined in the sum of Five dollars and that he be imprisoned for the space of Ten days in the Jail of Hawkins County and (p 248) that he there remain until Fine and costs are paid or good and sufficient security given therfor.

STATE of TENNESSEE)   Barrotry
     vs.   )   This day came the State by the Attorney Gen-
ISAIAH JONES   )   eral and the defendant in his proper person
and being charged on the Bill of Indictment plead not Guilty and put
himself on the Country and thereupon came a Jury, to wit, William Martin,
James Young, James Francisco, Daniel Chambers, Thomas Taylor, James Dodson, Robert Hensely, Thomas Monahon, James Jones, John McWilliams, William Young and George Argenbright who being elected tried and sworn upon
their oaths do say we find that the defendant is not Guilty in manner
and form as charged in the Bill of Indictment. Whereupon on motion of
the defendant by his attorney a rule is allowed him to shew cause why
the prosecutor should be taxed with the costs.

JOHN KING & others)   This day came the parties by their attornies
     vs.   )   and thereupon came a Jruy to wit, William
WILLIAM ALEXANDER)   Martin, James Young, James Francisco, Daniel Chambers, James Dodson, Thomas Monahon, James Jones, William Young,
George Argenbright (p 249) Samuel Henderson, Samuel Wilson Jr. & William Lipe who being elected tried and sworn upon their oaths do say we
find that the defendant is not Guilty of the Trespass as the Plaintiffs
in their declaration hath complained and we further find that the defendant is not entitled to any freehold as by pleading he hath alledged.
It is therefore considered by the Court that the defendant go hence without day and recover of the plaintiff the costs in this behalf expended
and that Execution issue accordingly.

ARCHIBALD McKINNEY)   On affidavit of the defendant. It is ordered
     vs.   )   by the Court that a Commission issue directed
LIJAH KINCHELOE   )   to any Justice of the peace of Hawkins County
to take the deposition of Jacob Surginer and Amy Surginer de bene esse and
that Ten days notice of the time and place of taking said depositions be
given to the Plaintiff.

STATE OF TENNESSEE)   On motion and by consent of the attorney Gen-
     vs.   )   eral. It is ordered by the Court that the
HEZEKIAH EMBERSON)   defendant be released from further imprisonment.

MICHAEL PEARSON)   This day came (p 250) the parties by their
vs.) Attack't)   attornies and thereupon came a Jury, to wit,
THOMAS JOHNSON)   Samuel McPheeters, Joseph McMinn, David Kearsner, John Laughmiller, Charles Stewart, James Bailey, James Sander,
Thomas Harmon, Thomas Hamblen, Preston Blevins, William Hensely and Stockley D. Luster who being elected tried and sworn upon their oath do say
we find that the defendant did not assume in manner and form as the plaintiff in his declaration hath complained. It is therefore considered by
the Court that the defendant go hence without day and recover of the Plaintiff his costs in this behalf expended and that Execution issue accordingly.

STATE of TENNESSEE)   This day personally appeared in open Court
     vs.   )   Joseph Beclor and James Bradley and acknowled-
JOSEPH BECLOR   )   ged themselves jointly and severally indebted
to the State of Tennessee in the penal sum of Two hundred and fifty dollars to be levied of their proper goods and chattels land and tenements to
the use of the State but to be void on condition that the said Joseph
Beclor make his personal appearance before the Honorable (p 251) Judge

of the Circuit Court at the Courthouse in Rogersville from day to day and answer a charge of the State exhibited against him and not depart without leave of Court.

STATE of TENNESSEE)   Recognizance to keep the peace.
vs.)   This day came into Court Lincoln Amis at
ROBERT BURTON)   whose instance the defendant had been bound
in recognizance and saus he does not further require the peace of the said defendant. Whereupon Robert Burton the defendant comes into open Court and confesses Judgment for the costs It is therefore considered by the Court that the State recover of the defendant the costs in this behalf expended for which Execution may issue.

PATRICK CAREY)   By consent of the parties by their attorniew this
vs.)   cause is continued until the next Term of this
JOHN S. HILL)   Court. And on motion of the plaintiff by his attorney. It is ordered by the Court that a Commission issue directed to any Justice of the peace of Washington County to take the deposition of Jacob Howard and Ten days notice of the time and place of taking said deposition be given to the adverse party.

JOHN CRITZ)   The death (p 252) of the defendant being sugg-
and)   estive in ababotement of this suit. In motion
MARY CROWBARGER)   of the plaintiffs by their attorney a rule is
Exr & EXx & c)   allowed them to shew cause why this suit should
vs.)   be revived against the legal representatives of
JACOB SEAVERS)   said deceased.

ISHAM REYNOLDS & wife)   This cause is continued until the next
vs.)   Term of this Court as on affidavit of the
JOHN A. ROGERS)   defendant.

JAMES BRADLEY)   By consent of the parties by their attornies this
vs)   cause is continued until the next Term of this
JOSEPH McMINN) Court.

JOHN BLEVINS)   This day came the parties by their attornies and
vs.)   thereupon came a Jury, to wit, William Martin,
JOHN BEAL)   James Young, Daniel Chambers, James Francisco, Dickerson Thurman, James Dodson, Thomas Monahon, George Argenbright, William James Jones, John Norman and Aeneas S. Galbreath who being elected tried (p 253) and sworn upon their oaths so day we find that the defendant is not Guilty of the Trespass as the plaintiff in his declaration alledged and we further find that the defendant was justified as in the second and third plea he hath alledged. It is therefore considered by the Court that the plaintiff take nothing by his writ and that the defendant go hence and recover of the plaintiff the costs in this behalf expended and that Execution issue accordingly.

Court adjourned until tomorrow 9 O'clock A. M.
Edw. Scott

Thursday 7th April 1825

Court met pursuant to adjournment.

Present The Honorable Edward Scott – Judge.

JOHN CANTRELL) This day came the plaintiff by his attorney and
by his next friend) with leave of the Court dismisses his suit and
THOMAS JOHNSON) thereupon the defendants come into open Court
vs.) in their prpper persons and confess Judgment
ANDERSON LAWSON) for the costs. It is therefore considered by
JESSE MANIS) the Court that the Plaintiff recover of the de-
and) fendant his costs in this behalf expended and
THOMAS LAWSON) that Execution issue accordingly.

ZACHARIAH STACEY) This day came the parties (p 254) by their att-
vs.) ornies and thereupon came a Jury, to wit, Will-
HIRAM CHARLES) iam Martin, James Young, Joseph McCullough, Daniel Chambers, Joseph Beclor, Preston Blevins, William Alexander, David
Kearner, William E. Hensely, William Giddens, Pleasant Mann and John Denny who being elected tried and sworn upon their oath do say we find that
the defendant is not Guilty of the Trespass as in the Plaintiffs declaration mentioned as by pleading he hath alledged. It is therefore considered
by the Court that the Plaintiff take nothing by his Writ but for his false
clamor be in mercy and that the defendant go hence without day and recover
of the Plaintiff the costs in this behalf expended and that Execution issue adcordingly.

STATE of TENNESSEE) Personally appeared in open Court Samuel Lee
vs.) and acknowledged himself indebted to the State
JOSEPH MORRISET) Of Tennessee in the sum of Two hundred and fifty dollars to be levied of his proper goods and chattels lands and Tenements to the use of the State but to be void on condition that he make his
personal appearance before the Honorable Judge of the Circuit Court at the
Courthouse in Rogersville on the Wednesday after the first Monday of October next and prosecute and give evidence on behalf of the State against
Joseph Morriset and not depart without leave of Court.

PATRICK CAREY) On motion (p 255) of the defendant by his attor-
vs.) ney. It is ordered by the Court that a Commission
JOHN S. HILL) issue directed to any Justice of the Peace of Knox
County to take the depositions of Capt John Boyd, Benjamin Boyd, Hiram
Barry and Samuel Pride and that Ten days notice of the time and place of
taking said depositions be given to the Plaintiff.

SAMUEL REYNOLDS) This day came the parties by their attornies and
and others) thereupon came a Jury, to wit, Samuel McPheeters,
vs.) Philip Critz, Hezekiah Hamblen, Joseph McMinn,
JAMES HAGAN) Thomas Monahon, George Tucker, James Jones, Robert Hensely, Joel Gillenwaters, Aeneas S. Galbreath, James Leeper and
James Mills who being elected tried and sworn upon their oaths do say we
find that the defendant did assume in manner and form as the Plaintiff in
his declaration hath complained and we further find that the Plaintiff did
not implead the defendandt in former suit for the same thing and assess
the Plaintiffs damage to One hundred dollars besides costs. Whereupon on
motion of the Defendant by his attorney a rule is allowed him to shew cause why a new trial should be granted.

WILLIAM WALKER) On affidavit (p 256) of the Plaintiff this
vs.) cause is continued until the next Term of this
JONATHON HENDERSON) Court and on motion of the defendant by his
attorney. It is ordered by the Court that a Commission issue directed
to any Justice of the peace of Washington County, to take the deposition of

David Thompson and that Ten days notice of the time and place of taking said deposition be given to the Plaintiff.

A Power of Attorney from Archibald McKinney and Anna McKinney his wife to Aphraine Pentland was proven in open Court by the oaths of Alexander F. McKinney and Robert J. McKinney and ordered to be certified.

STATE of TENNESSEE)   For Unlawful Gaming.
vs.   )   This day came the State by the Attorney Gen-
JOSEPH BEELER   )   eral and the defendant in his proper person
and being charged on the Bill of Indictment plead not Guilty and put himself on the Country and thereupon came a Jury, to wit, William Martin,
James Young, Joseph McCullough, Daniel Chambers, William Alexander, David
Kearsner, William Hensely, William Giddens, John Denny, James Williford,
Dickerson Thurman and James Charles who being elected tried and sworn upon
their (p 257) oaths do say we find that the defendant is Guilty in manner and form as charged in the Bill of Indictment.
Whereupon on motion of the Defendant by his attorney a rule is allowed him
to shew cause why a new trial should be granted.

BARNABAS KELLY)   This day came the Plaintiff and with leave of the
vs.) Appeal   )   Court dismisses his suit and confesses Judgment
JOHN PARK   )   for one half of the costs and thereupon the de-
Admr & c of   )   fendant came into open Court and confesses Judg-
JOHN KELLY Dec'd)   ment for the other half of the costs in this behalf expended. It is therefore considered by the Court that the plaintiff
recover of the defendant one half of the costs to be levied of the goods
and chattels of his intestate in the hand or possession of the said Administrator and that the defendant recover of the plaintiff the other half
of the costs in this behalf expended and that Executtions issue accordingly.

WILLIAM WALKER)   On affidavit of the Plaintiff these causes are con-
vs.   )   tinued until the next Term of this Court and that
JAMES WILLIS)   a Commission issue directed to any Justice of the
&   )   Peace of Knox County Kentucky to take the depos-
WILLIAM WALKER)   itions of Lewis Webb and Susannah (p 258) Webb
vs.   )   to be read on the trial of these causes on behalf
ASABEL JOHNSON)   of the Plaintiff and that Thirty days notice of
the time and place of taking said depositions be given to the adverse parties.

STATE of TENNESSEE)   This day personally appeared in open Court
vs.   )   James Bailey and acknowledged himself indebt-
MARTIN WOODS   )   ed to the State of Tennessee in the sum of
Five hundred dollars to be levied of his proper goods and chattels lands
and tenements to the use of the State but to be void on condition that
he make his personal appearance from day to day before the Honorable Judge of the Circuit Court at the Courthouse in Rogersville and prosecute
and give evidence on behalf of the State against Martin Woods and not depart without leave of the Court.

SPOTSWOOD LIPSCOMB)   This day came the parties by their attornies
vs.   )   and thereupon came a Jury, to wit, Samuel
JONATHON JONES   )   McPheeters, Hezekiah Hamblen, Thomas Monahon
George Tucker, James Jones, Robert Hensely, Joel Gillenwaters, Aeneas S.

Galbreath, James Leeper, James Mills, Robert Young and John Stokely who being elected tried and (p 259) sworn upon their oaths do say we find for the Plaintiff and assess his damage to Fifteen dollars besides costs. It is therefore considered by the Court that the Plaintiff recover of the defendant the sum of Fifteen dollars the damages aforesaid by the Jurors aforesaid together with the costs in this behalf expended and that Execution issue accordingly.

JOHN LONG   )   This day came the parties by their attornies and
   VS   √)   thereupon came a Jury, to wit, William Martin,
JACOB BURRIS)   James Young, Joseph McCullough, Dickerson Thurman, Preston Blevins, James Williford, William Alexander, John Denny, William Giddens, Hezekiah Hamblen, James Charles, and Daniel Chamber who being elected tried and sworn and progress having been made in the trial of this cause by the consent of the parties by their attornies and with the assent of the Court the Jurors aforesaid from rendering their Verdict in this cause are respited until tomorrow.

Court adjourned until tomorrow 9 O'clock A. M.
                   Edw. Scott

Friday 8th April 1825

Court met pursuant to adjournment.

Present - The Honorable Edward Scott Judge.

PATRICK CAREY)   On motion (p 260) of the defendant by his attorney
   vs.   )   It is ordered by the Court that a Commission issue
JOHN S. HILL   )   directed to any Justice of the peace of Roane County to take the depositions of Capt John Boyd, Benjamin Boyd, Hiram Barry and Samuel Pride and that Ten days notice of the time and place of taking said depositions be given to Plaintiff.

ARCHIBALD McKINNEY)   On motion of the plaintiff by his attorney and
   vs.   )   for reasons appearing to the satisfaction of
LIJAH KINCHELOE   )   the Court. It is ordered that each party pay his own witnesses who attended from the time the rule of reference was entered in this cause to the end of the present Term of this Court.

BETSEY HENDERSON   )   Petition for Divorce.
   vs.   )   This day came the plaintiff by her attorney
ROLLIN M. HENDERSON)   and the defendant being solemnly called to come into Court and answer the Petition of Betsey Henderson or the same would be taken as confessed and heard exparte and the Court proceed to decree accordingly came not but made default.

STATE of TENNESSEE)   This day (p 261) the State by the attorney
   vs.   )   General and with leave of the Court enters a
JESSE WALKER   )   Nollie prosequi in this cause.

STATE of TENNESSEE)   In this cause by consent of the attorney Gen-
   vs.   )   eral and with the assent of the Court. It is
ELIZABETH WALKER   )   ordered that the forfeiture entered against
JACOB RUSH   )   the defendants at a former Term of this Court
JESSE CREECH &   )   be set aside according to act of Assembly.

JOHN ROBINSON) And thereupon the defendants Elizabeth Walker, Jac-
bail for JESSE) ob Rush, Jesse Creech and John Robinson came into
WALKER   ) Court by their attorney Peter Parsons and assume and
take upon themselves the payment of the costs both of the Scire Facias and
of the original Bill of Indictment. It is therefore considered by the Court
that the State recover of the said defendants the costs both of the original Bill of Indictment and the costs arising on the Scire Facias and that
Execution issue accordingly.

STATE of TENNESSEE) On motion of the defendant by his attorney a
vs.) perjury   ) rule is allowed him to shew cause why the In-
MARTIN WOODS   ) dictment should be quashed.

JOHN LONG   ) This day came (p 262) the parties by their attor-
vs.   ) nies and thereupon came the Jury to wit, William Mar-
JACOB BURRIS) tin, James Young, Joseph McCullough, Dickerson Thurman, Preston Blevins, James Williford, William Alexander, John Denny, William Giddens, Hezekiah Hamblen, James Charles and Daniel Chambers the same
Jury that were on yesterday respited from rendering their verdict who being
elected tried and sworn upon their oaths do say we find that the defendant
is not Guilty of the Trespass as the Plaintiff in his declaration hath complained. Whereupon on motion of the Plaintiff by his attorney a rule is
allowed him to shew cause why a new trial should be granted.

JOHN BALCH   ) This day came the parties by their attornies and
vs.   ) thereupon came a Jury to wit, Joel Gillenwaters,
ALEXANDER SEVIER) John Laughmiller, Samuel McPheeters, James Mills,
GEORGE HOUSE   ) Markham Kenner, William Young, George Tucker,
and   ) William Armstrong,Jr., Christion Shanks, Absalom
JOHN RECTOR   ) Kyle, James Williams & Cleon Moore who being el-
his subt   ) ected tried and sworn upon their oaths do say we
find for the plaintiff and assess his damage to Fifty one dollars (p 263)
and forty cents besides costs. Whereupon on motion of the defendant by
his attorney a rule is allowed him to shew cause why a new trial should
be granted.

STATE of TENNESSEE) This day came the State by the Attorney Gen-
vs.   ) eral and with leave of the Court enters a Nol-
MARTIN WOODS   ) li prosequi in this cause. It is therefore
considered by the Court that the defendant be discharged and that the Clerk make out a Bill of the costs and present it to the County Court for
allowance.

STATE of TENNESSEE) This day personally appeared in open Court Jos-
vs.   ) eph Beelor and Hezekiah Davis and acknowledged
JOSEPH BEELOR   ) themselves indebted to the State of Tennessee
that is to say Joseph Beelor in the sum of One hundred dollars and Hezekiah Davis in the sum of Fifty dollars to be levied of their proper goods
and chattels lands and tenements to the use of the State but to be void
on condition that the said Joseph Beelor make his personal appearance before the Honorable Judge of the Circuit Court at the Courthouse in Rogersville from day to day and answer a charge of the State exhibited against
him and not depart without leave of Court.

STATE of TENNESSEE) This day (p 264) personally appeared in open
vs.   ) Court Hezekiah Davis and Joseph Beelor and ack-
HEZEKIAH DAVIS   ) nowledged themselves indebted to the State of

Tennessee that is to say Hezekiah Davis in the sum of One hundred dollars and Joseph Beelor in the sum of Fifty dollars to be levied of their proper goods and chattels lands and tenements to the use of the State but to be void on condition that the said Hezekiah Davis make his personal appearance before the Honorable Judge of the Circuit Court at the Courthouse in Rogersville from day to day – and answer a charge of State exhibited against him and not depart without leave of Court.

STATE OF TENNESSEE)   This day personally appeared in open Court
vs.)   Hezekiah Davis and Joseph Beelor and acknowledged themselves indebted to the State of
HEZEKIAH DAVIS)

Tennessee that is to say Hezekiah Davis in the sum of One hundred dollars and Joseph Beelor in the sum of Fifty dollars to be levied of their proper goods and chattels lands and tenements to the use of the State but to be void on condition that the said Hezekiah Davis make his personal appearance before the Honorable Judge of the (p 265) Circuit Court at the Courthouse in Rogersville from day to day – and answer a charge of the State exhibited against him and not depart without leave of Court.

STATE of TENNESSEE)   This day personally appeared in open Court
vs.)   Hezekiah Davis and Joseph Beelor and acknowledged themselves indebted to the State
HEZEKIAH DAVIS)

of Tennessee that is to say Hezekiah Davis in the sum of One hundred dollars Joseph Beelor in the sum of Fifty dollars to be levied of their proper goods and chattels lands and tenements to the use of the State but to be void on condition that the said Hezekiah Davis make his personal appearance before the Honorable Judge of the Circuit Court at the Courthouse in Rogersville from day to day – and answer a charge of the State exhibited against him and not depart without leave of Court.

WILLIAM BRANNON)   This day came the parties by their attornies
vs.)   and thereupon came a Jury, to wit, Andrew Galbreath, James Johnson, Samuel Wilson, John M.
ALEXANDER SEVIER)

Vaughan, John Mitchell, Lewis Click, Joseph Huffmaster, Larkin Willis, William Phipps, Thomas Armstrong (p 266) John Reynolds and William Martin who being elected tried and sworn upon their oath do say we find for the plaintiff and assess his damage to Two dollars and twenty five cents besides costs. It is therefore considered by the Court that the Plaintiff recover of the defendant the sum of Two dollars and twenty five cents the damages aforesaid by the Jurors aforesaid assessed also his costs by him about his suit in this behalf expended and that Execution issue accordingly.

JONATHON LONG)   In this cause on motion of the Plaintiff by Peter
vs.)   Parsons his attorney and it appearing to the satisfaction of the Court that the Plaintiff was compelled to pay as one of the securities of the defendant the sum of Twenty three dollars and two cents on a Judgment rendered in this Court at a former Term against the defendnat and John G. Winston, Robert Carden and the said Jonathon Long. It is considered by the Court that the Plaintiff recover of the defendant the sum of Twenty three dollars two cents and also the Interest theron from the 7th October 1823 together with the costs of this motion and that Execution issue accordingly.

Court adjourned until tomorrow 9 O'clock A. M.

Edw. Scott

Saturday 9th April 1825 (p 267)

Court met pursuant to adjournment.

Present - The Honorable Edward Scott - Judge

BETSEY HENDERSON) Petition for Divorce.
vs.) This day came the Plaintiff by her attorney
ROLLIN M. HENDERSON) and the defendant being solemnly called to
come into Court and answer the Petition of Betsey Henderson or the same would be taken as confessed and heard ex-parte and the Court proceed to decree accordingly came not but made default.

STATE of TENNESSEE) This day personally appeared in open Court Joseph
vs.) eph Morriset, John A. McKinney and Gabriel Mc-
JOSEPH MORRISET) Crow and Jointly & severally acknowledge themselves indebted to the State of Tennessee in the sum of Five hundred dollars to be levied of their proper goods and chattels lands and Tenements to the use of the State but to be void on condition that the said Joseph Morriset make his personal appearance before the Honorable Judge of the Circuit Court at the Courthouse in Rogersville on the Wednesday after the next Term of this Court and answer a charge of the State exhibited against him and not depart without leave of the Court.

STATE of TENNESSEE) This day (p 268) came on to be heard the rule
vs.) granted on a former day of this Term to tax the
ISAIAH JONES) prosecutor with the costs and after argument
of Counsel thereon as well for as against the rule and the premises seen and fully understood. It is considered by the Court that the rule be discharged & the Trustee of Green County pay the costs of this prosecution and that the Clerk of this Court issue certificates to those persons entitled to the same.

JOHN DEN LESSEE of) On affidavit of the defendant Thomas Hopkins.
JAMES MOSS) It is ordered by the Court that a Commission
vs.) issue directed to any Justice of the peace of
THOMAS HOPKINS and) Hawkins County to take the depositions of John
WALTER BEATY) Long, James Cooper and John Winegar de bene esse and that Ten days notice of the time and place of taking said depositions be given to Peter Parsons Plaintiff's attorney shall be deemed sufficient.

STATE of TENNESSEE) This day came the State by the Attorney Gener-
vs.) al and the defendant in his proper person and
HEZEKIAH DAVIS) being charged on the Bill of Indictment plead
Guilty and submit to the mercy (p 269) of the Court Whereupon the premises being seen and fully understood. It is considered by the Court that the said Hezekiah Davis for this his offence be fined in the sum of Five dollars and pay the costs of this prosecution and held in custody of the Sheriff until fine and costs are paid or security given therefor. Whereupon Absalom Kyle comes into open Court and offers himself as security for the fine and Costs. It is therefore considered by the Court that the State recover of the defendant and Absalom Kyle his Security the sum of five dollars the fine aforesaid assessed together with the costs of this prosecution and that Execution issue accordingly.

STATE of TENNESSEE)   For unlawful Gaming.
       vs.   )   This day came the State by the attorney General,
HEZEKIAH DAVIS &)   and the defendants in their proper persons and
JOSEPH BEELOR   )   being charged on the Bill of Indictment plead
Guilty and submit to the mercy of the Court. Whereupon the premises being
seen and fully understtod. It is considered by the Court that the defendants for their offence be fined the sum of Five dollars each and pay the
costs of this prosecution and held in custody until fine and costs are paid
or Security given therefor. Whereupon Absalom Kyle and Gabriel McCrow offer
themselves as Security for the fine and costs. It is therefore considered
by the Court that the (p 270) State recover of the defendants and Absalom
Kyle and Gabriel McCrow their securities the sum of Five dollars each the
fines aforesaid assessed together with the costs of this prosecution & that
Execution issue accordingly.

STATE of TENNESSEE)   This day personally appeared in open Court Hez-
       vs.   )   ekiah Davis and Absalom Kyle and acknowledged
HEZEKIAH DAVIS   )   themselves indebted to the State of Tennessee
Jointly and severally in the penal sum of Two hundred and fifty dollars to
be levied of their porper goods and chattels lands and tenements to the use
of the State but to be void on condition that Hezekiah Davis make his personal appearance before the Honorable Judge of the Circuit Court at the
Courthouse in Rogersville on the Wednesday after the first Monday of October next and answer a charge of the State exhibited against him and not
depart without leave of Court.

STATE of TENNESSEE)   This day personally appeared in open Court Jos-
       vs.   )   eph Beelor and Robert D. Young and acknowledged
JOSEPH BEELOR   )   themselves indebted to the State of Tennessee
Jointly and severally in the penal sum of Two hundred and fifty doblars to
be levied of their proper goods and chattels lands and (p 271) tenements
to the use of the State but to be void on condition that the said Joseph
Beelor make his personal appearance before the Honorable Judge of the Circuit Court at the Courthouse in Rogersville on the Wednesday of the next
Term of this Court and answer a charge of the State exhibited against him
and not depart without leave of Court.

STATE of TENNESSEE)   Writ of Error.
    vs.) Bastardy   )   The record and proceedings in this cause the
ALEXANDER BALLARD)   assignment of Errors and plea of Nullo est err-
atune having come on to be heard and argument of Counsel being heard thereon and the matters and things thereon being seen and inspected by the Court
here and fully understood. It is considered by the Court that there is
Error in the record and proceedings of the County Court and that the same
be in all things reversed annulled and for nothing held and that the defendant enter into recognizance in the sum of three hundred dollars with sufficient Security to appear at the Court of pleas and quarter sessions for
Hawkins County to abide the Judgement of the same in this behalf. Whereupon
personally appeared in open Court Alexander Ballard Jr. and Alexander Ballard Senr and jointly and severally acknowledged themselves indebted to the
State of Tennessee in the penal sum of Three hundred dollars to be levied
of their proper goods and chattels lands and tenements to the use (p 272)
of the State but to be void on condition that Alexander Ballard Jr. make
his personal appearance before the Justice of the Court of pleas and quarter session of Hawkins County at the Courthouse in Rogersville on the Wednesday after the fourth Monday of May next and answer a charge of the State

exhibited against him for Bastardy and enter into recognizance to save the Country harmless & c, and not depart without leave of Court.

STATE of TENNESSEE) The rule granted on a former day of this Term
      vs.   ) came on to be heard and after argument of cou-
JOSEPH BEELOR   ) nsel thereon as well for as against said rule
and the premises seen and fully understood. It is considered by the Court that the rule be made absolute and a new trial granted.

STATE of TENNESSEE) The record and proceedings of the County Court
      vs.   ) having been seen and inspected by the Court.
THOMAS MORRISON) It is considered by the Court that the Judgment
EDWARD KING   ) of the County Court in taxing William Alexan-
and   ) der the prosecutor with the costs of the pros-
ROBERT KING   ) ecution in this behalf be annulled and for nothing held and it is further considered by the Court that the County Trustee pay the costs in this behalf expended and that the Clerk (p 273)
of this Court issue certificates to those persons entitled to the same.

JOHN BALCH   ) This day came on to be heard and determined the
      vs.   ) rule granted on a former day of this Term and
ALEXANDER SEVIER) after argument of counsel thereon as well for as
against said rule and the premises seen and fully understood. It is considered by the Court that the rule be discharged and that the Plaintiff
recover of the defendant and George House, John Rector and Edward Y. Russell his securities the sum of Fifty one dollars and forty cents the damages by the Jurors aforesaid together with the costs in this behalf expended and that Execution issue accordingly.

WILLIAM BRANNON) On motion of the defendant by his attorney a
      vs.   ) rule is allowed him to shew cause why a new
ALEXANDER SEVIER) trial should be granted and after argument of
Counsel thereon as well for as against said rule and the premises seen
and fully understood. It is considered by the Court that the rule be
discharged and that the Plaintiff recover of the defendant and George
House and John Rector his securities the sum of Two dollars twenty five
cents the damages by the Jurors assessed together with the costs in this
behalf expended and that Execution issue accordingly.

ISHAM REYNOLDS) On affidavit (p 274) of the Plaintiff. It is
& wife   ) ordered by the Court that a Commission issue dir-
      vs.   ) ected to any Justice of the peace of Hawkins Co-
JOHN A. ROGERS) untly to take the deposition of Mary Hinton and
that Ten days notice of the time and place of taking said deposition be
given to the Plaintiff.

JOHN DEN LESSEE of) On motion of the Plaintiff by his attorney.
JAMES MOORE   ) It is ordered by the Court that Gabriel Mc-
      vs.   ) Crow survey the land in dispute and that he
WALTER BEATY and) return them a plot to the next term of this
THOMAS HOPKINS   ) Court.

ALEXANDER RICE by his) On motion of the Plaintiff by his attorney
father & next friend) and for reasons appearing to the satisfac-
WM RICE   ) tion of the Court. It is ordered that each
      vs.   ) party pay their own witnesses for their at-
OLIVER MILLER   ) tendance during the present Term.

GABRIEL McCROW)   This day came the plaintiff and with leave of Court
     vs.   )   dismisses his suit (p 275). Whereupon Absalom
JESSE COBB   )   Kyle personally appeared in open Court and confesses Judgment for the costs. It is therefore considered by the Court that
the Plaintiff recover of Absalom Kyle the costs in this behalf expended
and that execution issue accordingly.

SAUL REYNOLDS)   This day came on to be heard the rule for a new
& others   )   Trial granted on a former day of this term and af-
     vs.   )   ter argument of Counsel thereon as well for as ag-
JAMES HAGAN)   ainst said rule and the premises seen and fully understood. It is considered by the Court that the rule be discharged and
that the Plaintiff recover of the defendant the sum of One hundred dollars
the damages assessed by the Jurors together with the costs in this behalf
expended and that Execution issue accordingly.

JOHN LONG   )   This day came on to be heard and determined the rule
     vs.   )   granted on a former day of this term and after argu-
JACOB BURRIS)   ment of Counsel thereon as well in favor as against
the rule and the premises seen and fully understood. It is considered by
the Court that the rule be discharged and that the defendant go hence without day and recover of the Plaintiff his costs by him in this behalf expended and that Execution issue accordingly.

ISHAM REYNOLDS   )   Demurrer
& wife   )   This day came the parties by their attornies
     vs.   )   and the demurrer of the Plaintiff to the third
JOHN GRIGGSBY and)   plea of the defendant came on for argument and
CALEB J. PARKER   )   argument of Counsel being heard both on part
of the Plaintiff and defendant and the premises considered and fully understood. It is considered by the Court that the said third plea of the
defendant and the matters and things therein contained are not good and
sufficient in law and that the demurrer to the said third plea be sustained.

JOHN SHOUGH   )   This day came the parties by their attornies and the
     vs.   )   demurrer to the plea of the defendant came on for
JAMES SPENCER)   argument and argument of Counsel being heard as well
on behalf of the Plaintiff as defendant and the premises seen and understood. It is considered by the Court that the third plea of the defend-
antis good and valid in law and (p 277) that the demurrer be overruled
and on motion It is ordered that the defendant have leave to file a replication on his paying the costs of the demurrer.

JOHN DEN LESSE of)   By consent of the parties It is ordered by the
JOHN ELLIS   )   Court that a Commission issue directed to any
     vs.   )   Justice of the peace of Warren County in this
JOHN SMITH   )   State to take the deposition of Thomas Henderson and that Twenty days notice of the time and place of taking said deposition be given to the adverse party. And on application of the Plaintiff. It is ordered by the Court that the Plaintiff have leave to amend
his declaration by adding a Count on the demise of Thomas Henderson.

JOHN DEN LESSEE of)   On motion of the Plaintiff by his attorney it
ALEXANDER PORTER)   is ordered by the Court that a Commission iss-
     vs.   )   ue directed to any Justice of the Peace of
THOMAS COCKE   )   Washington County to take the depsotitions of

James Aiken & James V. Anderson and that ten days notice of the time and place of taking (p 278) said deposition be given & that a Commission issue directed to any Justice of the peace of Warren County in this state to take the deposition of Thomas Hopkins and that Twenty days notice of the time and place of taking said depositions be given to the adverse party.

GABRIEL McCROW) On motion of the Plaintiff by his attorney a rule
vs.) Certiorari) is allowed him to shew cause why the Certiorari
THOMAS JOHNSON) should be dismissed.

ARCHIBALD McKINNEY) On motion of defendants a rule is allowed him
    vs.   ) to shew cause why the Judgment by default in
GEORGE COX   ) the County Court should be set aside and after
argument of Counsel thereon as well for as against the rule and the premises seen and understood It is considered by the Court that the rule be discharged.

Court adjourned until Court in Course.
               Edw. Scott

Monday the 3rd day of October 1825

At a Circuit Court begun (p 279) and held for the County of Hawkins at the Courthouse in Rogersville in said County of Hawkins on the first Monday being the Third day of October in the Year of our Lord One thousand eight hundred and twenty five and the Fiftieth of American Independence.

Present --mThe Honorable Samuel Powel - Judge.

James P. McCarty Sheriff of Hawkins County returns now into open Court one Writ of Venire Facias returnable to the present Term of this Court Executed on the following persons being good and lawful men of Hawkins County and appointed by the Court of pleas and quarter sessions of said County - Viz.

James Williams
Willie B. Kyls
Absalom Kyle
Benjamin Davis
John Mitchell
Joseph McCullough Senr
William Smith
John Reynolds
John Johnston
Joseph Huffmaster
Jacob Miller
Samuel Wilson Esqr
Joel Gillenwaters
Wm Armstrong
John Critz
Thomas Stacey
Lewis Click
Abraham Hawk
Howel Brewer
William Crumly

Larkin Willis
William Nichols

from among whom the following persons being drawn in due form of law and compose the Grand Jury for the present Term of this Court, Viz

1. John Johnston Treas   (p 280)
2. Abraham Hawk
3. William Smith
4. Larkin Willis
5. Benjamin Davis
6. Joel Gillenwaters
7. Joseph McCullough
8. James Williams
9. Thomas Stacey
10 Samuel Wilson
11 William Crumley
12 John Critz
13 Howel Brewer

Whereupon the Court appointed John Johnston Foreman of the Grand Jury who were impanneled and sworn received their charge and withdrew from the Bar of the Court.

Robert W. Gillenwaters Constable was appointed by the Court officer to attend on Grand Jury for the present Term and was qualified in due form of law.

JOHN DEN LESSEE of)   By consent of the parties by their attornies
ALEXANDER PORTER)   this cause is continued until the next Term of
       vs.   )   this Court anf by consent It is ordered by the
THOMAS COCKE   )   Court that the deposition of Thomas Hopkins
heretofore taken in a former suit between the parties in this cause be read on the trial of this cause. And on motion of the Plaintiff by his attorney. It is ordered by the Court that a Commission issue directed to any Justice of the peace of Washington County in this State to take the depositions of James V. Anderson and James Aiker and that Ten days notice of the (p 281) time and place of taking said depositions be given to the adverse party.

NANCY MIDKIFF)   This day came the Plaintiff by her attorney and with
       vs.   )   leave of the Court dismisses her suit. It is there-
JOHN NORMAN)   fore considered by the Court that the defendant go
hence without day and recover of the Plaintiff his costs by him in this behalf expended and that Execution issue accordingly.

JOHN LONG   )   This day came the Plaintiff by his attorney and there-
vs. Slander)   upon Thomas Barrot comes into Court and confesses
THOMAS BARROT)   Judgment for the sum of Twenty five dollars the am-
and   )   ount of the fee paid by the plaintiff to his att-
WINNY BARROT)   orney and the costs, and the Plaintiff releases the
 his wife   )   defendants from all further damages on account of
the defamatory words spoken. It is therefore considered by the Court that the Plaintiff recover of the defendants Thomas Barrot the sum of Twenty five dollars and also the costs in this behalf expended as above confessed for which execution may issue.

JOHN DEN LESSEE of   ')   By consent of the parties by their attornies
JAMES McBEE & others)   (p 282) this cause is continued until the

vs.   )   next term of this Court. And on affidavit of
ETHELDRED WILLIAMS)   the defendant. It is ordered by the Court that
a Commission issue directed to any Justice of the Peace of Monroe County
State of Mississippi to take the depositions of William Cocke and that Forty days notice of the time and place of taking said deposition be given and
that A Commission issue directed to any Justice of the peace of Hawkins
County to take the deposition of Wm. Moffitt de bene esse and that Ten days
notice of the time & place of taking said deposition be given to the Plaintiffs.

WILLIAM CRUMLY)   This day came the parties by their attornies and
    vs.   )   thereupon came a Jury, to wit, Lewis Click, Will-
JOHNSON FRAZIER)   iam Nichols, William Armstrong Esq, John Mitchell,
Jacob Miller, Willie B. Kyler, James Johnson, John Reynolds, Lazarus Spiers, Cornelius Carmack, Isaad Lauderback and Jesse Howel who being elected tried and sworn upon their oaths do say we find for the defendant.
Whereupon on motion of the Plaintiff by his attorney a rule is allowed him
to shew cause why a new Trial should be granted & after argument of Counsel thereon as well for as against the rule the premises seen & fully understood. It is considered by the Court that the rule be discharged And
that the defendant go hence without day and recover of the Plaintiff the
costs in this behalf expended and that Execution issue accordingly.

LIJAH KINCHELOE)   By consent (p 283) of the parties by their
   vs.) No 1   )   attornies these causes are referred to the Arb-
JOHN A ROGERS   )   itration to the Honorable Thos. Emmerson, Absalom
   Same   )   Kyle, George Hale, John Miller and William Lyons
   vs,) No 2   )   and if any of the Above named referees refuse to
   Same   )   act the parties are to choose others in their
GABRIEL McCrow &)   stead and if the parties cannot agree the referees
ROBERT NALL   )   who are willing to act are to choose others in
   vs.   )   the place of them to act and their award return-
LIJAH KINCHELOE)   ed into Court under their hands and seals to be
the Judgments of the Court in said causes.

JOHN DEN LESSEE of)   On affidavit of the Plaintiff this cause is
WILLIAM BRADLEY   )   continued until the next Term of this Court.
    vs.   )
THOMAS SPROUL   )

Court adjourned until tomorrow 9 O'clock A. M.
                    S. Powel

Tuesday 4th October 1825.

Court met pursuant to adjournment.

Present - The Honorable Samuel Powel - Judge.

JOHN DEN LESSEE of)   This day came (p 284) the parties by their
WILLIAM WHITESIDES)   attornies and thereupon came on the rule for
    vs.   )   a new Trial in this cause for argument and
DAVID PROFFIT   )   after argument of Counsel being heard as well
in support of said rule as against it and it being admitted by both parties that the suit at law in the supreme Court of Errors and Appeals between John Den Lessee of Etheldred Williams & others Plaintiffs and David

Proffit defendant to which the agreement of the parties in this cause refers has been decided in favor of the Plaintiffs in the Court of law but it is admitted by the Plaintiffs attorney that a Bill of Injunction had been filed by the defendant in the said suit of John Den Lessee of Etheldred Williams & others against David Proffit which Bill is still depending. It is therefore considered by the Court that the Rule for a New trial be discharged.

JOHN DEN LESSEE of) On motion of the defendant by his attorney.
WILLIAM BRADLEY) It is ordered by the Court that a Commission
vs.) issue directed to any Justice of the peace
THOMAS SPROUL) of Hawkins County Tennessee to take the depositions of John Burris and John Marshall Senr de bene esse and that Ten days notice of the time and place of taking said depositions be given to the Plaintiff.

JOHN DEN LESSE of) This day came (p 285) the Plaintiff by his
RICHARD MITCHELL) attorney and with leave of the Court dismisses
vs.) his suit. It is therefore considered by the
WILLIAM JARVIS) Court that the defendant go hence without day
and recover of the Plaintiff his costs by him in this behalf expended and that Execution issue accordingly.

ROBERT C. CRAWFORD) Petition for Divorce.
vs.) This cause coming on to be heard and finally
SUSANNAH CRAWFORD) determined this 4th day of October 1825 on the
petition of the Petitioner and proof and it appearing to the satisfaction of the Court that the process has been regularly served on the defendant and the defendant having failed to appear and answer the Petition and it being proved to the Court that the defendant has been Guilty of Adultry as charged in the Petition & that the Petitioner is a man of Good moral character. It is therefore considered ordered adjudged and decreed by the Court that Bonds of Matrimony heretofore solemnized between the Petitioner and his said wife be and the same is hereby dissolved annulled and made void and that the said Robert C. Crawford be and he is hereby forever freed and separated from his said wife Susannah Crawford and that the Petitioner pay the costs of this Petition for which Execution may issue.

ABRAHAM B. TRIGG) This day (p 286) came the parties by their
vs.) attornies and thereupon came a Jury, to wit,
JOHN LYNN) Lewis Click, Jacob Miller, Joseph McCullough,
James Johnson, Willie B. Kyle, Thomas White, Aeneas S. Galbreath, Joseph Mooney, Arthur G. Young, Thomas Monahon, John Norman and David Kearsner who being elected tried and sworn upon their oaths do say we find that the defendant did assume as the Plaintiff in his declaration hath alledged and that he did not assume within three years as the defendant in his second plea hath alledged. It is therefore considered by the Court that the Plaintiff take nothing by his Writ but for his false clamor be in mercy and that the defendant go hence without day and recover of the Plaintiff the costs in this behalf expended and that Execution issue accordingly.

JOSEPH MORRISET) This day came the parties by their attornies
vs.) and thereupon came a Jury, to wit, William
OLLIVER JENKINS) Nichols, William Armstrong, John Mitchell,

Shadrach Epperson, Joseph Huffmaster, George Merrit, James Mills, Joseph Roberts, Preston Blevins, Solomon Seals, Elijah Herd and Henry Crowley, who being elected tried and sworn upon their oaths do say we find that the defendant hath kept and performed his Covenant (p 287) as in his plea he hath alledged. It is therefore considered by the Court that the Defendant go hence without day and recover of the Plaintiff & John A. McKinney his security the costs in this behalf expended and that Execution issue accordingly.

ARCHAIBALD McKINNEY)   On affidavit of Aeneas S. Galbreath agent
   vs.   )   for the defendant. It is ordered by the
LIHAH KINCHELOE)   Court that this cause be continued until
the next Term of this Court.

STATE of TENNESSEE)   This day Seviersfield Anderson who was bound
   vs.   )   in recognizance for the others for the person-
JAMES McKINNEY)   al appearance of the defendant at the present Term of this Court surrenders to Court the body of the said James Mc-
Kinney in discharge of himself and the others as appearance Bail.
Whereupon the Court ordered the said James McKinney in custody of the
Sheriff. And thereupon personally appeared in open Court James McKinney
and John A. McKinney and acknowledged themselves indebted to the State
of Tennessee in the penal sum One thousand dollars each to be levied of
their proper goods and Chattels lands and tenements to the use of the
State but to but to be void on condition that the said James McKinney
make (p 288) his personal appearance before the Honorable Judge of
the Circuit Court at the Courthouse in Rogersville from day to day and
answer a charge of the State exhibited against him and not depart without leave of the Court.

ISHAM REYNOLDS)   This day came the parties by their attornies,
& wife   )   and thereupon came a Jury, to wit, Lewis Click,
   vs.   )   Jacob Miller, Joseph McCullough Jr., James John-
JOHN GRIGGSBY)   son, Willie B. Kyle, Thomas White, Aeneas S.
CALEB J. PARKER)   Galbreath, Joseph Mooney, Arthur G. Young, Thomas Monahon, John Norman and David Kearsner who being elected tried and
sworn upon their oaths do say we find that the defendants have not kept
and performed the condition annexed to the obligation in Plaintiffs declaration mentioned as in their first and second pleas they have alledged
and they also say that the plaintiff did not put it out of the power of
the defendants to deliver the negroes in the Plaintiffs declaration mentioned to the Sheriff of Hawkins County as in the fourth plea they have
alledged and they assess the Plaintiffs damage to Five hundred and ninety seven dollars and fifty cents besides costs.

ISHAM REYNOLDS & wife)   On affidavit (p 289) of the defendant this
   vs.   )   cause is continued until the next Term of
JOHN A. ROGERS)   this Court on defendants paying the costs
of this Term. And on motion. It is ordered by the Court that a Commission issue directed to any Justice of the peace of Monroe County in this
State to take the depositions of Henry Reynolds, Henry Chestnutt and Sarah
Lawson on behalf of the defendant and that Ten days notice of the time and
place of taking said depositions be given to the Plaintiffs. And on motion of the Plaintiffs by their attorney. It is ordered by the Court that
a Commission issue directed to any Justice of the Peace of Hawkins County
to take the deposition of Mary Hinton de bene esse and that Ten days notice of the time and place of taking said deposition be given to the defend-

ant.

A Deed of Conveyance from John Marshall to Hohn McWilliams for one hundred acres of land was acknowledged in open Court and ordered to be registered.

PATRICK CAREY)   This day came (p 290) the parties by their att-
vs.) Cov't   )   ornies and thereupon came a Jury, to wit, William
JOHN S. HILL)   Nichols, William Armstrong, John Mitchell, Shadrach Epperson, Joseph Huffmaster, Joseph Roberts, Samuel Henderson, James Young, Wilson Roach, James Carden, James Griggsby and Solomon Seals
who being elected tried and sworn amd prpgress having been made in the
trial of this cause by consent of the parties by their attornies and with
the assent of the Court the Jurors aforesaid from rendering their Verdict
are respited until tomorrow.

The Court adjourned until tomorrow 9 O'clock A. M.
                        S. Powel

Wednesday 5th October 1825.

Court met pursuant to adjournment.

Present - The Honorable Samuel Powel - Judge.

STATE of TENNESSEE)   On motion of Michael McCann Esqr attorney for
        vs.   )   the defendants a rule is allowed them to shew
JOHN REESE &   )   cause why the Indictments in these cause should
JOHN NUTTY   )   be quashed.
)
)
STATE   )
     vs.   )
ELIJAH FALKNER   )
& ABRAHAM BLEVINS)

ROBERT McGINNIS   )   By consent (p 291) of the parties by their
Admr & c of   ⨯)   attornies this cause is continued until the
LAWRENCE STONE Dec'd)   next Term of this Court.
        vs.   )
JOHN COCKE & JOHN)
F. JACK   )

STATE of TENNESSEE)   On motion of the defendants by James P. Taylor
        vs.   )   their attorney a rule is allowed them to shew
WILLIE B. KYLE &)   cause why the Indictments should be quashed.
SHADROCH EPPERSON)
)
Same   )
     vs.   )
RICHARD GAMMON   )

JAMES BRADLEY)   By consent of the parties this cause is referred to
     vs.   )   the arbitration of Jacob Miller, James Francisco,
JOSEPH McMINN)   John McWilliams and Richard Mitchell and if they can-

not agree they are to call on William Lyons and their award returned into open Court under their hands and seals to be the Judgment of the Court.

WILLIAM WALKER) George Rogers who had been legally summoned as a
    vs.   ) witness on behalf of defendant Asabel Johnson in
ASABEL JOHNSON) this cause and being now solemnly called to come into Court came not but made default (p 292). It is therefore considered by the Court that the defendant Asabel Johnson recover of the said George Rogers the sum of One hundred and twenty five dollars agreeable to act of Assembly in such case made and provided unless sufficient cause of his disability to attend be shewn at the next Term of this Court after notice of this Judgment.

WILLIAM WALKER) David S. Rogers who had been legally summoned as
    vs.   ) a Witness on behalf of the defendant in this cause
ASABEL JOHNSON) and being now solemnly called to come into Court came not but made default. It is therefore considered by the Court that the defendant Asabel Johnson recover of the said David S. Rogers the sum of One hundred and twenty five dollars agreeable to Act of Assembly in such case made and provided unless sufficient cause of his disability to attend be shewn at the next Term of this Court after notice of this Judgment.

STATE of TENNESSEE) Assault & Battery with intent to kill and murder.
    vs.   ) On affidavit of the defendant this cause is con-
ISAIAH JONES   ) tinued until the next Term of this Court. Where-upon personally appeared in open Court Isaiah Jones, Cornelius Smith and James Jones and acknowledged themselves (293) indebted to the State of Tennessee that is to say Isaiah Jones in the sum of Five hundred dollars and Cornelius Smith and James Jones in the sum of Two hundred and fifty dollars each to be levied of their proper goods and chattels lands and tenements to the use of the State but to be void on Condition that the said Isaiah Jones make his personal appearance before the Honorabel Judge of the Circuit Court at the Courthouse in Rogersville on the Wednesday after the first Monday of April next and answer a charge of the State exhibited against him and not depart without leave of Court.
Whereupon personally appeared in open Court Hugh Carter and acknowledged himself indebted to the State of Tennessee in the sum of Two hundred and fifty dollars to be levied of his proper goods and chattels lands and Tenements to the use of the State but to be void on condition that he make his personal appearance before the Honorable Judge of the Circuit Court at the Courthouse in Rogersville on the Wednesday after the first Monday of April next and prosecute and give evidence on behalf of State against Isaiah Jones and not depart without leave of Court.

STATE   ) For Obstruction of lawful prowess.
    vs.   ) On affidavit of the defendant (p 294) this cause
ISAIAH JONES) is continued until the next Term of this Court. Whereupon personally appeared in open Court Isaiah Jones, Cornelius Smith, and James Jones and acknowledged themselves indebted to the State of Tennessee that is to say Isaiah Jones in the sum of Five hundred dollars and Cornelius Smith and James Jones in the sum of Two hundred and fifty dollars each to be levied of their proper goods and chattels lands and Tenements to the use of the State but to be void on condition that the said Isaiah Jones make his personal appearance Before the Honorable Judge of the Circuit Court At the Courthouse in Rogersville on the Wednesday after the first Monday of April next and answer a charge of the State exhibited ag-

ainst him and not depart without leave of Court.

And thereupon personally appeared in open Court Hugh Carter and acknowledged themselves indebted to the State of Tennessee in the sum of Two hundred and fifty dollars to be levied of his proper goods and chattels lands and Tenements to the use of the State but to be void on condition that he make his personal appearance before the honorable Judge of the Circuit Court at the Courthouse in Rogersville on the Wednesday after the first Monday of April next and prosecute and give evidence on behalf of the State against Isaiah Jones and not depart without leave of the Court.

STATE of TENNESSEE)   For Harbouring (p 295) a Negro Slave.
      vs.   )   This day personally appeared in open Court
  ISAIAH JONES   )   Isaiah Jones and James Jones and acknowledged themselves indebted to the State of Tennessee in the penal sum of Five hundred dollars each to be levied of their proper goods and chattels lands and tenements to the use of the State but to be void on condition that the said Isaiah Jones make his personal appearance before the honorable Judge of the Circuit Court at the Courthouse in Rogersville on the Wednesday after the first Monday of April next and answer a charge of the State exhibited against him and not depart without leave of Court. And thereupon personally appeared in open Court John Kennedy and acknowledged himself indebted to the State of Tennessee in the penal sum of Two hundred and fifty dollars to be levied of his proper goods and chattels lands and Tenements to the use of the State but to be void on condition that the said John Kennedy make his personal appearance before the Honorable Judge of the Circuit Court at the Courthouse in Rogersville the Wednesday after the first Monday of April next and prosecute and give Evidence on behalf of the State against Isaiah Jones and not depart without leave of the Court.

STATE of TENNESSEE)   This day (p 296) came the State by the
      vs.   )   attorney General and the defendant in his
  JOSEPH MORRISET)   proper person and being charged on the Bill
of Indictment plead not Guilty and put himself on the Country and thereupon came a Jury, to wit, Jacob B. Groves, James Willis, Samuel Bishop, James Chestnut, Asa David, Francis Kenner, Lazarus Spears, William Lipe, William Giddens, Robert Burton, George Stipe and Meredith Williford who being elected tried and sworn well and truly to try the issue of traverse upon their oath do say we find the Defendant Guilty in manner and form as charged in the Bill of Indictment. It is therefore considered by the Court that the defendant Joseph Morriset for this his offence be fined Twenty five dollars and pay the costs of this prosecution and that he be imprisoned in the Jail of Greene County for the space of Two Calendar months, it being represented to the Court that the common prison of this County is insecure and that he there remain until fine and costs are paid or good and sufficinet Security given therefore. And that the Sheriff of this County deliver the said defendant Joseph Morriset into the custody of the Sheriff of Greene County accordingly.

A Deed of Conveyance (p 297) from Samuel Nicholson to Walter Allen for Fifty acres of land was proven in open Court by the oaths of Thomas Lawson and Thomas Epperson and ordered to be registered.

PATRICK CAREY)   This day came the parties by their attornies and
    vs.   )   thereupon came a Jury, to wit, William Nichols,
  JOHN S. HILL) William Armstrong, John Mitchell, Sahdroch Epperson,

Joseph Huffmaster, Joseph Roberts, Samuel Henderson, James Young, Wilson Roach, James Carden, James Griggsby and Solomon Seals the same Jury that were respited on yesterday from rendering their verdict who being elected tried and sworn upon their oaths do say we find that the defendant has not kept and performed the covenant in the Plaintiffs declaration mentioned as he in pleading hath alledged & that he hath broken the covenant & that he did not discharge the obligation and assess the plaintiffs damage to One dollars besides costs. It is therefore considered by the Court that the Plaintiff recover of the defendant the sum of One dollar the damages aforesaid by the Jurors aforesaid assessed and also the costs by him in this behalf expended and that Execution issue accordingly.

Ordered by the Court that James P. McCarty Sheriff of this County be fined the sum of Five dollars (p 297) for being absent on the meeting of the Court this morning for which Execution may issue.

STATE of TENNESSEE) For Robbery.
    vs.   ) This day came the State by the Attorney General and the defendant in his proper person
JAMES McKINNEY)
and being charged on the Bill of Indictment plead Not Guilty and put himself on the County and thereupon came a Jury, to wit, John Reynolds, William Armstrong, John C. Gillenwaters, Joseph Beelor, Lewis Click, John McWilliams, Grief B. Huntsman, Willie B. Kyle, Shadroch Epperson, Daniel Carmichael, Christion Shanks and Jesse Howel who being elected tried and sworn upon their oaths do say we find that the defendant is not Guilty in manner and form as charged in the Bill of Indictment. It is therefore considered by the Court that the defendant be discharged. And on motion of the defendant by his attorney and for reasons appearing to the satisfaction of the Court. It is considered that John Wallen the prosecutor pay the costs of this prosecution and that Execution issue accordingly.

WILLIAM WALKER) This day came the parties by their attornies and
    vs.   ) thereupon (p 298) came a Jury, to wit, Jacob
ASABEL JOHNSON) Miller, Joseph McCullough jr., Lewis Click, James
Johnson, George Smith, John Hagan, Thomas Monahon, George W. Thompson, Willie B. Kyle, Horace Rice, John Stokeley and Joseph McMinn who being elected tried and sworn upon their oaths do say we find that the defendant did assume in manner and form as the plaintiff in the first Count of his declaration hath complained and we further find that the defendant did not assume in manner and form as the plaintiff in the second count of his declaration hath complained and assess the plaintiffs damage to One hundred and twenty eight dollars and seventy cents besides costs. It is therefore considered by the Court that the Plaintiff recover of the defendant the sum of One hundred and twenty eight dollars and seventy cents the damages aforesaid by the Jurors aforesaid assessed together with the costs in this behalf expended and that execution issue accordingly.

Court adjourned until tomorrow 9 O'clock A. M.
            S. Powel

Thursday 6th October 1825.

Court met pursuant to adjournment.

Present - The Honorable Samuel Powel - Judge.

On motion and for reasons appearing to the satisfaction of the Court.
It is ordered that the fine assessed against James P. McCarty Sheriff on
yesterday be set aside.

JAMES LOVIN and)   The Court assigns   (p 299)   John A. McKinney Coun-
FRANCES LOVIN)   sel for the Plaintiffs under the act of Assembly
his wife   )   passed for the benefit of paupers. It appearing
   vs.   )   to the Court that the oath required by law is en-
JESSE COBB   )   dorsed on the Writ.
and   )
EMEL MOORE   )

A Deed of Mortage from John Hale & Isaac Hale to the Bank of the State of
Tennessee for Two hundred and nine acres of land was proven in open Court
by the oaths of Jacob Hackney and Michael McCann and ordered to be registered.

POLLY MORRISET)   Petition for Divorce.
   vs.   )   This cause coming on to be heard and finally de-
GEORGE MORRISET)   termined and the petition being read and evidence
heard. And It appearing to the satisfaction of the Court that a Subpoena
and Copy of the Petition had been regularly served on the defendant. And
the Court being fully satisfied touching the premises. It is considered
ordered adjudged and decreed by the Court that the Bonds of Matrimony
heretefore subsisting between the Petitioner Polly Morriset formerly Polly
Rork and her husband George Morriset be and the same is hereby declared
null and void and for nothing held and that the said Polly Morriset be
(p 300) and she is hereby forever freed and separated from her said husband George Morrissett and it is further considered by the Court that the
defendant pay the costs of this Petition for which Execution may issue.

JOHN ROLLER   )   By consent of the parties by their attorney this
   vs.   )   cause is continued until the next Term of this
JOSEPH ROBERTS)   Court and on affidavit of the defendant It is ordered by the Court that a Commission issue directed to any Justice of the
Peace of Scott County Virginia to take the deposition of Abraham Bledsoe
and that a Commission issue directed to any Jusitce of the peace of Lee
County Virginia to take the deposition of Stockley Lawson and David Lawson on behalf of the defendant and that Ten days notice of the time and
place of taking said depositions be given to the Plaintiff.

JUDITH SMITH   )   Petition for Divorce.
by her next friend)   This cause coning on to be heard this 6th day
ASHBY GRIGGSBY)   of October 1825 and the petition of the Petit-
   vs.   )   ioner & proff and it appearing to the Satis-
SAMUEL SMITH   )   faction of the Court that proclamation and publication had been made according to law (p 301) and the defendant who
is not an inhabitant of this State having failed to appear and answer and
it having been proved to the satisfaction of the Court that the Defendant
Samuel Smith had absented himself from the Petitioner and failed to return
and live with her for more than two whole years before the Petition was
filed as stated in said petition, and it further appearing to the Court
that the Petitioner is a woman of good moral character and has conducted
herself as such since the said Defendant left her. It is therefore consid-

ered ordered adjudged and decreed by the Court that the Bonds of Matrimony heretofore solemnized between the said Samuel Smith and the Petitioner Judith Smith formerly Judith Griggsby be and the same is hereby dissolved annuled and made void and that the said Judith Smith be and she is hereby forever freed and separated from her said husband Samuel Smith and it is further considered by the Court that A shby Griggsby pay the costs of this Petition and that Execution issue accordingly.

WILLIAM CARROLL)
Govr for the use)
of ISAIAH JONES)
        vs.   )
ROBERT MALONY)
and   )
JACOB T. WYRICK)

By consent of the parties by their attornies this cause is continued until the next term of this Court.

WILLIAM WALKER)
        vs.   )
JONATHON HENDERSON)

This day (p 302) came the parties by their attornies and thereupon came a Jury, to wit, Lewis Click, William Armstrong, John Mitchell, William Nichols, Moses Rice, William Lipe, John Griggsby, Thomas Cox, Joseph Reese, Simson Williford, Meredith Williford and David Kearsner who being elected tried and sworn upon their oaths do say we find that the defendant is Guilty in manner and form as the plaintiff against him in his declaration hath complained and assess the plaintiffs damage to Twenty five dollars beside costs.

Whereupon William Cloud surrenders to Court the body of the said Jonathon Henderson in discharge of himself as appearance Bail. And thereupon personally appeared in open Court Jonathon Henderson, Moses McGinnis, William Giddens and William Cloud and confess Judgment for the sum of Twenty five dollars the damages aforesaid by the Jurors aforesaid assessed and also the costs. It is therefore considered by the Court that the plaintiff recover of the said Jonathon Henderson, Moses McGinnis, William Giddens and William Cloud the sum of Twenty five dollars as above confessed being the damages assessed by the Jurors aforesaid assessed together with the costs in this behalf expended and that execution issue accordingly. Which Judgment is assigned to John A. McKinney.

JOHN A. ROGERS)
        vs.   )
SAMUEL WILSON Junr.)

This day (p 303) Lazarus Spiers surrenders in open Court the body of Samuel Wilson Junr the defendant in this suit in discharge of himself as appearance Bail for said Samuel Wilson Junr and thereupon the Plaintiff personally appeared in open Court and says he does not require the defendant to be held in custody.

WILLIAM WALKER)
        vs.   )
JAMES WILLIS)

This day came the parties by their attornies and thereupon came a Jury, to wit, Jacob Miller, Joseph Huffmaster, James Johnson, John Reynolds, Willie B. Kyle, Joseph McCullough, Abraham Blevins, Elijah Falkner, John Nutty, John Stokeley, John Hagan and Meridith Williford who being elected tried and sworn upon their oaths do say we find that the defendant is Guilty in manner and form as the Plaintiff in his declaration hath alledged and we further find that the defendant is not justified as in his second plea he hath alledged and assess the Plaintiffs damage to Seventy two dollars and sixty cents besides costs. It is therefore considered by the Court that the Plaintiff recover of the defendant James Willis & Robert W. Gillenwaters his security the sum of seventy two dollars (p 304) and sixty cents the damages aforesaid by the Jurors aforesaid assessed together with the costs in this behalf expended and that Execution issue accordingly.

MARKHAM KENNER)   On affidavit of the defendant this cause is con-
        vs.   )   tinued until the next Term of this Court.
PETER ELROD   )

Court adjourned until tomorrow half past 8 O'clock A. M.
                                        S. Powel

Friday 7th October 1825

Court met pursuant to adjournment.

Present - The Honorable Samuel Powel Judge.

PHEBE KING)   The Court assign Peter Parsons Counsel for the Plain-
    vs.   )   tiff under the act of Assembly passed for the Benefit
JOHN BLAIR)   of paupers. It appearing to the Court that the oath
required by law be endorsed on the Writ.

STATE of TENNESSEE)   For unlawful Gaming.
        vs.   )   This day came the State by the Attorney Gen-
RICHARD GAMMON   )   eral and with leave of the Court enters a
Nolli prosequi in cano. Whereupon personally appeared in open Court Richard Gammon and confesses (p 305) Judgment for the costs. It is therefore
considered by the Court that the State recover of the defendant the costs
of this prosecution and that execution issue accordingly.

STATE of TENNESSEE)   For unlawful Gaming.
        vs.   )   This day came the State by the attorney Gen-
MORGAN WILDS   )   eral and with leave of the Court enters a
)   Nolli prosequi in these causes. It is there-
Same   )   fore considered by the Court that the defend-
    vs.   )   ants be discharged.
THOMAS COLLY &   )
JAMES McNIGHT   )
)
Same   )
    vs.   )
HEZEKIAH DAVIS &   )
JOSEPH BEELOR   )

WILLIAM HAGOOD   )   Demurrer.
vs.) In Equity   )   This day came on for argument the Demurrer of
ROBERT YOUNG Senr.)   the defendant to the Bill of Complainant and
after argument of Counsel thereon as well for as against the demurrer and
the premises seen and fully understood. It is considered by the Court
that the Demurrer be sustained. And on motion of the Complainant by his
attorney. It is ordered that he have leave to amend his Bill by making the
Trustee a party.

WILLIAM BRADLEY   )   By consent of the parties by their attornies
vs.) in Equity   )   this cause is set for hearing at the next Term
GEORGE ARCENBRIGHT)   of this Court. And by consent of the parties

(p 306) by their attornies. It is ordered that they have four months to take the Depositions.

STATE of TENNESSEE) This day came the State by the Attorney Gen-
        vs.   ) eral and with leave of the Court enters a
JOHN NUTTY   ) Nolli prosequi in this cause. And thereupon
personally appeared in open Court John Nutty and confesses Judgment for the costs. It is therefore considered by the Court that the State re-cover against the defendant the costs of this prosecution and that Ex-ecution issue accordingly.

STATE of TENNESSEE) For unlawful Gaming.
        vs.   ) This day came the State by the attorney Gen-
RICHARD MORRISET   ) eral and with leave of the Court enters a
Nolli prosequi in this cause. And thereupon personally appeared in open Court Richard Morriset and confesses Judgment for the costs. It is there-fore considered by the Court that the State recover of the defendant the costs of this prosecution and that Execution issue accordingly.

STATE of TENNESSEE) For unlawful Gaming.
        vs.   ) This day came the State by the Attorney Gen-
WILLIE B. KYLE   ) eral and with leave of the Court enters a
Nolli prosequi in this cause. And thereupon personally (p 307) app-eared in open Court Willie B. Kyle and confesses Judgment for the costs. It is therefore considered by the Court that the State recover of the de-fendant the costs of this prosecution and that Execution issue accordingly.

STATE of TENNESSEE) For unlawful Gaming.
        vs.   ) This day came the State by the Attorney Gen-
SHADROCH EPPERSON) eral and with leave of the Court enters a Nol-
li prosequi in this cause. And thereupon personally appeared in open Court Shadroch Epperson and confesses Judgment for the costs. It is therefore considered by the Court that the State recover of the defendant the costs of this prosecution & that Execution issue accordingly.

JOHN DEN LESSEE of) On affidavit of John Kennedy Defendant's attor-
JAMES MOORE   ) ney. It is ordered by the Court that this
        vs.   ) cause be continued until the next Term of this
THOMAS HOPKINS &   ) Court and that a Commission issue directed to
WALTER BEATY   ) any Justice of the peace of Grainger County
Tennessee to take the deposition of John Long and that Fifteen days notice be given and that a Commission issue directed to any Justice of the peace of Hawkins County to take the depositions of James Cooper and John Winegar de bene esse and that ten days notice of the (p 308) time and place of taking said depositions given to Peter Parsons shall be deemed sufficient.

WINGATE & JONES   ) This day came the parties by their attor-
        vs.   ) nies and thereupon came a Jury, to wit,
GEORGE & PHILIP S. HALE) Joel Gillenwaters, John Johnston, Abraham
Hawk, Larkin Willis, Benjamin Davis, James Williams, Thomas Stacey, Will-iam Crumly, John Critz, Howel Brewer, William Smith and Lewis Click who be-ing elected tried and sworn upon their oaths do say we find that the de-fendants did assume in manner and form as plaintiffs have complained and assess the Plaintiffs damage to One hundred and eleven dollars and thirty nine cents besides costs. It is therefore considered by the Court that the Plaintiffs recover of the defendants the sum of One hundred and eleven

dollars and thirty nine cents the damages aforesaid by the Jurors aforesaid assessed together with the costs in this behalf expended and that Execution issue accordingly.

JOHN DEN LESSEE of) This day came the Plaintiff by his attorney
OWEN SISEMORE) and with leave of the Court dismisses his suit.
vs.) And thereupon personally appeared in open Court
WILLIAM STAPLETON) William Stapleton and confesses (p 309) Judgment for the costs. It is therefore considered by the Court that the Plaintiff recover of the defendant the costs in this behalf expended and that Execution issue accordingly.

JOHN G. ROBERTS) This day came the parties by their attornies and
vs.) thereupon came a Jury, to wit, John Mitchell,
ROBERT NALL) William Nichols, William Armstrong, Joseph Huffmaster, Willie B. Kyle, Aeneas S. Galbreath, John Hagan, Preston Blevins, James Griggsby, Joseph Reese, John Nutty and Robert Wright who being elected tried and sworn upon their oaths do say we find that the defendant did assume as the Plaintiff in his declaration hath alledged and assess the plaintiffs damage to Sixty six dollars besides costs. It is therefore considered by the Court that the plaintiff recover of the defendant the sum of Sixty six dollars the damages aforesaid by the Jurors aforesaid assessed together with the costs by him in this behalf expended and that Execution issue accordingly.

AGNES RICE assesse & c) This day came the parties by their attornies and thereupon came a Jury, to wit,
vs.) nies and thereupon came a Jury, to wit,
WILLIAM YOUNG) Joel Gillenwaters, John (p 310) Johnston, Abraham Hawk, Larkin Willis, Benjamin Davis, James Williams, Thomas Stacey, William Crumly, John Critz, Howel Brewer, William Smith and John Reynolds who being elected tried and sworn upon their oaths do say we find that the defendant has paid the debt in the declaration mentioned except the sum of Nine dollars and thirty one cents. It is therfore considered by the Court that the Plaintiff recover of the defendant the sum of nine dollars thirty one cents the Balance of the debt in the declaration mentioned as found by the Jurors aforesaid and also the costs in this behalf expended and that Execution issue accordingly.

STATE OF TENNESSEE) For unlawful Gaming.
vs.) This day came the State by the Attorney General and with leave of the Court enters a Nolli in these causes. It is therefore considered by the Court that the defendants be discharged.
JOHN REESE)
)
Same)
vs.)
ELIJAH FALKNER)
)
Same)
vs.)
GEORGE MORRISET &)
ASA DAVIS)
)
Same)
vs.)
GEORGE MORRISET)

JESSE ALLEN) This day came the parties by their attornies and thereupon came a Jury, to wit, William Nichols (p 311)
vs.) debt)

PETER BURAM) Joseph Huffmaster, Willie B. Kyle, William Armstrong James Johnson, Lewis Click, Samuel Wilson, George McCullough, Jesse Howel, John Norman, Joseph McCullough and Philip Laughmiller who being elected tried and sworn upon their oaths do say we find that the defendant has not paid the debt in the declaration mentioned except the sum of Sixty dollars and assess the plaintiffs damage to Fifty seven dollars forty seven cents besides costs. It is therfore considered by the Court that the plaintiffs recover of the defendant and Thomas Hopkins his security the sum of One hundred and forty one dollars twenty five cents the Balance of the debt in the declaration & also the sum of Fifty seven dollars forty seven cents the damages aforesaid assessed together with the costs by him in this behalf expended and that execution issue accordingly.

Court adjourned until tomorrow 9 O'clock A. M.
                    S. Powel

Saturday 8th October 1825

Court met pursuant to adjournment.

Present - The Honorable Samuel Powel - Judge.

JAMES FORD ") On motion of the Plaintiff by his attorney
    vs.) and for reasons appearing to the satisfaction
ORVILLE PAINE &) of the Court. It is ordered by (p 312)
RICHd G. WATERHOUSE) the Court that the Execution issued in this
    Esqrs & c.) cause be quashed and that Execution issue
against the goods and chattels of William Paine Deceased in the hands of Orville Paine and Richard G. Waterhouse Executors of the Estate of said deceased.

STATE of TENNESSEE) On motion of Sterling Cocke attorney General
    vs.) and it appearing to the satisfaction of the
HEZEKIAH EMBERSON) Court that the defendant has no goods & chattels whereby the costs can be made. It is considered by the Court that the County Trustee pay the costs of the prosecution and that the clerk of the Court issue certificated to those persons entitled to the same/

WILLIAM WALKER) This day came the plaintiff and acknowledged satisfaction of Seventy eight dollars sixty five
    vs.) cents of the damages assessed by the Jurors on
ASABEL JOHNSON) a former day of this Term/

WILLIAM WALKER) This day came the defendant by his attorney and
    vs.) releases George Rogers and David S. Rogers witnesses for him in this suit from forfeiture tak-
ASABEL JOHNSON) en against them on a former day of this Term. Whereupon the said George Rogers and David B. Rogers (p 313) came into Court and assume the costs. It is therefore considered by the Court that they pay the costs of entering the forfeitures & c and that Execution issue accordingly.

PLEASANT M. MILLER for) This day personally appeared in open Court
JAMES P. McCARTYS use) Thomas Cocke and confesses Judgment for
    vs.) the sum of One hundred and eight dollars
THOMAS COCKE) and fifty cents and the costs. It is there-

fore considered by the Court that the plaintiff recover of the defendant the sum of One hundred and eight dollars and fifty cents as above confessed and also the costs in this behalf expended & that Execution issue accordingly. The Plaintiff James P. McCarty agrees to take good current Tennessee money in discharge of this Judgment & stays Execution six months.

THOMAS INGRAM) On affidavit of the defendant. It is ordered by the
    vs.) Court that a Commission issue directed to any Jus-
JOSEPH REESE) tice of the peace of Davidson County in this State
to take the deposition of John Neighbours and that Twenty days notice of the time and place of taking said deposition be given to the plaintiff.

A Deed of Conveyance from (p 314) James P. McCarty Sheriff of Hawkins County to John A. McKinney for Four hundred and eighty acres of land was acknowledged in open Court and ordered to be registered.

CHARLES KING) On affidavit of the Plaintiff. It is ordered by
    vs.) the Court that a Commission issue directed to any
SAMUEL CHESTNUTT Justice of the peace of Battetourt County in the
State of Virginia or Hawkins County in this State to take the deposition of Elias Boyers and that Thirty days notice of taking in Virginia and Ten days notice of taking in Hawkins County in this State of the time and place of taking said deposition be given to the defendant.

ISHAM REYNOLDS & wife) On motion of the defendants by their attor-
    vs.) nies a Rule is allowed them to shew cause
JOHN GRIGGSBY & CALEB) why a new trial should be granted and after
W. PARKER) argument of Counsel thereon as well on be-
half of the rule as against it and the premises seen and fully understood
It is considered by the Court that the rule be made absolute and a new trial granted, and that the Plaintiff have leave to amend his replications, if he thinks proper.
And on motion of the Plaintiff by his attorney. It is ordered by the Court that a Commission issue directed to any Justice (p 315) of the peace of McMinn County in this state to take the deposition of Henry Reynolds and that Fifteen days notice of the time and place of taking said deposition be given to the Plaintiffs.

JAMES HAGAN) On motion of the Plaintiff by his attorney. It is
    vs.) ordered by the Court that the Rule of Reference en-
JOHN A. ROGERS) tered on a former Term of this Court in this suit
be set aside and that it stand for trial at the next Term.

JOHN MILLER) This day came on for argument the demurrer of the de-
    vs.) fendant to the replication of the Plaintiff to the
ELIJAH JONES) first second and third pleas of the defendant and
after argument of Counsel being heard on both sides and the premises seen and fully understood. It is considered by the Court that the demurrer to said Replications be overruled and on motion of the Defendant he has leave to rejoin to said replications and that this cause stand for trial at the next Term of this Court.

ALEXANDER RICE by) Demurrer.
WILLIAM RICE his) This day came on for argument the Demurrer
father & next friend) to the plea of the defendant (p 316) coming
    vs.) on to be heard and after argument of Counsel
OLLIVER MILLER) thereon as well for as against it and the pre-

mises seen and fully understood. It is considered by the Court that the demurrer be overruled and that the defendant go hence without day and recover of William Rice the costs by him in this behalf expended and that Execution issue accordingly.

WINGATE and JONES) On motion of the defendants by their attorney a rule is allowed them to shew cause
vs.)
GEORGE & PHILIP S. HALE) why a new trial should be granted and argument of Counsel being heard as well for as against the rule and the premises seen and fully understood. It is considered by the Court that the rule be made absolute and a new trial granted and it is further considered by the Court that Plaintiffs pay the costs of this Term for which Execution may issue.

C. ESKRIDGE KENNER) In this cause it appearing to the satisfaction
vs.) of the Court that the order of the County Court
JAMES WILLIFORD) of Hawkins County in laying out a ferry and appointing James Williford keeper of said Ferry. It is therefore considered by the Court that said order be quashed and that all the proceedings, relative (p 317) thereto be set aside and that the said C. Eskridge Kenner recover of the said James Williford the costs by him in this behalf expended & that Execution issue accordingly.

WILLIAM CRUMLY) In the progress of the trial of this cause the
vs.) plaintiff by his attorney tenders a Bill of Ex-
JOHNSON FRAZIER) ceptions which is signed sealed and ordered to be made part of the record, in this cause.

JOHN DEN LESSEE of) In this cause the defendant by his attorney
WILLIAM WHITESIDES) prays an appeal in the nature of a Writ of Er-
vs.) ror to the Supreme Court of Errors and Appeals
DAVID PROFFIT)) to be held at the Courthouse in Knoxville on the second Monday of July next gave bond and Security according to law and the appeal by the Court granted.

JOHN SHOUSE) On motion. It is ordered that the time for amend-
vs.) ment be enlarged so as not to delay trial.
JAMES SPENCER)

JESSE HOWEL) On motion (p 318) of the defendant by his at-
vs.) torney. It is ordered by the Court that a Com-
SAMUEL McCULLOUGH) mission issue directed to any Justice of the peace of Union County State of Indiana to take the deposition of Simeon Perkins and that Thirty days notice of the time and place of taking said deposition be given to the Plaintiff.

BETSY HENDERSON) Petition for Divorce.
vs.) On motion. It is ordered by the Court that
ROLLIN M. HENDERSON) publication be made in the Greenville Economist four successive weeks calling on the defendant to appear and answer the Petition otherwise the same will be taken for confessed and the Court will proceed exparte and decree accordingly.

The Court adjourned until Court in Course.
S. Powel

www.ingramcontent.com/pod-product-compliance
Lightning Source LLC
Chambersburg PA
CBHW080616270326
41928CB00016B/3077